Dan Flavin

Dan Flavin New Light

Edited by Jeffrey Weiss

Essays by Briony Fer,

Hal Foster,

Jeremy Gilbert-Rolfe,

Alex Potts,

Anne M. Wagner,

& Jeffrey Weiss

Yale University Press

New Haven & London

National Gallery of Art

Washington

Set in Cycles and Scala Sans types by BW&A Books, Inc.
Printed in the United States of America by Thomson-Shore,
Inc.

Library of Congress Cataloging-in-Publication Data
Dan Flavin : new light / edited by Jeffrey Weiss ; essays by
Briony Fer ... [et al.].
      p. cm.
Includes bibliographical references and index.
ISBN-13: 978-0-300-11409-6 (alk. paper)
ISBN-10: 0-300-11409-5 (alk. paper)
1. Flavin, Dan, 1933–1996—Criticism and interpretation.
2. Light art—United States. I. Weiss, Jeffrey S. II. Fer, Briony.
N6537.F55D36 2006
709'.2—dc22   2006007568

A catalogue record for this book is available from
the British Library.

The paper in this book meets the guidelines for permanence
and durability of the Committee on Production Guidelines for
Book Longevity of the Council on Library Resources.

10 9 8 7 6 5 4 3 2 1

Contents

vii Preface

xi Acknowledgments

1 Dan Flavin: "in . . . cool white" and
"infected with a blank magic"
Alex Potts

25 Nocturama: Flavin's Light Diagrams
Briony Fer

49 Blunt in Bright Repose
Jeffrey Weiss

82 Space and Speed in Flavin: Minimalism,
Pop Art, and Mondrian
Jeremy Gilbert-Rolfe

108 Flavin's Limited Light
Anne M. Wagner

133 Dan Flavin and the Catastrophe of Minimalism
Hal Foster

153 Contributors

155 Photograph Credits

157 Index

Preface

Although widely acknowledged by historians of the art of the 1960s as central, the work of Dan Flavin has been subjected to very little serious monographic study. The dearth of historical and critical literature is perhaps not mysterious, for despite its obvious significance, Flavin's work has always literally been difficult to find. To be sure, there exist a handful of semipermanent installations in the United States and Europe. But correctly showing Flavin's work requires more space than museums are generally able (or willing) to devote to a single artist, a condition that is exacerbated by the deleterious impact fluorescent light has on neighboring art. Only recently has this problem been prominently redressed at the Dia facility in Beacon, New York, where a group of works is perpetually on view in a dedicated space, although only a narrow portion of the range of the oeuvre can be represented at any one time.

The recent, first-ever career retrospective, mounted at the National Gallery of Art and touring as I write, was intended to bring a broad range of Flavin's work to new audiences. While the exhibition's tour will eventually run its course, it has produced two important volumes, both written by Michael Govan and Tiffany Bell, who also organized the exhibition and have had long, hands-on experience with Flavin's art (part of it in connection with Dia's support of various projects): the exhibition catalogue itself, which includes an authoritative account of Flavin's career, and the catalogue raisonné of the "lights," which addresses the many complicated technical matters surrounding the work. The exhibition represents the first opportunity for students of the art of Flavin's generation to behold the development of his career as a chronological and typological narrative. On the occasion of the Washington show, I invited a group of critical historians (none of them Flavin specialists per se, yet each a distinguished scholar in relevant fields) to present papers about the issues raised by the work—its historical formation and its life in the realm of art since 1960. Subsequently revised, these papers make up the contents of the present volume, further including an essay of my own.

The ontological nature of Flavin's work is difficult to define, a peculiarity that represents one unifying theme of these papers. Each author addresses the significance of the work, at least in part, through notions of duality or dichotomy. To be sure, these qualities belonged to Flavin criticism from the beginning. Neither painting nor sculpture (although it possesses elements of both), Flavin's work was famously placed by Donald Judd within the domain of the "specific object," a term Judd devised in 1965 to account for the peculiar hybrid nature of much new art in the United States. It could be rightly argued that Flavin's lights are only insecurely identified as either of these things—as objects or as specific. The fluorescent lamp was characterized by the artist more often as medium than as sculptural entity, its chief role being the emission of color as light, which washes walls and spreads through ambient or actual space. Color-light, in turn, along with a pronounced dependence on the wall as support (in two senses of the word), brings us close to painting, or to the pictorial, although, again, the light will not be constrained by painting's physical or perceptual limitations—by surface or frontality. But an emphasis on what Flavin called the "situational" nature of his work as installation, especially after the mid-1960s, will always beg us to recall the opposite: that the lamp is, after all, a prefabricated object drawn from the commercial culture of utility—that is, a readymade, which brings us back to the "sculptural," or at least the "object," nature of the work.

The present authors might be said, however, to demonstrate that the ambiguities of Flavin's work actually represent something like ambivalence. Indeed, from the vantage of forty years, it is now possible to recognize that the formal and critical narratives of the 1960s, while framed by ambition, were underwritten by doubt. The significance of Duchamp for young artists during this period signals the emergence of a form of skepticism—relating above all to the philosophy of medium—wholly alien to artists of the preceding generation. Specifically, the certainties—or pieties—attending abstract expressionist painting (especially the near-mythology of the self) came to make up a kind of closed system, driving Flavin, Judd, Carl Andre, and Sol LeWitt (all of whom began as painters) out of the arena of heroic faith and into the warehouse, the machine shop, and the stockroom, where the high subjectivity of paint was traded for the deliberately banal certainty of hardware and the materials of industrial fabrication. As the expansiveness of the later work of most "minimalists" attests, this move would eventually beget its own sort of quasi-heroic faith, but not before it first, during the sixties, managed to express a kind of loss.

As is often observed in this volume, the role of painting—or of the pictorial—for Flavin is especially significant, given the optical quality of fluorescent light. We might even attribute to Flavin's work a species of nostalgia in this respect, especially as he often saw fit, over time, to distance his work from that of most of his contemporaries, positioning himself more closely instead to high modernism: to Matisse and Brancusi, for example, and to Russian constructivism (the icons and the "monuments" to Tatlin)—to an art of faith, after all. Yet (and this is also discussed elsewhere in these essays) Flavin was often apt to deploy irony as the voice of his work; that is, as he well knew, his proximity to modernism was historically checked. Ultimately, Flavin's medium was itself inherently elusive, and the conceptual condition of his work was fully prepared by the "discovery" or designation of the fluorescent lamp (an act which he described in epiphanic terms), and by the fact that, in his work, as opposed to the work of other light-based artists such as Robert Irwin and James Turrell, the lamps are always exposed. In this way, Flavin's lamp is, art historically, an acutely—and almost uniquely—critical object. Not only does it implicate multiple aesthetic media (therefore escaping medium specificity), but, in its banal and ephemeral nature—the lamps will eventually burn out—it represents the technological in almost unmediated, decidedly nonutopian terms.

So it is the lamp as medium that concerns us. Light, object, diagram, color, situation: in this book, Flavin's work is addressed as a function of each of these things, and conclusions about the philosophy and legacy of the work are drawn from formalist considerations. Interestingly, we find that Flavin's practice appears less quantifiable with time, something that is perhaps truer of Flavin than of any of his contemporaries. It is a quality that, more than anything else, might even be credited with Flavin's relevance, so far, to subsequent generations. Or, to reverse this formulation, if interpretations of Flavin's work now openly address its complexities and its properties of opposition or ambivalence, then this may be because the nature of art since Flavin allows us to articulate what was only intuitively available to contemporary observers. For many of those observers, Flavin's fluorescent lamp was largely one of two things: unfit to be art or possessed of mesmerizing presence and the unmistakable aura of the aesthetic. Between hardware and aura lies fetishization, a risk that Flavin recognized (when he referred to the tube as a "common industrial fetish"). But Flavin put the readymade to work: even as medium, the lamp negotiates the very identity of art. This consideration is one that concerns Flavin's work surely as much as it does that of Warhol (an artist whose conceptual company he keeps at least as much as Judd's and LeWitt's). And it is one that, ever commemorative, Flavin might now be said to have addressed from well within the precincts of a modernism that was soon to expire.

Acknowledgments

This book is the result of a collaborative effort. The essays were first presented as papers at a conference at the National Gallery of Art in Washington, D.C., held in 2005 on the occasion of the exhibition *Dan Flavin: A Retrospective.* For her enthusiastic and unflagging support of this project—as a conference, above all, and as a book—I thank Faya Causey, Head of Academic Programs in the Division of Education at the National Gallery. I would also like to acknowledge Lynn Russell, Head of Education. For their key roles in organizing and managing the conference, thanks go to Ana Maria Zavala and Allison Benedetti, along with Jeannie Bernhards, Hugh Colston, John Conway, and Karl Parker. Judy Metro, Editor in Chief in the Publishing Office at the National Gallery, worked with Patricia Fidler, Publisher of Art and Architecture at Yale University Press, to make this book a co-publication between the two institutions.

In my own department, my gratitude goes to Jennifer Roberts, Research Associate, who has worked in various capacities on the exhibition, the conference, and the book. Marcie Hocking, Staff Assistant to the Curator, also contributed to all three and has looked after the myriad details relating to preparation of manuscripts and picture research for this book with tireless resourcefulness and outstanding efficiency.

At Yale University Press: Susan Laity, Senior Manuscript Editor, edited the manuscript with superb expertise, sensitivity, and tact. All the authors join me in thanking her for her contribution. I would also like to thank: Michelle Komie, Associate Editor; Mary Mayer, Art Book Production Manager; and John Long, Photo Editor and Assistant Production Coordinator.

Throughout the preparation of the book, we have relied on Tiffany Bell, Director of the Dan Flavin Catalogue Raisonné, whose expertise in the work of Dan Flavin is unmatched by that of anyone else in the field. Tiffany's devotion both to the work and to the accuracy of the historical record, along with her great goodwill, has made her an essential resource for this project, and I cannot overstate my gratitude. Thanks also go to Michael Govan, who first proposed a volume of studies in conjunction with the Washington retrospective.

And to Stephen Flavin, the artist's son, we also owe our warmest thanks. His commitment to his father's legacy is exemplary, and his support of this project has been generous and ever gracious.

A final thanks, of course, goes to the authors. As participants in the symposium and contributors to this book, their enthusiasm has been gratifying. The essays in this volume have certainly exceeded my expectations for new literature about Flavin's work.

Alex Potts   **Dan Flavin** "in . . . cool white" and "infected with a blank magic"

Both Flavin and his apologists agree that a major breakthrough occurred in his work in the early 1960s—the moment when he discovered the fluorescent tube as his basic medium and abandoned his earlier symbolically loaded and at times expressionistically romantic practice for the radically abstract and often serially based minimalist work for which he is best known. In this essay, my aim is to shift the focus from later, "mature" work to the earlier work and to that produced in the moment of transition, and thus draw attention to the affinities as well as the differences between what are usually seen as radically disparate facets of Flavin's oeuvre, the earlier usually left out of account as minor late–abstract expressionist juvenilia—a mere prelude to, and largely irrelevant for understanding, the art by Flavin that really matters. At issue here is not just a complicating of what might at first seem to be a clear-cut break between the early, overtly symbolically loaded works and the full-fledged, categorically abstract fluorescent works. I am arguing that a close consideration of the former is important for understanding the complex poetic affect and political resonance of Flavin's early experiments with fluorescent light fixtures.

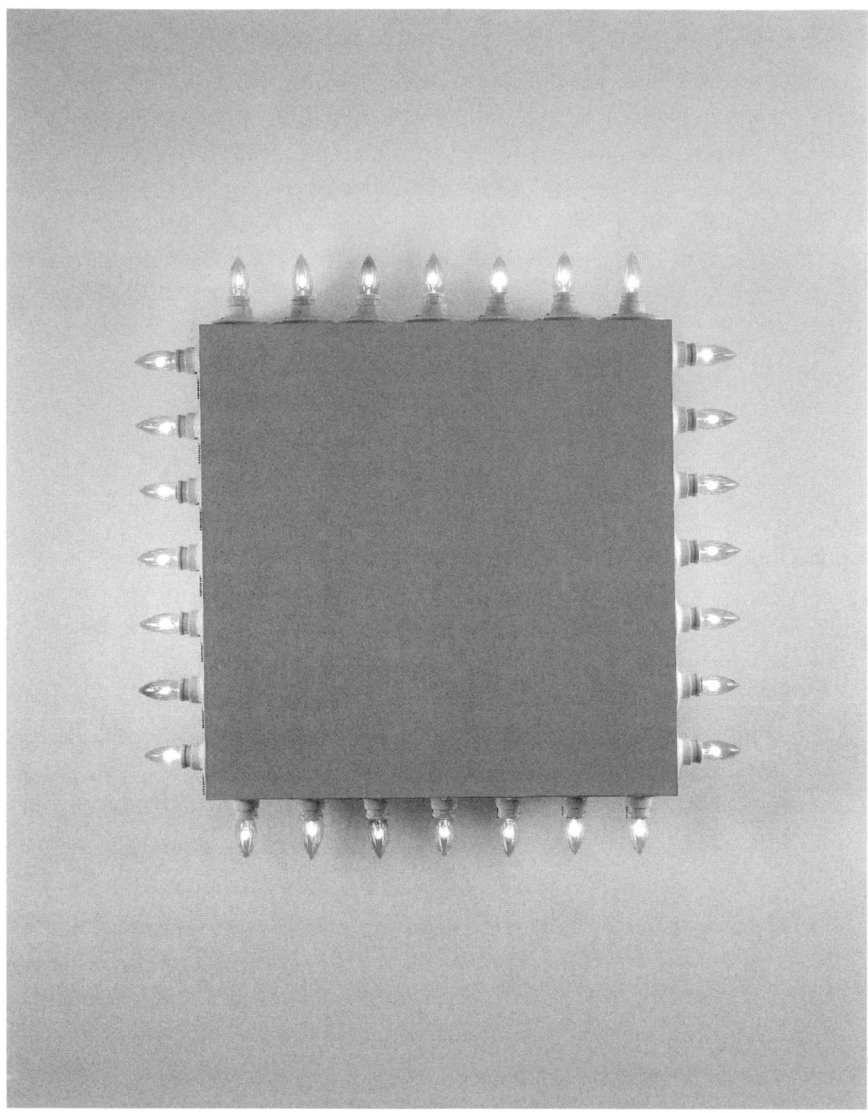

Fig. 1. Dan Flavin, *icon V (Coran's Broadway Flesh)*, 1962, oil on cold gesso on Masonite, porcelain receptacles, pull chains, and clear incandescent "candle" bulbs, 41⅝ × 41⅝ × 9⅞ in. (105.9 × 105.9 × 25.1 cm). Private collection, New York.

There is a striking contrast in both the visual conception and the titling of two works that straddle the divide in Flavin's oeuvre, *icon V (Coran's Broadway Flesh)*, dating from 1962, and *daylight and cool white (to Sol Le Witt)*, dating from two years later (figs. 1, 2). Both these works featured prominently in his first one-man show in a major commercial gallery, *some light* held at the Kaymar Gallery in New York in March 1964, when the artistic public was introduced

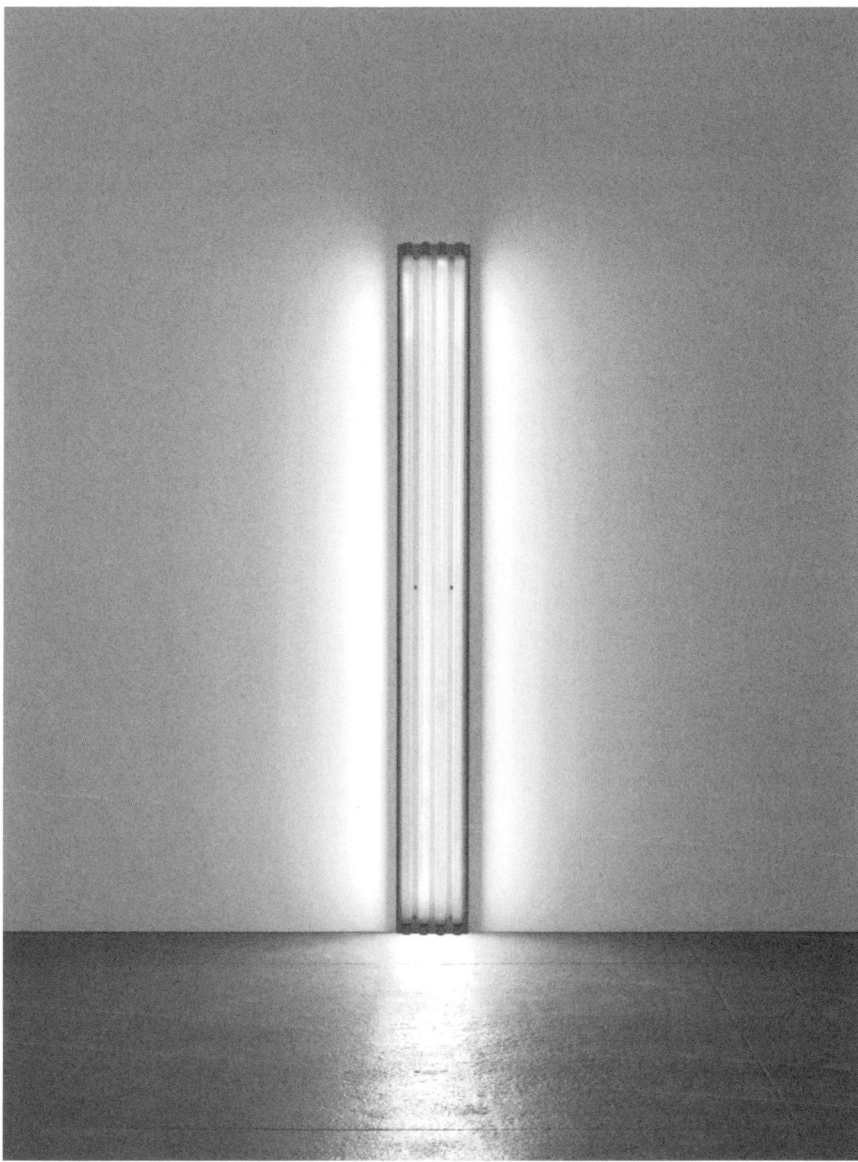

Fig. 2. Dan Flavin, *daylight and cool white (to Sol LeWitt)*, 1964, daylight and cool white fluorescent light, 8 ft. (244 cm) high. Photo courtesy of Dia Art Foundation.

to his new minimal fluorescent light mode. The later work, *daylight and cool white*, nicely epitomizes his breakthrough to a radically new approach to art—simple, self-evident proposals using standard fluorescent lighting units, unburdened by existential or poetic or techno-utopian pretensions, and in this case dedicated to the up-and-coming master of cool, conceptually rigorous statement, Sol LeWitt. Yet responses to the show at the time indicate that the situation is not quite so straightforward. Donald Judd may have emphasized the "simple, unstressed, unconcluded placing of the adjacent lines," but Lucy Lippard was struck by how even this work had powerful emotive resonances. As she put it, the "four vertical white tubes—warmer bulbs on the outside and cooler within—create an extraordinarily sensuous and romantic pillar."[1]

Similar dichotomies continue to emerge in critical responses to Flavin's fluorescent light works during the late 1960s and early 1970s, often within texts by the same writer, and occasionally even with reference to the same work. For Lippard, it was not that the matter-of-fact formation of the later work expunged any romantic charge but rather that it carried a charge that was less disturbing, less raw in its psychic provocations, than the earlier *icon V*. With the latter, she was deeply disturbed by the "jewel case" effect of the "small pointed bulbs with sparkling filaments," and no doubt would have been even more concerned had Flavin carried out his initial plan of surrounding the central block with a Christmas tree–like array of lights in red and green as well as clear white.[2] If this is a light piece, and hence has certain affinities with the slightly later works composed solely of fluorescent light fittings, it is still very different in conception, as Flavin made clear in a now much-quoted comment to a prospective buyer. The work, he explained, was envisioned as "an emblem. . . . [I]t stands for a young English homosexual who loved New York City. What I have made for him is a square block loaded with flesh tint, mechanized by lamps, and bounded by excurrent tips of clear glass glister. But beyond structure and phenomena, I have tried to infect my icon with a blank magic which is my art. I know that this is hard to cope with, but if I have succeeded, *Coran's Broadway Flesh* will hold you simply, succinctly."[3]

Flavin's comment nicely sums up the impact of the work—the plain painted block does acquire a darkened blankness when surrounded by the dazzle from the sparkling glass bulbs. At the same time there is in Flavin's titling and commentary a gratuitous expressiveness—a psychologically charged frisson that straight society would have associated at the time with male homosexuality. This piece is perhaps as close as Flavin ever came to an aesthetics of camp, but the work comes from the point of view of an outsider, intrigued and vaguely troubled by a sexuality seen as deviating from the masculine norms of simplicity and succinctness he was seeking to cultivate in his new fluorescent light work, norms explicitly announced in a manifesto piece he devised in the summer of 1963, *the nominal three (to William of Ockham)* (figs. 3, 4).[4]

A critic, commenting on the Flavin retrospective held at The Jewish Museum in New York in 1970 after its initial showing at the National Gallery of Canada in Ottawa, was struck by the "oppositions between the cold arrangements and sentimental dedication titles and a submerged religious content."

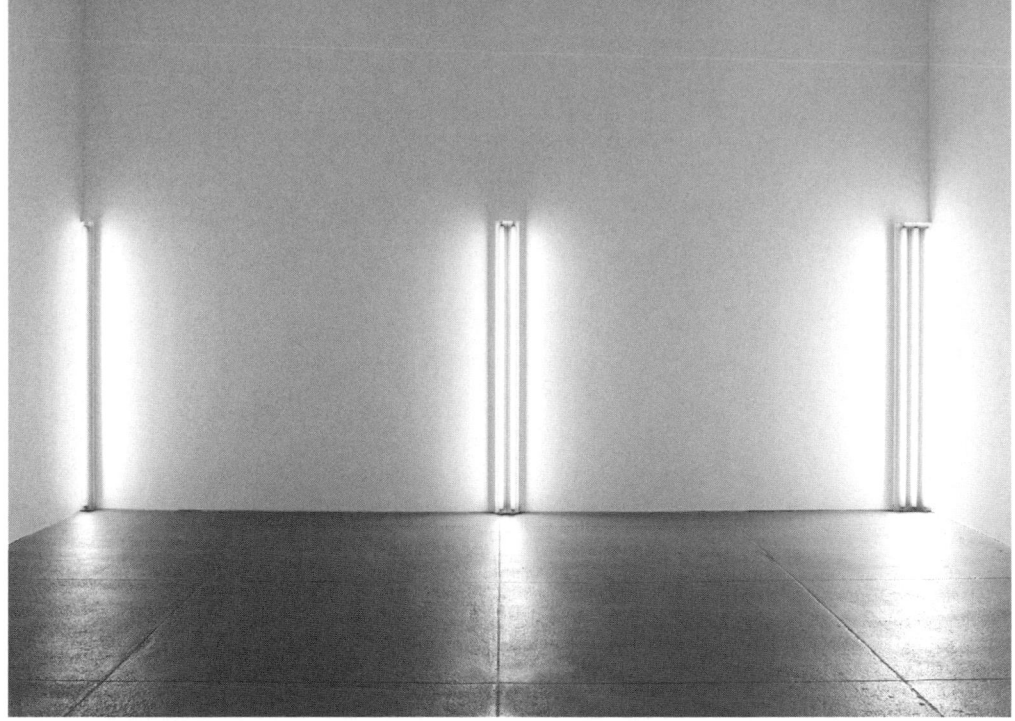

Fig. 3. Dan Flavin, *the nominal three (to William of Ockham)*, 1963, cool white fluorescent light, 8 ft. (244 cm) high. Dia Art Foundation.

Fig. 4. Dan Flavin, *three from meditation (for William of Ockham)*, 1963, and *three (to William of Ockham)*, 1963, two drawings in pencil on paper mounted on cardboard, each 4⅞ × 2¹⁵⁄₁₆ in. (12.5 × 7.5 cm). Collection Stephen Flavin.

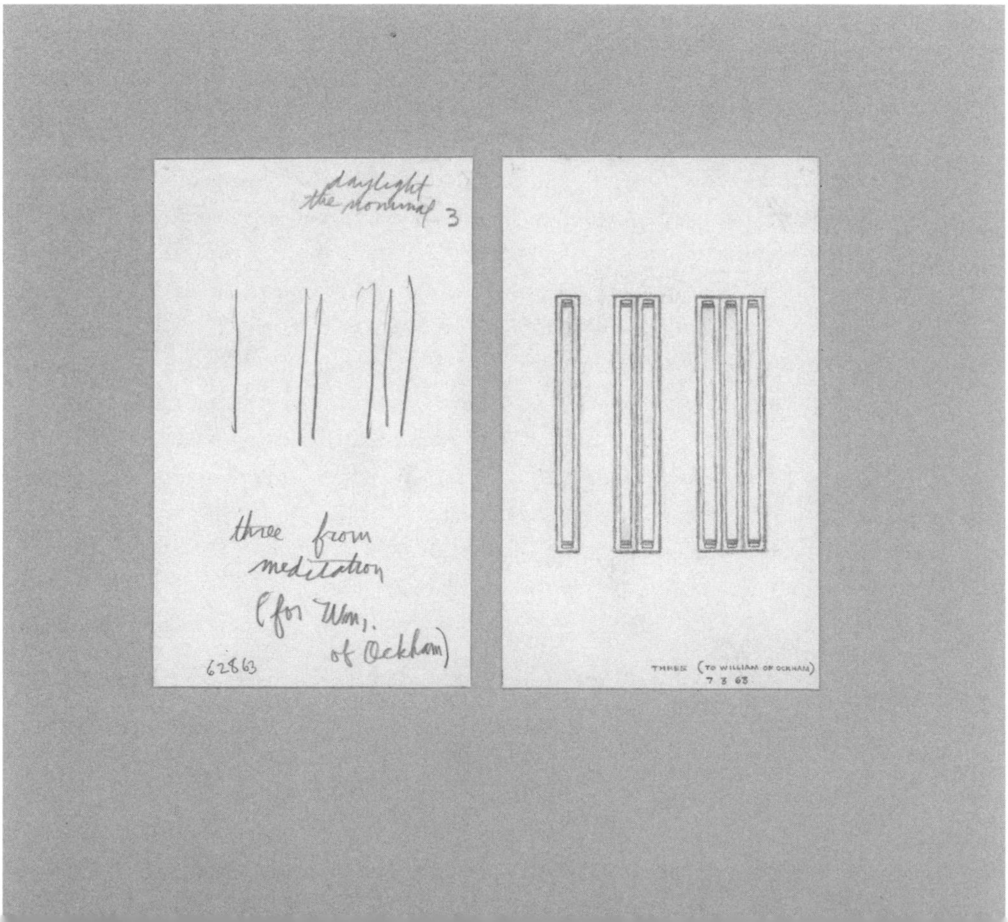

Two years earlier Philip Leider had similarly noted how, despite Flavin's apparent commitment to a radical anti-illusionism in his recent proposals in fluorescent light, he "seemed to make no effort to rid the works of a rich romanticism with religious and atmospheric overtones quite out of keeping with these ideas." Flavin's early icon series, and above all the junk assemblages and poetic drawings with which he began his career and which were abundantly represented, with Flavin's endorsement, in the National Gallery of Canada retrospective, are explicitly symbolic in a manner that one could call poetic, expressive, and even at times sentimental.[5] A number consisted of handwritten poetic texts extracted from both traditional and modern sources, with the script surrounded by informal abstract painterly markings in ink and water color. One dating from 1959 (fig. 5) featured a passage from Solomon's Song of Songs: "Come my beloved, let us go / forth into the field, let us / abide in the villages. / Let us get up early to the / vineyards, let us see if the / vineyard will flourish, if the flowers / be ready to bring forth fruits / if the pomegrantes [sic] flourish: / there I will give thee my breasts."

Even after his breakthrough moment, Flavin would give titles to his light pieces that suggested a continuing attachment to highly charged affect, nowhere more evident than in the work with which he chose to represent himself at the *Primary Structures* show held at The Jewish Museum in the spring of 1966, *monument 4 those who have been killed in ambush (to P.K. who reminded me about death)* (fig. 6). "P.K." is Paul Katz, a photographer and friend of the artist. The work has prompted certain recent critics to give such free rein to their imagination that they envisage "P.K." as a possible reference to the death of Dan Flavin's brother in Vietnam—even though Flavin's brother actually died several years before the war.[6]

Unusually for Flavin's fluorescent light works, the expressiveness of the title is carried over into the visual conception of the work. Flavin himself commented in an interview in 1972 that this was exceptional among his light works in that its form was clearly bound up with its symbolic dedication.[7] The effect was particularly marked when it was shown on its own in a darkened room at the Flavin exhibition in Washington, D.C., in 2004—by contrast, in the original installation in the 1966 *Primary Structures* show, it was set off in the corner of a large open area filled with works by other artists. As a visual/sculptural phenomenon, it comes across as a somewhat threatening conjuncture of a red glow and red shaft. One of the light fixtures juts directly out at the viewer, inclined slightly upward and balanced somewhat precariously between the horizontal fitting straddling the corner and the juncture between the two fittings set on the walls, as if it were a shaft about to be shot from a crossbow or a deadly ray about to zap an adversary.

The political references here are quite complex—the immediate associa-

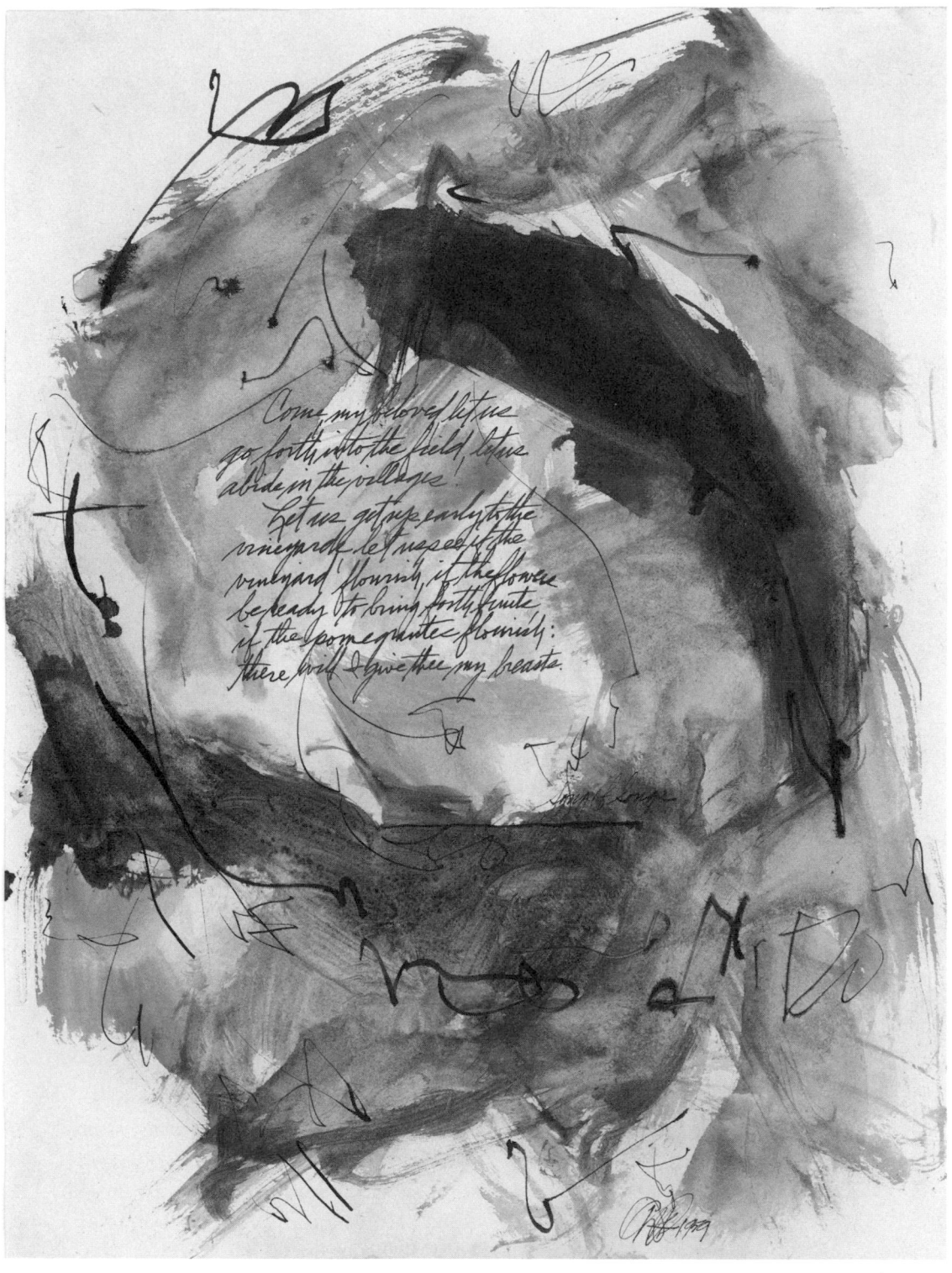

Fig. 5. Dan Flavin, *Song of Songs*, 1959, watercolor and carbon ink on paper, 11¹⁵⁄₁₆ × 9 in. (30.4 × 23 cm). Collection Stephen Flavin.

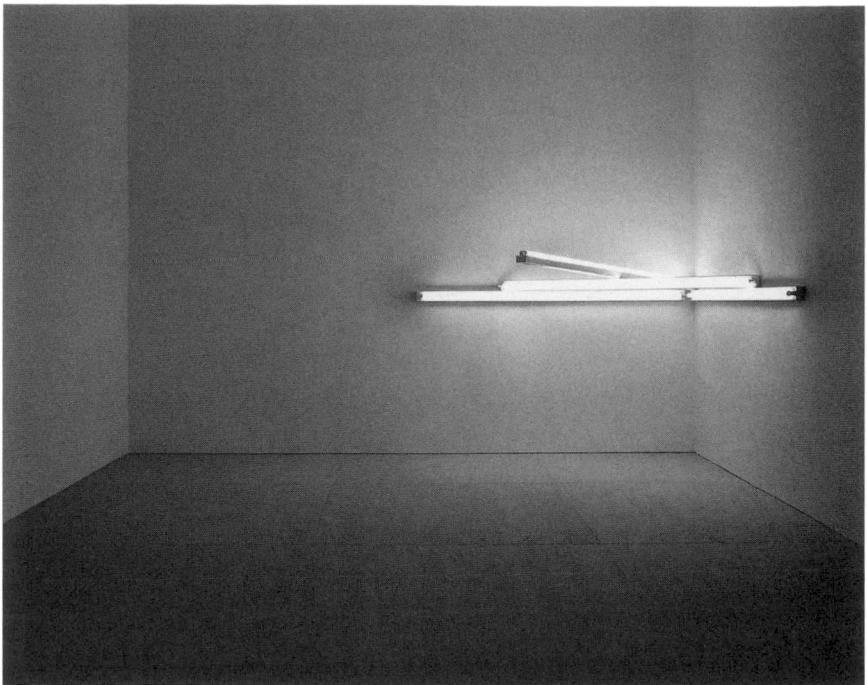

Fig. 6. Dan Flavin, *monument 4 those who have been killed in ambush (to P.K. who reminded me about death)*, 1966, red fluorescent light, 8 ft. (244 cm) wide, 8 ft. (244 cm) deep. Dia Art Foundation.

tion of the title would have been to the threat of ambush that became a big concern as U.S. troops were deployed in active combat in Vietnam and were beginning to suffer heavy casualties, for example at Ia Drang Valley in the late fall of 1965, where one unit lost 151 men after stumbling into an ambush. While the title itself does not clearly align the work with the emergent anti-war movement, this still is hardly a standard war memorial, and the second International Day of Protest took place in late March 1966, just before the opening of *Primary Structures* in late April. The work does nothing to mitigate the crude, blood-red violence of war, the blood red here operating in quite a different register from the red glow of *icon I,* titled *(the heart)* and dedicated *to the light of Sean McGovern which blesses everyone,* where a single red fluorescent tube rests on a red painted square Masonite block.[8] If Flavin had had his way, and the statement he proposed for the catalogue of the *Primary Structures* exhibition had been published, the effect would have come close to symbolic overload. Among the quotes he assembled for his statement were these lines from a poem, "A rhyme about an electrical advertising light," by Vachel Lindsay:

I look on the specious electrical light
Blatant, mechanical, crawling and white,
Wickedly red or malignantly green
Like the beads of a young Senegambian queen.[9]

I have insisted on the political charge of this work because Flavin had produced, and continued to produce into the early 1970s, a number of works with
a sharp political content. In 1960 he conceived a piece made up of a crushed
can on thickly painted Masonite inscribed *Africa (to seventy-two negroes)* in response to the notorious Sharpeville massacre, in which police fired on and
killed seventy-two people who had been protesting South Africa's apartheid
passbook law. Soon afterward, in February 1961, he dedicated one of his drawings that combined handwritten text with gestural abstraction "to those who
suffer in the Congo," in response to the murder of Patrice Lumumba in January that year. The previous autumn, Lumumba, the democratically elected
prime minister of the Congo and the first black leader of the newly independent state, had been deposed in a military coup that enjoyed tacit support
from the U.S. government, and soon afterward the CIA had tried, unsuccess-
fully, to assassinate him. The passage from Psalm 21:16–19 (Douay-Rheims
version) that Flavin inscribed on the drawing includes the lines:

My strength is dried up like a potsherd,
And my tongue hath cleaved to my jaws:
And thou has brought me down
Into the dust of death.
For many dogs have encompassed me:
The council of the malignant hath besieged me
They have dug my hands and feet
They have numbered all my bones
And they have looked
And stared upon me.[10]

A rather different political charge informs the famous series of light
pieces styled as monuments to the Russian revolutionary artist Vladimir
Tatlin that Flavin initiated in 1964. A statement he published in 1965 commenting on the seventh work in this series suggests a richly evocative, almost
poetic, identification on Flavin's part with Tatlin's uncompromisingly utopian
project: "*Monument 7* in cool white fluorescent light memorializes Vladimir
Tatlin, the great revolutionary, who dreamed of art as science. It stands, a
vibrantly aspiring order, in lieu of his last glider, which never left the ground."
Crucial here is the characterization of Tatlin as a "great revolutionary," a
"vibrantly aspiring" dreamer, whose last impossible project, a human-

propelled flying machine, never took off. The deep-felt affinities with Tatlin's vision of "art as science" expressed here might seem to contradict Flavin's categorical distancing of himself elsewhere from the futuristic, techno-utopianism of his contemporaries, who like him were working with artificially generated light and other modern-seeming technical devices.[11] The contradiction only remains, however, if one fails to take account of the somewhat one-dimensional, apolitical enthusiasm for the progressive potential of modern technology in many of the "art and technology" initiatives of the 1960s, or to appreciate Flavin's complex investment in the fusion of revolutionary politics and highly charged, almost romantic poetic vision that he saw embodied in the "vibrantly aspiring order" of Tatlin's lost and largely unrealized works.

Explicit references to topical political issues in Flavin's work continued to surface from time to time during the period of intense protest in the United States against the Vietnam War in the late 1960s and early 1970s. He planned a work commemorating the students killed at Kent State University and Jackson State College in May 1970 during the violent suppression of the widespread protest sparked by Nixon's announcement of his disastrous policy of incursion into Cambodia. Though never realized, a drawing for this work was exhibited at the Whitney Museum Sculpture Annual that opened in December 1970, bearing the inscription "(to the young women and men murdered in Kent State and Jackson State Universities and to their fellow students who are yet to be killed)."[12]

Flavin's attentiveness to the concrete politics of the situation is demonstrated by his giving equal status to the killings at Jackson State, a predominately black college in Mississippi, which did not receive the same public attention and symbolic status as the killings of white students at Kent State. One of his last pointedly political pieces was a light work devised in 1972 as a tribute to George McGovern, the antiwar presidential candidate who lost to Richard Nixon. The piece consisted of two triangular arrays of white circular fluorescent tubes set at separate corners of an otherwise empty room. The inscription Flavin placed on the preparatory sketch suggests the deep investment he had in the McGovern campaign and his bitterness over its failure: "to beset to abuse the complete room (to a man George McGovern)."[13]

Several of Flavin's more charged political pieces, including the one shown at the *Primary Structures* exhibition, drew on associations with death and the commemoration of the dead. The latter was a central theme in Flavin's work. In 1962 Flavin, like Warhol, planned a memorial to Marilyn Monroe that he would have titled "The Blonde painting (I'm still I suppose alone) to Marilyn Monroe." Among the more richly invested of his commemorative pieces is a work from his crushed-can series, *Apollinaire wounded*, dating from 1959–60. The physical fabric of the work here powerfully evokes the head wound the

French poet and art critic suffered when serving as a soldier in the First World War in 1916, and also puts the viewer in mind of his death soon afterward. In a poem written slightly later, in February 1961, in which Flavin amplified on the resonances of this work, he directly conflated Apollinaire's war injury with his death in the Spanish influenza epidemic two years later: "Apollinaire wounded/killed at can cadence/his gleaming head crushed/tar blood/rusting dead."[14]

This poem featured in the 1969 Ottawa retrospective alongside another emblematic poem of the same date that is often cited as an iconic statement by Flavin on his use of fluorescent light: "fluorescent/poles/shimmer/flick/out/dim/monuments/of/on/and/off/art."[15] One would clearly be travestying the tenor of Flavin's subsequent experiments in fluorescent light were one to see the latter as expressing, or even perhaps connoting, some poetic cliché about the affinity between the vulnerability of mortal existence and the on-off ephemerality of shimmering fluorescent light poles. Still, the association cannot entirely be dismissed. If Flavin's poem dates from a couple of years before he moved into his mature fluorescent light mode, he himself featured it prominently in his later published writings and commentaries on art.

This is a good point to examine Flavin's complex narrativizing of his trajectory from symbolically loaded poetry to clean-cut, quasi-literalist statements in common hardware. Like so many other artists' autobiographical narratives of self-discovery, Flavin's essay "'. . . in daylight or cool white,'" published in *Artforum* in 1965, is structured around an epiphanic moment when he supposedly discovered the true way—or saw the light, as it were. The moment was dated by him very specifically to May 25, 1963, the day when he claimed he made a crucial discovery by setting diagonally against a blank wall a single eight-foot fluorescent strip—its color could be described as yellow or gold, depending on whether one wanted it plain or just a little mystical. Suddenly, Flavin's story ran, he was seized by the sight of something extraordinary—a plain, simple phenomenon that held its own, powerfully and amply, without laying claim to any symbolic intent. The discovery presented him with the model for making a new kind of art, one that would enable him to leave behind the physical and emotional messiness of his earlier, small-scale, deliberately poetic work. His understanding of this moment of entry to a new arena of artistic practice, however, was hardly divested of psychological charge—he inscribed the drawing created in conjunction with this work "the diagonal of personal ecstasy."[16]

The terms in which he celebrated his conversion to this new way of working in his 1965 essay are clearly not straightforward or emotionally sanitized. No laid-back literalist he, when he described how the "radiant tube . . . implanted itself directly, dynamically, dramatically in my work-room wall—a buoyant and relentless gaseous image which, through brilliance, betrayed its physical presence into approximate invisibility." Note also the curious choice of words with which he introduced this passage: "The radiant tube and the shadow cast by its pan seemed ironic enough to hold on alone." The use of the word *ironic* refers us back to a statement he made two years earlier about his declaratively reductivist *nominal three*, dedicated to the antischolastic William of Ockham: "Such an elemental system becomes possible (ironic) from the context of my previous work." [17] *Ironic* here refers to a distancing and negating, a negating that does not totally expunge, however, but to an extent incorporates that which it negates. Flavin is implying that his new work is ironic to the extent that it becomes significant by, paradoxically, eliminating those features of his earlier work that had sought to project a larger significance, most notably expressive or poetic content. But just as, in some deeply ambivalent way, Flavin remained cathected to the highly charged symbolic and poetic meanings of his earlier work, so a residual trace of these meanings continued to make their presence felt, ironically perhaps, in his new practice.

These complexities tend to be edited out in Flavin's later statements about his art. Already in the first of his "excerpts from a splenetic journal" published a year later, in 1966, he envisaged himself as operating a self-perpetuating system that needed no personal investment or input on his part, one that would be true to the plain, objectified qualities of the mass-produced elements that it utilized. The burden of the past had supposedly been cast off—it was as though the conversion to a systematic process of making enabled him to dispel the doubts and anxieties that had burdened and weakened his earlier efforts. If he continued to append an occasional poetic dedication to his work, he would, when pressed—as in an interview he gave in 1972—claim that the dedications were not to be seen as having any real bearing on the significance and logic of his work as art. They were "trifling," purely personal additions, an indulgence he allowed himself of a kind that "makes life easier to take from time to time" [18] However, such trifling might be seen as a necessary trifling, which at some level gave sustenance to an artistic project whose results were only ostensibly at odds with the affective self-indulgence of his titles.

It would hardly be far off the mark to suggest, as a critic did in response to Flavin's show at the Saint Louis Art Museum in 1973, that Flavin continued to have "a romantic sense of academic responsibility, of carrying on the flame," that manifested itself in, among other things, the hypercharged intensity of his splenetic denunciations of critics and art institutions in his writings from the late 1960s. In Flavin's case, as with several of his minimalist or literalist contemporaries, the driving sense of purpose that could be seen in the commitment to producing art divested of easy expressive resonance and true to the hardnosed skepticism of a factual, positivistic age was operating in collusion with a suppressed existentially and romantically charged belief in the

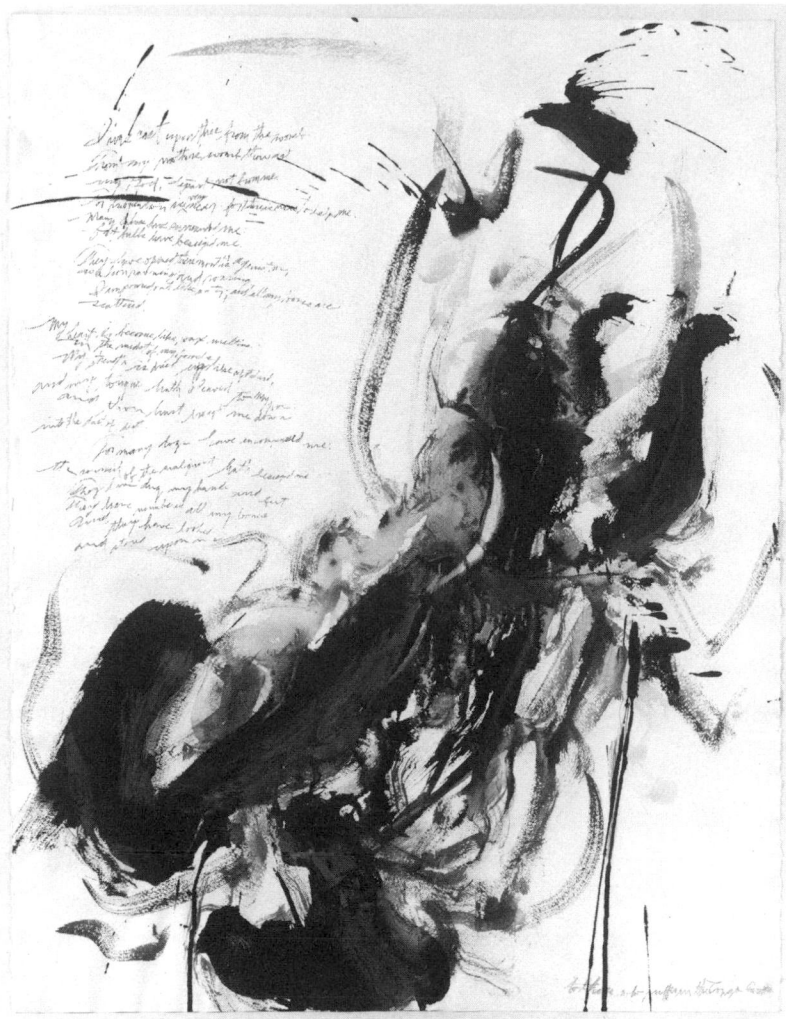

Fig. 7. Dan Flavin, *to those who suffer in the Congo*, 1961, watercolor and black waterproof drawing ink on paper, 26 × 20 in. (66 × 50.8 cm). Collection Stephen Flavin.

higher purpose of art.[19] While Flavin entertained the illusion of moving beyond and transcending such belief, it continued to shadow and animate his enterprise, at least during the first few years of his work with fluorescent light.

It is important to remember that unlike most postwar artists who prided themselves on having forged a true path to radical abstraction, Flavin, in his first major retrospective, the Ottawa exhibition of 1969, did not edit out his earlier work. On the contrary, he ensured that his earlier poetic drawings and junk assemblages were fully represented (figs. 5, 7, 8), much to the consternation of some critics, who found the inclusion of "so many inferior early works

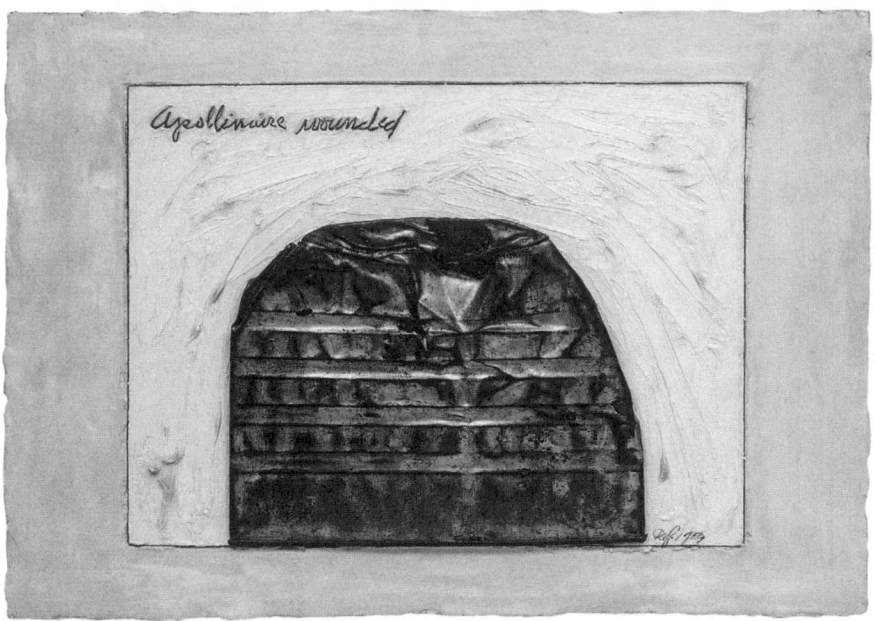

Fig. 8. Dan Flavin, *Apollinaire wounded (to Ward Jackson)*, 1959–60, crushed can, oil and pencil on Masonite, and plaster on pine, 13½ × 19⅜ × ⅞ in. (32.7 × 49.2 × 2.2 cm). Collection Stephen Flavin.

. . . although interesting . . . wholly depressing,"[20] and irrelevant to Flavin's mature achievements as an artist. Moreover, he was far from being prepared to abandon the use of commemorative or evocative titles once he started working exclusively with fluorescent light tubes. A particularly striking recognition on his part of the complex relationship between his commitment to a radically abstract and quasi-literalist way of working and his earlier thematizing of affective and ideologically charged, sometimes almost sentimental, poetic meaning occurs in his tribute to Donald Judd, an artist with whom he had particularly close affinities.

His contribution to the catalogue of Judd's first one-man retrospective, held at the Whitney in 1968, *Several Quotations for Don Judd . . .* , included a telling passage from a letter the painter Juan Gris wrote to his dealer Daniel-Henry Kahnweiler in 1915 about his new-found commitment to a rigorously abstract, formal approach to painting: "Sometimes I feel my way of painting is wholly mistaken. I can't find room in my pictures for that sensitive and sensuous side which I feel should always be there. . . . I find my pictures excessively cold. But Ingres too is cold, and yet he is good. Seurat also. Yes, Seurat also, although I dislike the meticulous element in his pictures almost as much as my own. Oh, how I wish I could convey the ease and charms of the unfinished!

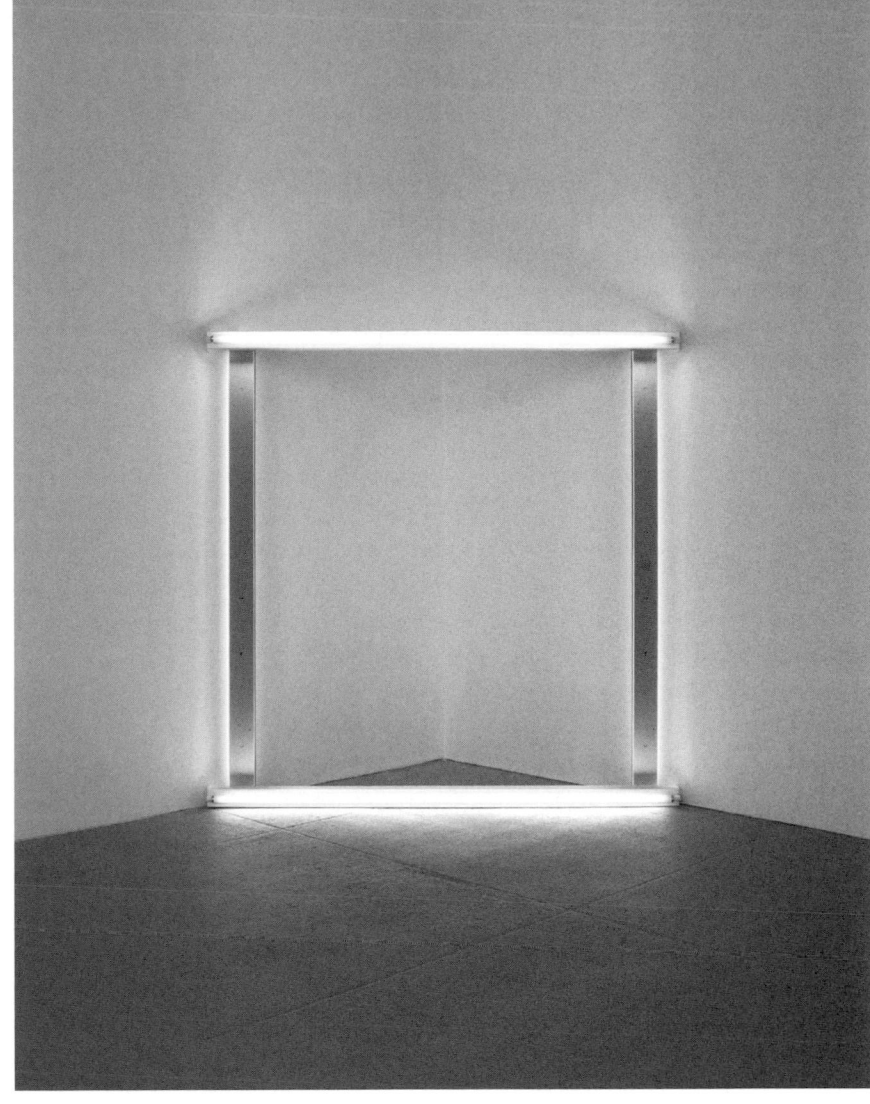

Fig. 9. Dan Flavin, *untitled (to the "innovator" of Wheeling Peachblow)*, 1966–68, daylight, yellow, and pink fluorescent light, 8 ft. (244 cm) square across a corner. Photo courtesy of Dia Art Foundation.

Well it can't be helped. One must after all paint as one is oneself." That Flavin had for some time felt a particular affinity with Gris is demonstrated in an early crushed-can work dating from 1960–62 devised as a tribute to Gris entitled *Juan Gris in Paris. Adieu Picabia*.[21]

The reference to the "sensitive and sensuous" brings to mind a work Flavin completed in 1968, *untitled (to the "innovator" of Wheeling Peachblow)* (fig. 9). The "untitled" title may reference in deadpan literalist fashion an invention by a nineteenth-century American firm called Wheeling—the "Peachblow" glass that simulated the coloring of Peachblow Chinese porcelain. But

Flavin indicated that he was not entirely averse to the work being seen as having a lyrical, painterly effect. As he put it, the "installation was intended to be beautiful, to produce the color mix of a lovely illusion," a color mix that the critic Philip Leider noted created a "kind of orange/salmon strikingly reminiscent of the impudent and delightful palette of Willem de Kooning." The peach color recalls Flavin's earlier fascination with the poetics of peach blossom evident in a series of drawings from 1960 that accompany two Chinese poems. Among the phrases he singled out there were those evoking "the flowering peach after rain" and the way "inside this door/her pretty face/the peach flowers /each to each/reflected pink/Pretty Face."[22]

It seems that Flavin, even in his later, hardnosed phase, was mindful of the lyrical effects created by work such as the *Peachblow* piece, in which the pale pink and gold/yellow coming from fluorescent bulbs mingles with a secondary peach or orange hue that these generate by being set together. However, to isolate these effects as being the essence of the work would be to smother its clear, plainspoken, and subtly tuned rhetoric in a treacly poetry of pretty pink and peach. As so often with Flavin, the implied poetics gains its power precisely from its incongruous presence in a literalist environment, where suggestions of poetic symbolism or expressivity are almost completely blanked out and displaced. This partly suppressed lyrical strain is important to bear in mind when one is being assaulted by the aggressively macho vituperation that dominates Flavin's later essays and statements or ponders his (ironic?) attachment to a dictum attributed to Hermann Göring, "I am in the habit of shooting from time to time, and if I sometimes make mistakes, at least I have shot." This quotation was selected by Mel Bochner for his 1966 tribute to Flavin, "Less Is Less," and then reused by Flavin with the "author's name withheld" in his 1968 tribute to Judd. For all its deeply contaminated source, the dictum, laid out bare as it is here, can seem less baldly authoritarian and more tempered by the complexities of the real than a lot of mainstream politic discourse these days.

In his review of the Flavin retrospective held in New York in 1970, Lawrence Alloway made a suggestive point about the peculiar significance of the moment of transition in Flavin's work, before the new fluorescent light mode became fully stabilized as a system that could be deployed in ever more elaborate combinations over ever more extensive spatial settings. As he noted, "Initially [Flavin] condensed his early diffuse interests, with a brilliant intuition, into his single bar of light. He did it, moreover, without losing his sense of art's sacredness. Later the problem arises—as it has for others who have clenched their art into one thing—how to keep working. Often this has meant relaxing and a gradual return to a traditional canon of complexity."[23]

Certainly with Flavin's more expansive later installations, there is a move

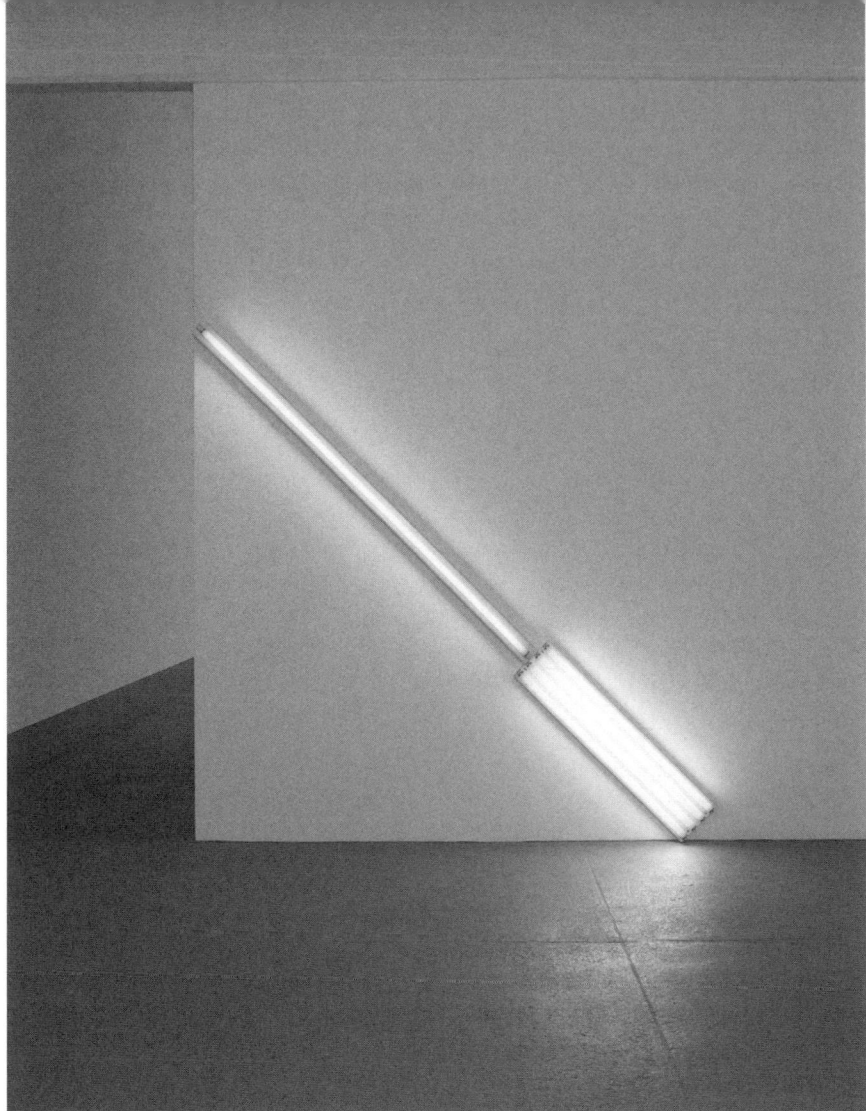

Fig. 10. Dan Flavin, *alternate diagonals of March 2, 1964 (to Don Judd)*, 1964, daylight and cool white fluorescent light, 12 ft. (366 cm) long on the diagonal. Dallas Museum of Art.

into a new arena, where the elaborate and striking architectonic and lighting effects efface the sense one might have of the strange materiality of the lit fluorescent tube. Almost incongruously, it is where the materiality of the individual units still looms large, where the work is not so much a light installation as an object, that it seems to acquire the densest affective charge—with the tubes striking one simultaneously as pulsatingly and slightly precariously alive, and as perfectly ordinary hardware. In *alternate diagonals of March 2, 1964 (to Don Judd)* (fig. 10), the long bright daylight tube thrusting out beyond the cluster of more muted, yellowish, almost fleshlike cool white tubes, its presence given a further resonance by the shadow it casts against the wall, has an erotic, almost phallic charge not be found in the later work.[24]

These early works often prompt us, as they did critics at the time, to consider the curious nature of fluorescent light fixtures, their odd physical substance and their deceptively simple light effects, and to puzzle the diffuse resonances they both suggest and seem to deny through their instantaneous immediacy. Flavin himself commented on the disjuncture between the hard objectivity of the units' forms and the less graspable light effects they generate —a disjuncture that occurs in the first instance between the solidly anchored metal pans and the glow emanating from the units and shadows they cast, and then within the tubes themselves between the gaseous-seeming illumination emanating from the fluorescent material lining the inside of the tubes and the clear cylindrical outline of their shiny glass outsides.[25] As David Bourdon put it, "the light has an intangible fluidity that contrasts sharply with the rigid contours of the tubes themselves." Mel Bochner, a particularly subtle and appreciative admirer of Flavin's work, made the point that while "the fascination resulting from the gaseous fluorescent glow is undeniable . . . any attempt to posit the objects with a transcendent nature is disarmed by the immediacy of their presence."[26] It is through dichotomies like these in Flavin's work that the focusing of the viewer's attention on fluorescent light fixtures as facts and presences becomes particularly intriguing. We are presented with a cool, precise matter-of-factness, at the same time that we are prompted to sense something in the lighting that is a little diffuse and vague.

The collage of citations that Bochner devised as a tribute to Flavin in the 1969 catalogue of Flavin's retrospective in Ottawa, which clearly must have had Flavin's imprimatur, included several where simplicity and forthright precision are to the fore. But many of the quotations evoke almost the opposite: a "liquid elemental scattering," "the gloom calm of idle vacancy," "immense and insatiable desires, an atrocious ennui and continuous yawns," "those stagnant expanses where all movement is vibrationless and immobilized." Such phrases put one in mind of the statement with which Flavin signed off his first "excerpt from a spleenish journal": "I can hardly keep coherent. Fatigue encompasses my wandering ballpoint"—and this, after beginning his article by staking out his claims for a new art that would shed its "vaunted mystery for a common sense of keenly realized decoration." The most intensive and creative moment of Flavin's career lay perhaps at the moment of passage from vaunted mystery to keenly realized decoration, when he was producing work that prompted the viewer to focus on very simple arrangements of fluorescent light tubes, shadowing and casting a diffuse glow on the surrounding wall. The wayward poetics integral to the conception of this body of work struck a strong chord with close colleagues of Flavin's such as Bochner and Robert Smithson, who clearly saw in his efforts affinities with their own artistic projects. Such a poetics features explicitly and vividly in the quotations that Bochner assembled for his tribute to Flavin, as well as in Smithson's wildly melodramatic locutions about the suggestions of "final dissolution" to be found in "the sullen electricities of Flavin's 'lighting.'"[27]

Smithson, as usual, overloads the pessimistic collapse into entropic immobility. But his comments lead us to consider a crucial point about the temporal associations to be made with the limited lifespan of the tubes deployed in the "dim monuments" of Flavin's "on and off art." To dwell overmuch on the connotations of death and decay and disposability would be to immerse ourselves in the kind of easy poetic affect that Flavin was at pains to keep at one remove. At the same time, we are compelled to recognize that these lights are not particularly long-lasting, let alone eternal. The unrelenting yet also slightly softened luminescence of the tubes and the hard, resistant, shiny enamel painted surfaces of the pans seem in the first instance utterly clean and new, even with their fading manufacturer's label attached. Immediately apprehended, they look momentarily eternal. Yet we know that they will burn out, that the glass tubes sustaining the luminescent glow and the flow of electricity through their gas-filled interiors are physically fragile, and that the glow is easily extinguished with the flick of a switch. And when the tubes burn out, they are dead, useless, mere rubbish.

Flavin's work is more mortal than most in that it will not be able to survive the inevitable obsolescence of the particular manufactured lighting elements he used. This situation both obsessed and fascinated him. As he commented in a much-quoted journal entry dating from 1962, just before his breakthrough into the world of fluorescent light: "I can take the ordinary lamp out of use and into a magic that touches ancient mysteries. And yet it is still a lamp that burns to death like any other of its kind," adding in a tone reminiscent of Smithson's entropic imaginings: "In time the whole electrical system will pass into inactive history. My lamps will no longer be operative; but it must be remembered that they once gave light." Or take the comment with which he concluded an interview conducted much later, in 1982, that refers back to a poem about an on-and-off art he had written twenty years previously: "I go with that," he emphasized, "And rust and broken glass. I mean you really have no choice."[28]

Looking at the multitube architectonic light installations for which he became best known in his later years, we find it hard to see suggestions of this temporal decay. Such suggestions are more evident in the simpler, objectlike light works of the mid- to late 1960s. A good example is his ironic *a primary picture* (fig.11), with its bright yellow and boiled-sweet red and artificial pastel blue tubes, which at first seems so much more instantaneously fresh than any picture painted on canvas. Looking at the individual tubes, vague and barely perceptible tonal variations or imperfections soon become apparent, however,

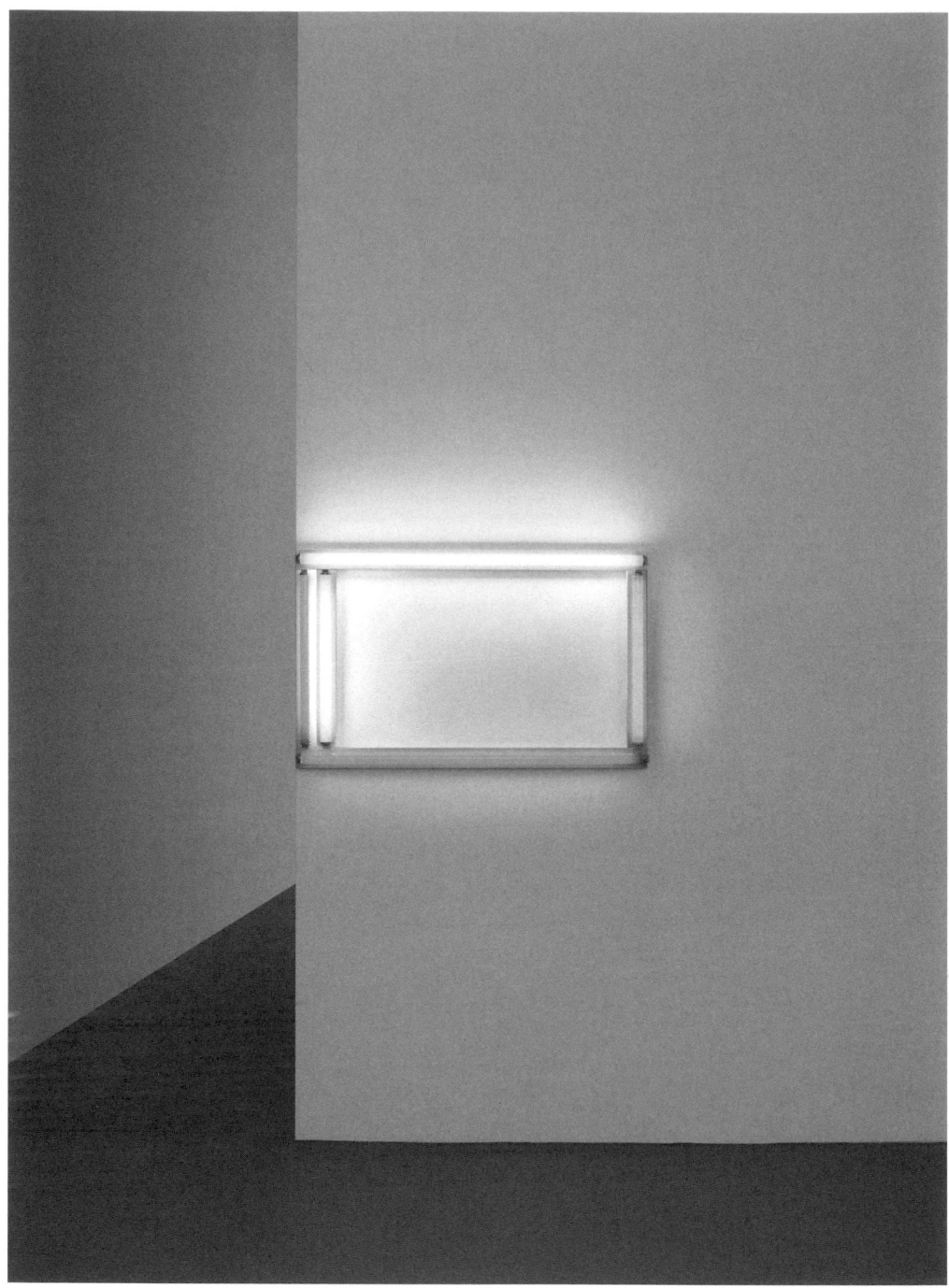

Fig. 11. Dan Flavin, *a primary picture*, 1964, red, yellow, and blue fluorescent light, 2 ft. (61 cm) high, 4 ft. (122 cm) wide. Hermes Trust, United Kingdom. Photo courtesy of Dia Art Foundation.

of the kind that are also very noticeable in the monochrome works assembled from a few cool white tubes, such as the earlier "monuments" to Vladimir Tatlin.[29] One cannot but become aware that though the light never dulls, it must at some point come to an abrupt end—the light tubes do not age like paint but rather suddenly die out. As it happened, when *primary picture* was on display in the Washington, D.C., exhibition in 2004, a tube was beginning to flicker at one end, indicating that it would soon go dead, a phenomenon that attracted a great deal of attention from visitors passing through the gallery.

If ones goes back even further in Flavin's career, to the junk-tin-can art from the years around 1960, the vulnerability, and the decay into rubbish and rust, comes right to the fore, the damaged materials almost ostentatiously and indulgently expressive, as in the incinerated can of his *Washington Street sculpture* (the street in the meatpacking district of Manhattan where Flavin lived) and in the crushed, rust-color paint of another early work, *Vincent at Auvers,* dating from 1960. Dedicated to van Gogh, and explicitly invoking the painter's mental torments that led to his suicide, the pages of drawings inside the latter work spell out the motto: "As for my work, I do it at my life's risk and half my reason has foundered on it." For this to resonate in a way that would be appropriate to the elusive intensity of Flavin's intriguingly contradictory project, one would need to balance the late-romantic tragic poetics here with the more deadpan but in its own way equally charged resonances of a comment Flavin recorded in 1963 when devising one of his more emphatically minimal works, *the nominal three (to William of Ockham):* "With *the nominal three* I will exult primary figures and their dimensions. Here will be the basic counting marks (primitive abstractions) restated long in the daylight glow of common fluorescent tubes."[30]

Notes

1. Paula Feldman and Karsten Schubert, eds., *it is what it is: writings on Dan Flavin since 1964* (London: Thames and Hudson, 2004), 20, 21. The arrangement of the bulbs at the Kaymar Gallery show in 1964 (see also Dan Flavin, *fluorescent light, etc. from Dan Flavin/lumière fluorescente, etc. par Dan Flavin,* exh. cat. [Ottawa: National Gallery of Canada, 1969], no. 86) was the reverse of that recorded in recent illustrations, where the warmer cool white bulbs are placed on the inside and the brighter daylight ones on the outside.

2. See the drawing *untitled (icons V, VI, VII)* dating from 1962 (collection Stephen Flavin), listed in Michael Govan and Tiffany Bell, *Dan Flavin: A Retrospective,* exh. cat. (New Haven: Yale University Press, 2004), 202.

3. Dan Flavin, *three installations in fluorescent light/drei Installationen in fluoreszierendem Licht,* exh. cat. (Cologne: Kölnische-Verlagsdruckerei, 1973), 83.

4. A streak of homophobia emerges from time to time in Flavin's more dyspeptic comments on his contemporaries, as in the following statement in a 1968

letter to Enno Develing in which Flavin was complaining about the group show Robert Morris had organized at the Castelli Warehouse: "What was represented was the most preciously effete and affected obviously arty, delicate art décor that I have seen together for some times [*sic*]. Almost all of it appeared to possess the excessively careful compositioning (but sometimes seemingly random-like, of course) of dilettanted dada homosexuals" (Flavin, *three installations*, 110). For details of *the nominal three,* see *fluorescent light . . . from Dan Flavin*, no. 78. That the cool literalism of works such as *the nominal three* was not, initially at least, seen by Flavin as requiring him to dissociate himself from works that carried an explicit psychic charge, such as *Coran's Broadway Flesh,* is indicated clearly in a letter he wrote in February 1963 to the president of the Albright-Know Art Gallery in which he set out an equally intensely wrought account of both works (Flavin, *three installations*, 83).

5. Feldman and Schubert, *it is what it is* 97, 44 (review of Flavin's show in the Dwan Gallery in 1968). See also Jack Burnham, "A Dan Flavin Retrospective in Ottawa," *Artforum* (December 1969): 55: "The 'hardware' quality of his proposals and the sentimentality of his titles are again ramifications of a double-edged logic." Leider interestingly failed to make a clear distinction between the icons and the early fluorescent tube pieces, referring to the latter at one point in his 1968 review as "icons."

6. The claim was made in the publicity for the Flavin show held at the Villa Panza in 2004. Flavin devised at least two memorials to his brother, *icon IV (the pure land) (to David John Flavin)* dating from 1962–69 (Govan and Bell, *Flavin: A Retrospective*, p. 25, fig. 11), and a work from the series of East New York Shrines that carries the inscription, "Holy Mother of God loaded with grace please help David Sonja-Dan Flavin—1962," which was included in the Washington, D.C., show. One of these shrines is illustrated in Govan and Bell, *Flavin: A Retrospective*, p. 28, fig. 14. The former, a radically simplified piece comprising a white Formica square with a single white fluorescent tube running along the top edge, hovers between a total evacuation of symbolic content and suggestions of a purified "heavenly light," while the latter tempers the overt Catholic religiosity with flagrant irony—the body of the shrine consists of a can of Pope brand tomatoes.

7. Govan and Bell, *Flavin: A Retrospective*, 194.

8. The work is illustrated in Govan and Bell, *Flavin: A Retrospective*, p. 24, fig. 7.

9. Flavin, *three installations*, p. 89. The poem, from Vachel Lindsay, *Collected Poems* (New York: Macmillan, 1925), 339–40, like *icon V* makes reference to Broadway lights. The poem begins with the passage quoted by Flavin. After continuing with further evocations of the "specious" electrical lights of the advertising displays projected over the "millions" hurrying by—"By maggotry motions in sickening line" / Proclaiming a hat or a soup or a wine"—it finishes in a whimsical flight of fancy, imagining how these Broadway lights might at some time in the future be transformed into a "marvelous stair" leading beyond "the steep cliffs of the street" to the stars singing their "message elusive and sweet" in the sky above.

10. Crushed can on thickly painted Masonite, 1960, illustrated in Flavin, *fluorescent light . . . from Dan Flavin*, no. 40; see Flavin, *fluorescent light . . . from Dan Flavin*, no. 42.

11. *Art Voices* (Summer 1965): 72; see, for example, Dan Flavin, "some remarks . . . excerpts from a spleenish journal," *Artforum* (December 1966): 27.

12. The drawing (collection Stephen Flavin) is listed in Govan and Bell, *Flavin: A Retrospective*, 202.

13. Govan and Bell, *Flavin: A Retrospective*, p. 116, fig. 102 (collection Stephen Flavin). Also illustrated there is a view of half the final light piece (p. 76, fig. 60). Flavin planned another explicitly political piece at this juncture— a pink fluorescent light work for a tunnel between the Mall and the Hirshhorn Museum in Washington, D.C., recorded in a drawing dating from 1973 that is inscribed "to the thinkers and lovers of America now unknown to most of their politicians" (*Dan Flavin: tall cornered fluorescent light* [New York: Pace Wildenstein Gallery, 1993]).

14. The drawing listing the proposed memorial to Marilyn Monroe is entitled *Inventory of work sketches for the doors (to M. Antonioni)* and dated 1962. Listed in Govan and Bell, *Flavin: A Retrospective*, 202 (collection Stephen Flavin). Flavin's image of Apollinaire wounded/killed was probably inspired by passages from a volume of letters by Juan Gris that he knew well and from which he quoted (see William C. Agee, ed., *Donald Judd* [New York: Whitney Museum of American Art, 1968]). On April 16, 1916, Gris reported seeing Apollinaire in hospital, "with a head wound, but not serious. Clearly he owes his life to his tin helmet, which I saw. There's an enormous hole (in the helmet). He's not trepanned." A subsequent letter, written on May 7, however, indicated that the wound was having such "appalling after-effects," including paralysis and serious loss of memory, that Apollinaire was having to be trepanned after all, an operation that should have been carried out when the wound was fresh. Finally, on May 15, Gris notes that the trepanning had been successful in improving Apollinaire's condition (*Letters of Juan Gris*, collect. Daniel-Henry Kahnweiler; trans. and ed. Douglas Cooper [London: Percy Lund, Humphries, 1956], 36–38).

15. Flavin, *fluorescent light . . . from Dan Flavin*, nos. 46, 47 (both collection Stephen Flavin). The poem on fluorescent light is illustrated in Govan and Bell, *Flavin: A Retrospective*, p. 112, fig. 99.

16. Dan Flavin, "'. . . in daylight or cool white.' an autobiographical sketch," *Artforum* (December 1965): 21–24. The drawing (collection Stephen Flavin) is illustrated in Govan and Bell, *Flavin: A Retrospective*, p. 33, fig. 18, and the final work on p. 108, fig. 96.

17. Flavin, "'. . . in daylight or cool white,'" 24; Flavin, *three installations*, 83.

18. Flavin, "some remarks . . . ," 27; Govan and Bell, *Flavin: A Retrospective*, 194.

19. Feldman and Schubert, *it is what it is*, 136. The more self-consciously modern American artists of Flavin's generation would have been particularly attuned to Clement Greenberg's contention that the positivistic temper of the present time, with its narrowing "conception of what constitutes an indisputable fact of experience," demanded "of aesthetic experience an increasingly literal order of effects" (Greenberg, "The New Sculpture" [1949], in *The Collected Essays and Criticism*, vol. 2 [Chicago: Chicago University Press, 1986], 314). See also "Our Period Style" (1949), in the same volume (322–26).

20. Feldman and Schubert, *it is what it is*, 96.

21. Quoted in Agee, *Donald Judd*, 6–7. The crushed-can work is illustrated in

Govan and Bell, *Flavin: A Retrospective*, p. 135, fig. 124 (collection Stephen Flavin). What Flavin had in mind when he added the inscription "Juan Gris in Paris. Adieu Picabia" is hard to decipher. A distaste for the neodada currents in the art of his own time is evident in splenetic comments he made later on (see, for example, note 4, above), so he may have been wanting to suggest that Gris's art, the very visual formal rigor of which he clearly admired, displaced the dada tendencies of artists such as Picabia. On the other hand, he could have been registering an awareness of the close connections between Gris and Picabia during Gris's early days in Paris, before a split emerged between the dadaists and the artists who continued to be committed to the formal values of painting, evidenced in Gris's painting *Maisons à Paris—Place Ravignan* (1911) carrying the dedication "A mon cher ami Picabia, avec toute l'admiration de Juan Gris." See Douglas Cooper, *Juan Gris: Catalogue raisonné de l'oeuvre peint établi avec la collaboration de Margaret Potter* (Paris: Berggruen Editeur, 1977), no. 9.

22. Flavin, *fluorescent light . . . from Dan Flavin*, 238; Feldman and Schubert, *it is what it is*, 45; Flavin, *fluorescent light . . . from Dan Flavin*, 96.

23. Feldman and Schubert, *it is what it is*, 100

24. In the original installation in the 1964 Kaymar Gallery show, the tones were reversed: the single long tube was cool white and the cluster of shorter ones were brighter daylight. When the piece was shown at the Green Gallery later in the same year, the long bulb was gold and the cluster of shorter ones were red. See Flavin, *fluorescent light . . . from Dan Flavin*, no. 87. The recent arrangement, with the long bulb daylight, is the one recorded in certificates for the work. See Michael Govan and Tiffany Bell, *Dan Flavin: The Complete Lights, 1961–1996* (New Haven: Yale University Press, 2004), 226.

25. Govan and Bell, *Flavin: A Retrospective*, 192 (from a previously unpublished interview conducted in 1972). See also the comment Flavin made about "this unfocused source coming out of a well-defined instrument" in "some remarks . . . ," 28.

26. Feldman and Schubert, *it is what it is*, 29 (from a review published in 1966).

27. Flavin, *fluorescent light . . . from Dan Flavin*, 32–34. Several of these passages had already been published in a tribute to Flavin devised by Mel Bochner that came out in 1966; it similarly consisted of a series of texts quoted from different sources. See "Less Is Less (for Dan Flavin)," in Feldman and Schubert, *it is what it is*, 30–31; Flavin, "some remarks. . . ," 29, 27; Robert Smithson, "A Museum of Language in the Vicinity of Art" (1968), *Robert Smithson: The Collected Writings* (Berkeley: University of California Press, 1996), 78–79.

28. Quoted in a review published in 1970 in the *Christian Science Monitor*. See Feldman and Schubert, *it is what it is*, 103; Govan and Bell, *Flavin: A Retrospective*, 199.

29. See, for example, *"monument" 1 for V. Tatlin*, 1964, illustrated in Govan and Bell, *Flavin: A Retrospective*, p. 47, fig. 32.

30. Burnt can (opened) preserved with Krylon Clear plastic spray, 1959–60. Illustrated in Flavin, *fluorescent light . . . from Dan Flavin*, no. 19; see no. 78 (the finished work is illustrated in Govan and Bell, *Flavin: A Retrospective*, pp. 38–39, fig. 23, and the drawing listed there on p. 202).

Briony Fer   **Nocturama** Flavin's Light Diagrams

In his fluorescent light works Flavin creates an artificially lit world that brings
to mind W. G. Sebald's description of the Nocturama at Antwerp Zoo, situated
immediately next to the Centraal Station, at the beginning of his novel *Austerlitz*. A nocturama is not an altogether dark place—at least not once you have
acclimatized to its uncanny light. After your eyes become used to "the
artificial dusk" it is possible to see the nocturnal creatures going about their
sombrous lives. Sebald's narrator remembers the creatures' strikingly large
eyes, which remind him of the inquiring gaze of certain writers and thinkers
who seek to penetrate the darkness "purely by means of looking and thinking"
He wonders whether the electric light is turned off once the zoo closes and
real night sets in—so that, as he puts it, "as day dawned over their topsy turvy
universe they could fall asleep with some degree of reassurance."[1] By suspending the normal experience of night and day, a nocturama skews and distorts
our temporal markers. And while Flavin's "situations" (as Flavin preferred to
call his installations) are anything but dark, they also have the effect of skew-
ing our sense of time. Do the lights get turned off, we might wonder.

Sebald began by plunging his narrator into a twilight world. It is, fittingly,
the opening sequence of a novel in which the narrator travels through various

European cities, where every sojourn is temporary, a pause between journeys elsewhere. The nocturama is merely the first of a series of temporal and spatial disorientations and adjustments. It is a place of limbo within the city rather than outside of it. Although as a natural world it might seem exempt from the city, it is the city's most intimate core. Sebald's narrator confuses it in his memory with the station waiting room, or salle des perdus, that he goes to on leaving the zoo, with its mirrors and reflected lights and emptiness— as if in this confusion are distilled all the daily routines and habits of a technologized subject in an artificially lit world.

It may seem perverse to begin an essay that is first and foremost about Flavin's drawing and diagramming with an evocation of the spectacular *affect* of the situations and their capacity to disorientate us. But it seems important to lay the stress there at the outset, to emphasize how far the experience of the situations departs from the experience of the drawings—which seem slight and deliberately inconsequential by comparison. To some, the drawings might seem like the "thinking" bit as opposed to the "looking" involved in the experience of the lights, but that would be a false distinction. Yes, many are working drawings, often done in ballpoint in a notebook and including shorthand notations with brief directions. But there is more to be said about the space between the apparently inconsequential jottings and the resulting installations, which can be dazzlingly bright and at times vertiginous in their effects. If we use the term "working" or even "technical" drawing, or if we call these drawings matter-of-fact or factual, then we need to take into account the *fact* of their unpredictability. The kind of thinking *and* looking that goes on in drawing is not reducible to that of the engineer or the mathematician— although drawing and diagramming may historically have been part of the rhetoric of both. The temporal disordering of vision shall concern me as much in the discussion of Flavin's drawings as of his situations.

The phenomenological experience of a room of fluorescent light is not to look *at* it but to be *in* it. The fluorescents may be ready-made objects, but they cease to be discrete objects as soon as they are arranged in a situation. They cast light and shadow all around, onto the walls and onto the spectators who are there. They can cast over the body of the viewer an uncanny glow of color, or they can drain the flesh of color. If you look at people looking at Flavin's lights, they mostly seem to be washed out and in something like the dreamworld that Elaine de Kooning attributed to the effect of color cast from a Rothko painting onto the viewers in front of it; they "assume a dream-like clarity and glow . . . as though the painting emptied the space before it." Flavin was not the first to make this space count, and most directly we could relate his effects to those of Barnett Newman. Mel Bochner had noted how Newman's *Vir Heroicus Sublimis* shed a red glow over the bodies of the spectators who were looking at it.[2] What Flavin did was to dramatize that space as empty of objects but full of colored light. And rather than the ideal clarity that de Kooning imagined, Flavin drains bodies of substance in the dreamworld of a technologized subject.

This may seem a long way from the organic world of a nocturama, but of course the nocturama is entirely artificial: a miniaturized world of diverse habitats available only through the manipulation of light. As I have said, these uncanny effects hardly seem compatible with the idea of a diagram or technical drawing understood as the apparently neutral vehicle for a set of instructions. But it's worth remembering that the diagrammatic mode had been deployed by Marcel Duchamp and Francis Picabia as the mechanism of the erotic and the bodily; and that it is not only scientists or mathematicians who make diagrams but Doctors Freud and Lacan, too, who liked to make diagrams of the unconscious. Here I want to try to extend the idea of diagramming from Flavin's drawing to his approach to art making in general—to see the situations from the point of view of his drawing.

Flavin's drawings were a means to an end. He said they were "instruments" not "resultants"—that is, they were not ends in themselves. They certainly did not substitute for the works. In one sense the idea of a purely technical drawing seems to fit with the idea of using ready-made, standard-length fluorescent tubes. The artist does not make or even assemble the work; this is done by a technician to the artist's instructions. So far so good. This sounds like minimalism, like Donald Judd sending off specifications to Bernstein Brothers. But despite Flavin's admiration for and friendship with Judd throughout most of his career, it also differs pretty markedly. For one thing, as Judd himself acknowledged, Flavin was more interested than he was in making phenomena rather than objects. Flavin's spectacular light situations transform whole rooms. For another, Flavin loved drawing, and drew throughout his career, while Judd, though he produced working drawings for use, was also "antagonistic to drawing," as his former fabricator Peter Ballantyne has put it. Flavin had a far more positive sense of drawing. In his last interview with Tiffany Bell he confessed, "I really do like little and least art. It has nothing to do with 'minimal' at all. That's at the bottom of the garbage can. That's why I've liked drawing."[3]

"Little and least art": this is hardly the most likely way to describe Flavin's increasingly spectacular installations. He may have used the same ready-made standard-color standard-length fluorescent tubes bought from a hardware store throughout his career, but the effects were anything but standard. His lights started out transforming small rooms of domestic scale in the Green and Kornblee galleries, but by the beginning of the seventies he was transforming entire architectural spaces of monumental proportions like the Guggenheim. The posthumous installation of his sixteen corridors in eight old artillery huts at Marfa is a complex, cumulative experience of dazzling optical effects. However ambitious the projects became, they existed first for Flavin as drawings and diagrams—as if the epic experience were never quite cut loose from the little and least of drawing.

Of course, it would be wrong to cast all Flavin's situations as dazzling spectacle. He knew well that a room of green fluorescents produced a different effect from a room full of white ones, which could be understated and cool. Just as Mondrian had excluded green, Flavin used it as the color that heightened the pitch of his installations. Green is the least "natural," least relaxing color in fluorescent light: it dramatically assaults the eye like an artificial irritant. Ranging between these extremes seems to interest Flavin. Or, rather, as Bell has pointed out, Flavin seems to have discovered that this was what interested him when he saw his fluorescents first grouped together in his early shows.[4] This is something he had to see in situ, which could not be predicted either in drawings and plans or in the individual pieces. The little and least of drawing is rather like the little and least of the plain fluorescent light, which is just a light against which to set the uncontrollable, unexpected, unpredictable effects of the lights in an ensemble and in a particular situation.

Flavin's interest in drawing is the beginning of his interest in art and in being an artist. And although his early drawings seem like the antithesis of his later working drawings, they show his first investigations into how to control the medium, while seeming to seek out the random effect. The drawings from the late 1950s are expressive and gestural. His series of ink washes of 1959 entitled *untitled (tenements in the rain)* (fig. 1) are made of large, paint-filled strokes of extreme liquidity. At this time, Flavin was interested in Franz Kline's work; he later owned one of Kline's calligraphic watercolors painted over newsprint. There is a book dedicated to van Gogh that combines words ("half my reason foundered in it") with van Gogh's palette of turquoise, yellow, and orange in ample, gestural pools of color.[5] It was made out of a Japanese foldout book which opened up to create an almost serial effect.[6] It is of course dangerous to project too much on the early works. These are not serial in the more fundamental sense that his later work would become. But they do show, I think, that what Flavin took from abstract expressionism was the idea that gesture is not so much opposed to repetition as grounded in it. There is a series of drawings from 1960 of a thunderstorm as seen from the Gansevoort Pier (fig. 2). They capture the most ephemeral effects of a thunderstorm in the most ephemeral medium: a tiny sketch on paper. And another. And another. The repetition is not so much ordering the fugitive experience as registering it in the only way possible.

Flavin always drew, throughout his career. And he drew in not one but

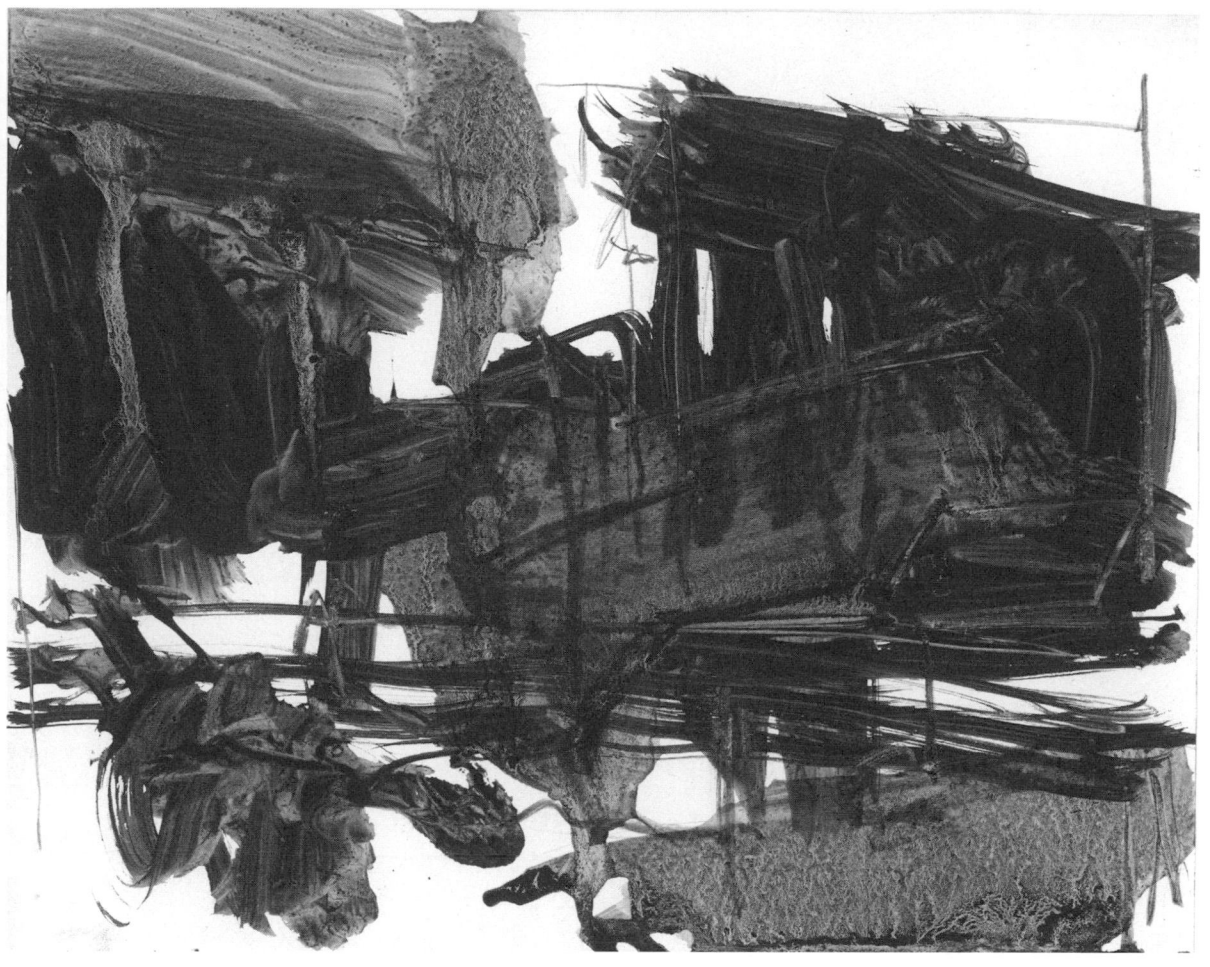

Fig. 1. Dan Flavin, *untitled (tenements in the rain)*, 1959, carbon ink and charcoal on paper, 10^{15}/$_{16}$ × 13^{7}/$_{8}$ in. (27.9 × 35.3 cm). Collection Stephen Flavin.

several different idioms, both figurative and abstract, gestural and mechanical. This was not motivated by stylistic concerns; it had more to do with what I want to call the temporal modes of drawing. There is a quick time of drawing—the speedy execution of an ink sketch, like his early gestural drawing or his portrait sketches—and a slow time of drawing, the continuous, daily habit that is drawing for many artists, not all artists, but certainly Flavin. Quick-slow: this is an important dynamic in Flavin's work and suggests that an interest in temporality is not confined to the situations but stems from his own habit of drawing. In his autobiographical sketch ". . . in daylight and cool white," he recalled these early drawings, dismissing some of them as "ejacula-

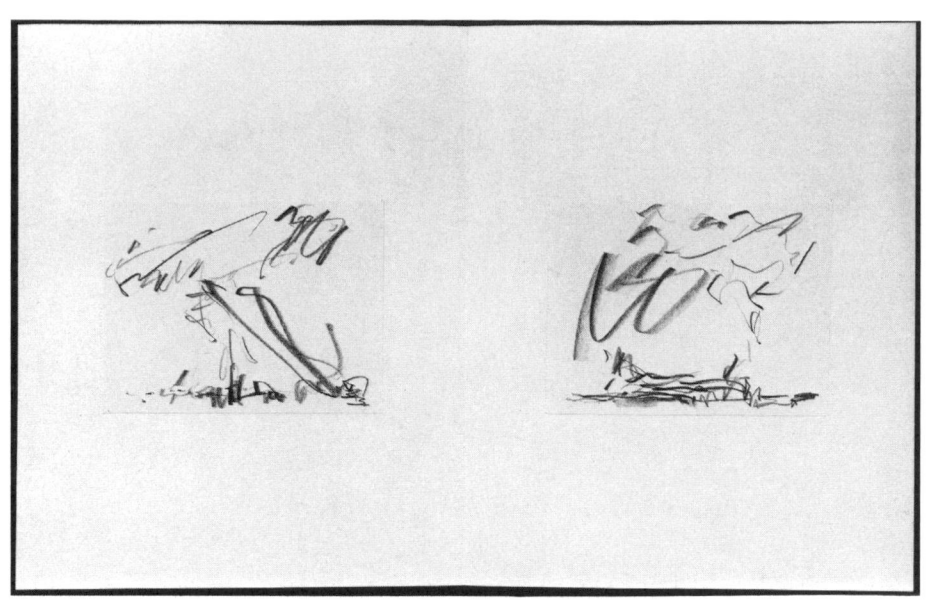

Fig. 2. Dan Flavin, *untitled*, 1960, pencil on paper, 3¾ × 5 in. (9.5 × 12.7 cm). Collection Stephen Flavin.

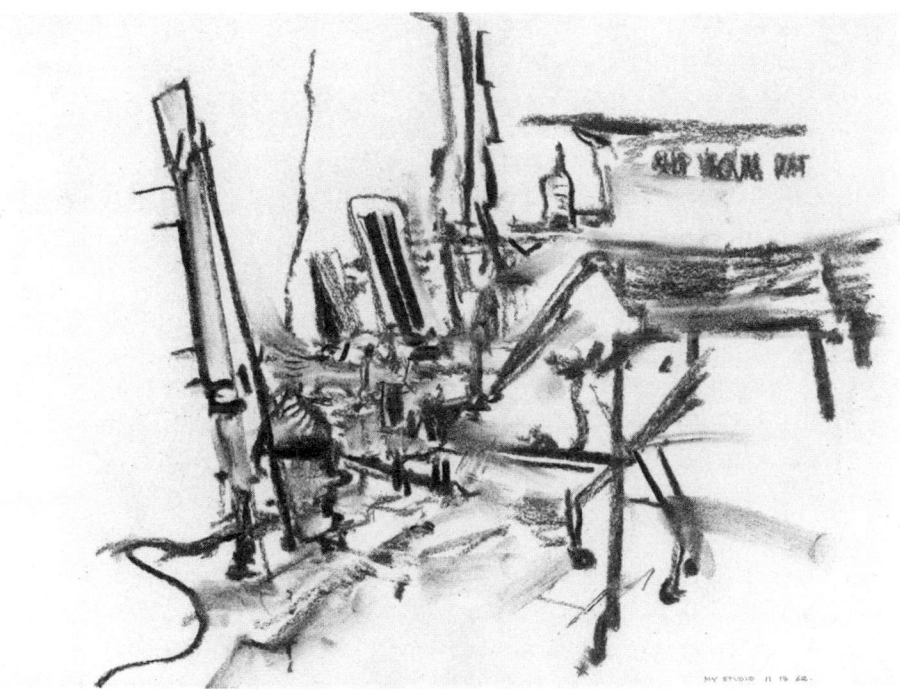

Fig. 3. Dan Flavin, *my studio*, 1962, charcoal on paper, 8¾ × 11¹³⁄₁₆ in. (22.2 × 30 cm). Collection Stephen Flavin.

tions" of watercolor and ink, condemning the "funereal black ink." "By 1961," he went on, "I was tired of my three-year-old romance with art mainly as tragic practice." Looking back with hindsight—from December 1964, when he first presented these thoughts as a lecture—he felt that it all seemed rather directionless: "I celebrated just about anything: crude Cézanne's self-portrait mask ennobled in a whirl of charcoal; drab tenements on the waterfront." In retrospect, finding a crushed olive oil can in the gutter and attaching it to a textured golden box in his *mira mira* (1960) seemed part of the same aesthetic of sentimental attachment to the city—and certainly many artists were engaged at the time in scouring the city for its debris in this way. Of his cluttered studio he wrote, "Most materials deposited there were found during wanderings near piers."[7] We might imagine Flavin drawing a storm off the Gansevoort Pier in the meatpacking district and on the same day picking up old crushed cans off the street for his assemblages. Although for Flavin the link between the drawings and the assemblages seemed part of an aesthetic he had to overcome in some way, I think that what is interesting about these early drawings concerned with ephemeral and fugitive effects of weather is how formative they were: as though from that moment drawing came to stand as a model of the ephemeral and the random and the temporary.

Despite the dismissive tone, Flavin certainly did not give up making drawings of his surroundings after this. In 1961 he moved to a new studio in Williamsburg, Brooklyn, and he went on to make a number of charcoal sketches of it. They coincide with his icon series—and they also shed light on the development the icons represented for him. Figure 3 is a quick, expressive sketch of Flavin's studio done in charcoal. It records the clutter of the studio, including two of the icons that the artist was working on at the time. That this is a figurative sketch of a monochrome object puts paid to many of the assumptions that see abstraction and figuration as mutually exclusive. That Flavin would not care much for the distinction is borne out in his diagrammatic and technical drawings of his lights. A charcoal sketch may look more like the kind of drawing that belongs in the studio than a technical drawing. It may look like the kind of drawing that Flavin would have to give up in favor of the ready-made objects that are his fluorescent tubes. But that does not seem to have been the case. There is a very similar drawing, dated 1964, entitled *the mechanical interior,* which shows him continuing to draw like this after he had begun his project with fluorescents. The title, neatly written in pencil, adds a twist. *This* is mechanical, a term he never uses for his diagrams.

It is significant that Flavin gave up the studio in favor of an office. There is a photograph from 1966 of Flavin in his office with his son Stephen on his lap (fig. 4), the table scattered with annotated plans but also with reproductions of a Mondrian and a Cézanne drawing, a self-portrait, propped against the wall (the same "crude" Cézanne that had hung over his "tragic practice": he had not given it up). The move from studio to office did not mean that he gave up thinking about Mondrian. An office is all you need for drawing and dia-gramming. Other minimalists abandoned the studio in the sense that they stopped making work there and had it made by fabricators instead. Flavin was not alone in using ready-made materials, although his small, cluttered office was different from the large loft spaces that others worked in. Flavin's move marked a radical shift away from a studio-based practice, but in a way we could also say that drawing had also always had an ambivalent relation to the studio, both of it and not of it. There was always an aspect of drawing that was outside the studio and portable: the sketchbook. Flavin's sketchbook became a notebook. He gave up the handmade papers he had used when he began draw-ing for a small, loose-leaf, ring-bound notebook. Not an artist's sketchbook, but an ordinary notebook in which he drew and made notes. Drawing went

Fig. 4. Dan Flavin with his son Stephen Flavin in his office, Cold Spring, 1966. Photo courtesy of Stephen Flavin.

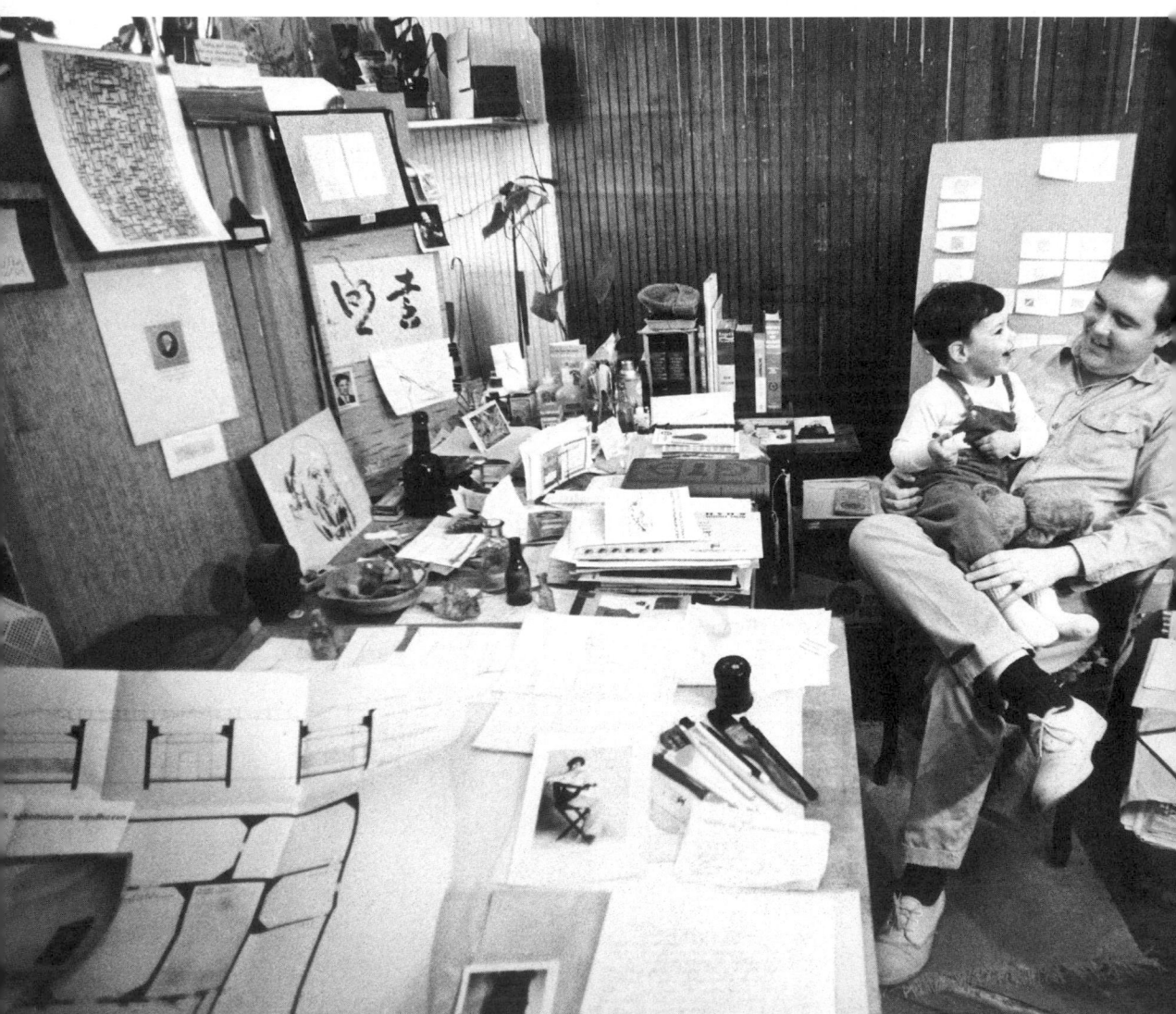

hand in hand, then, with his move out of the imaginative space of the studio. Its impermanence, and the ephemeral world of paper that it involved, could come to seem not so different from—even quite like—the impermanent and temporary installations that he made in light.

By October 1962, when Flavin wrote an "inventory of work," he was "in progress" on *icon IV* and *icon V* and had various ideas for future projects, including a series of doors dedicated to the Italian film director Michelangelo Antonioni, whose *La notte* Flavin had recently seen. He made a number of drawings of the doors, through which the viewer would enter into a darkened space, but these were never made. The connection between the icons and the doors seems to have been clear to Flavin—as if to work with night and day, light and dark, was the way forward from his *icons*. There is a dynamic of lighting up and dimming or darkening in both. In the *icons*, just as the lights around the edge seek attention, none more so than the one with the bulb flashing on and off, so the monochrome surfaces, though colored, tend as readily to blank out that mode of address and block off access. In the doors, a viewer was invited to enter—just as a viewer was invited into a lit or a darkened space, both of which would have amounted to an invitation to a dead end. Rather than light up the color of the monochrome panels as we might expect, the competition of the lights tends to deaden the color.

It was during 1962, when he was working on the *icons*, that Flavin developed a mechanical method of drawing in addition to his more gestural technique. The charcoal sketches of the studio with the icons coexist at this point with the sheet of "iconostases"—the simple pencil drawings demonstrating the different permutations in the series as well as the different possible arrangements of the icons, showing that the order of the icons was entirely variable (fig. 5). A fairly sudden and sharp divergence in various kinds of drawing he produced seems to be symptomatic of the radical shift Flavin's work undergoes at this time. The variety proliferates just at the point where he narrows his focus to concentrate exclusively on fluorescent light. The working drawings trace that shift to ready-made lights, but they also function as a kind of inventory or archive. Flavin had made drawings of his earlier assemblages, rough little drawings, as if to jog his memory. With the icons, making drawings had become more systematic, with a more careful exposition and meticulous attention to the titles and dates of each. It is as though making and saving and ordering these drawings was another way for Flavin to figure out what he was doing at what in retrospect was an important turning point for him. Flavin was already taking a great deal of care to keep records of his work, as he would throughout his life. His schemes and projects were inventoried before they were even made.

I doubt Flavin made such hard distinctions between the different kinds of

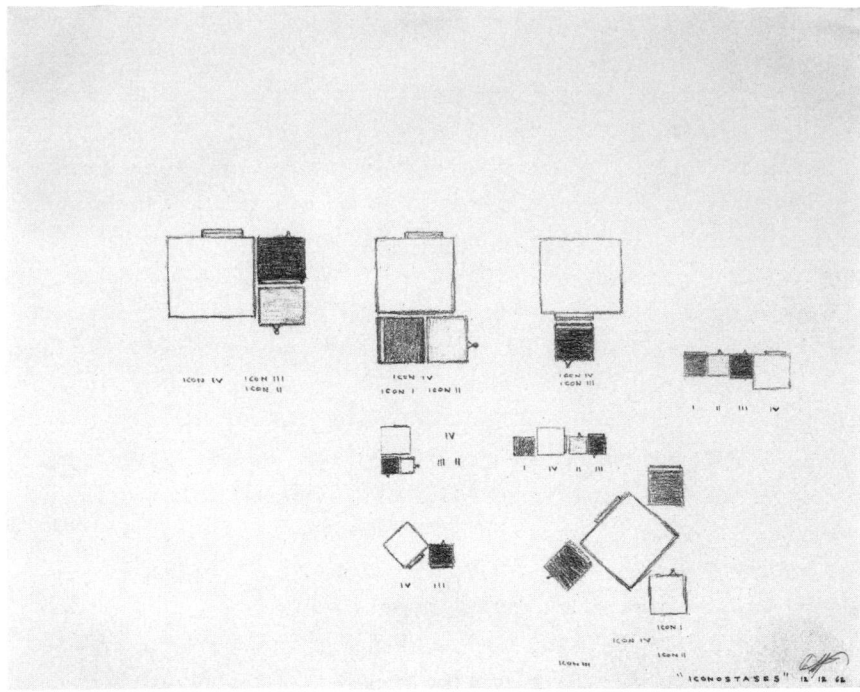

Fig. 5. Dan Flavin, *iconostases (for icons I, II, III and IV)*, 1962, pencil on paper, 11 × 13¹⁵⁄₁₆ in. (27.9 × 35.4 cm). Collection Stephen Flavin.

drawings he made—they were just drawings: the gestural sketch, the simple section, the deadpan technical drawing, a rough projection. All except the sketches of friends or sailboats were working drawings in one way or another. But even then, as an avid collector of drawings, especially the nineteenth-century work of the Hudson River School, he liked those that were like "working drawings," in which the colors were scribbled on the sheet and the painter's thinking and looking showed through in such annotations. And as a collector of drawings as well as of paintings and decorative arts and crafts, Flavin was disposed to archiving as well as accumulating a highly eclectic group of work. When Flavin writes his own notes on his drawings, his writing, in a wiry staccato hand, serves this double purpose—as both graphic trace and archival document.[8]

The differences between the types of drawing are not insignificant; rather, the ones that initially appear most important may not be the ones that count in the end. There is a knot that needs unraveling here, and it involves the move from the *icons* of 1962 to the first fluorescent of May 1963. The *icons* take a different direction from the representation of modernity through the ephemeral effects and debris of the city. Flavin himself compared them to

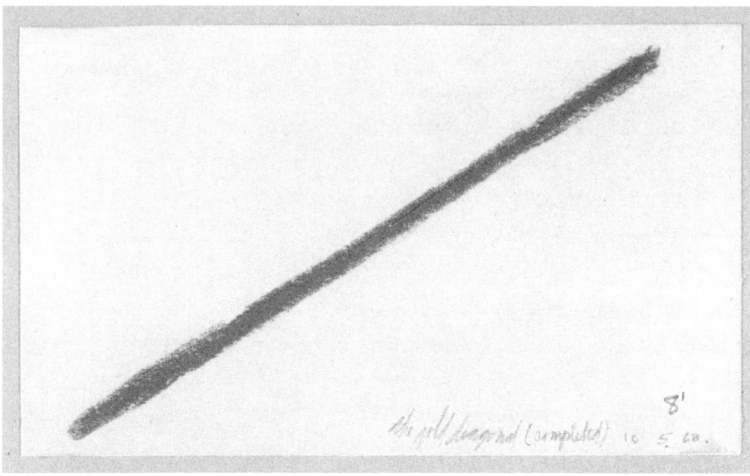

Fig. 6. Dan Flavin, *the gold diagonal (completed)*, 1963, grease pencil on paper mounted on cardboard, 3 × 5 in. (7.6 × 12.7 cm). Collection Stephen Flavin.

Russian icons of the Novgorod school that had struck him at an exhibition at the Metropolitan Museum in New York in 1962. The brooding gold ground or scintillating silver encasement of the icon seemed to offer Flavin a way of thinking beyond *mira mira* to something closer to the intense, even hallucinatory, aura of an icon painting. Flavin wanted to keep the aura without the mystical dimension or spiritual meaning. The gold and silver literally blank out the possibility of a contemplative gaze and displace attention onto the heightened intensity of the lights.

I don't think it is accidental that Flavin's first fluorescent light tube, which was attached diagonally to the wall, was gold. It was a standard yellow light, but Flavin called it "the gold diagonal," which linked it to the brooding gold ground of the icon. This is a long way from the "busily textured golden box," as he described the ground of *mira mira*.[9] Part of the charge of Flavin's simple arrangements of fluorescent lights is the combination of the literal light fixture attached to the wall with the intense phenomenological experience of colored light, which seems excessive by comparison. The simple pencil drawings he did of *the diagonal of personal ecstasy* make this same leap between a deadpan manner of drawing and "ecstatic" affect. The last in a series of drawings that Flavin put together in a single frame is a simple yellow line, captioned "the gold diagonal (completed)" and dated October 5, 1963, after the original light that he made on May 25 (fig. 6). To call these technical drawings makes them sound more complicated than they are. They are not even particularly precise: the rulered lines are drawn over in softer, shorter pencil strokes. But they deliberately adopt the tone of technical drawings, a deliberate muteness, an air of indifference.

Although Flavin was clear about the look he wanted for his situations he did not fix up the lights himself. His first electrician was his wife, Sonja, who seems to have been an important collaborator throughout their marriage. But although Flavin delegated the light installations to others, first Sonja and then to a series of technicians, he was intensely physically involved in making his drawings. If the lights eschewed the handmade, his drawings brought the hand back. Or perhaps it is more accurate to say that the hand never went away but came to be redefined in a new configuration of what the role of the artist could and should be. There were precedents for this, not least Duchamp's extensive notes and drawings, which had been published as facsimiles in the various editions of the Green and White Boxes. There were also the plans and projects of the Russian constructivists, which mattered to Flavin more directly. Camilla Gray's *The Great Experiment: Russian Art, 1863–1922*, which Flavin owned, was published in 1962, and Flavin was drawn more to the Russians than he was to Duchamp. He later owned a Kasimir Malevich drawing, though it was Vladimir Tatlin who seemed most to capture his imagination, demonstrated in the series of lights that Flavin dedicated to him. And it was Gray who described the extent to which Tatlin himself had started out in thrall to the schematic formal devices of icon painting.[10] She showed how Tatlin's corner reliefs had hung across corners as icons traditionally had. Fittingly, and in a way that must have appealed to Flavin, the materialist relief and the religious icon were not so much at opposite ends of the artistic spectrum as might be imagined.

Part of the radical project of the Russian avant-garde was the importance given to drawing as a vehicle for thinking into the future. For constructivists like Tatlin and Alexander Rodchenko, technical drawings and diagrams became a vital mode of making art that was both experimental and in many cases impractical, given the constraints of postrevolutionary Russia. Drawings on graph paper were "laboratory research," as they termed it. Rodchenko's line was a basic component in a new system, a new revolutionary visual culture that would ultimately transform consciousness. This is a huge claim for a line drawn in pencil diagonally across a small piece of graph paper—but in a way that is the point. This was a line that unlocked a whole graphic system that would infiltrate mass culture from candy wrappers to posters to city planning.

Flavin described *"monument" 7 for V. Tatlin* as a memorial to a revolutionary who dreamed of art as science. What becomes clear is that it is not the science claim that draws him but the capacity to dream. *"monument" 7* stands, he wrote, " a vibrantly aspiring order, in lieu of his last glider, which never left the ground." Flavin saw himself as trying to build on the constructivist precedent, what we now call the historic avant-garde. His work, he continued, "tries to build from that 'incomplete' experience as I see it."[11] This is Flavin identifying with Tatlin the visionary materialist (or is it a materialist visionary?). It is a startling way of thinking about both Tatlin's project and his own and reveals a twin impulse within his work. That a scrap of paper, a line on a page, could unlock a huge utopian vision, that temporary exhibitions of models built in a fairly provisional manner could radicalize the art of the century —that was the avant-garde legacy to lay claim to, and it seems more vivid to him than the more distant respect in which he held Duchamp.

Of course, what did not interest him was the scientific aspect, just as he was not interested in the spiritual significance of the icons. Rather, the opposition between a brooding gold ground and a technical drawing of a glider becomes harder to maintain. Both are schematic in the end. Both are reasonably small and artisanal but templates of something bigger than themselves. Rather than a way of returning the avant-garde to "tradition," for Flavin this presented a potent mixture. It answered to his own interest in the literal, material thing and the intense, almost hallucinatory set of effects that could be had from it. The first part of the equation fitted with Judd's idea of a specific object—the second did not. Flavin's sense of the hybridity of Russian art left little use for a conventional opposition of irrational color versus a rational line. In the same way, it is hard to hold in place a distinction between the icon as all aura (no object) and the technical drawing as all object (no aura).

The word *diagram* entered Flavin's vocabulary with his fluorescents— mainly, to start with, I think, as a way of saying what the drawings were not. They were not preparatory "sketches" in the art sense. Rather, they were like a paper pattern or template that could be used more than once. Yet they were not "designs" either—although he sometimes called them proposals or plans. Perhaps he preferred the word *diagram* because it did not have the connotations of preparatory work but implied the kind of working drawing that could be reused. When he gave a talk in 1964 that later became his *Artforum* autobiographical sketch "'. . . in daylight or cool white,'" he related how "from a recent diagram, I declared 'the diagonal of personal ecstasy.'"[12] How much further could one be from the "tragic" connotations of his earlier art endeavors? *Diagram:* the word erupts on the page, plucked from the world that is not art. It jostles oddly with the other key terms in Flavin's vocabulary like *icon* and *fetish*. Rather than cast the work in a strictly utilitarian light—as the constructivists wished to do—the word *diagram* operates more like a spanner in the works. It takes on real significance for Flavin and transforms his sense of the other terms: he turns it into a verb, "drawing and diagramming," when he describes what he does.

Flavin had two exhibitions at the Kornblee Gallery during 1967. The first opened in January and consisted of all cool-white fluorescents. The second show, held in the fall, was very different: an all-green room. Flavin made two diagrams for that installation. They are done in ballpoint, and although they look quite rough they are meticulously dated, as was his custom. On the first sheet there are two drawings, "both of 8.21.67," and on the second, "8.22.67/2" (fig. 7). These were done over two days in August and show how he developed the arrangement of green fluorescents. They are working drawings. Next to the first projection there is a note which says, "progression much too easily understood." In this version, from the entrance to the gallery, the lights are placed vertically but at an angle of about 30 degrees, all slanted in the same direction. In the second version he has placed them not diagonally but hori-

Fig. 7. Dan Flavin, *second diagram for Kornblee Gallery installation 7 October–8 November 1967*, ballpoint ink on paper, 8½ × 11 in. (21.6 × 27.9 cm). Collection Stephen Flavin.

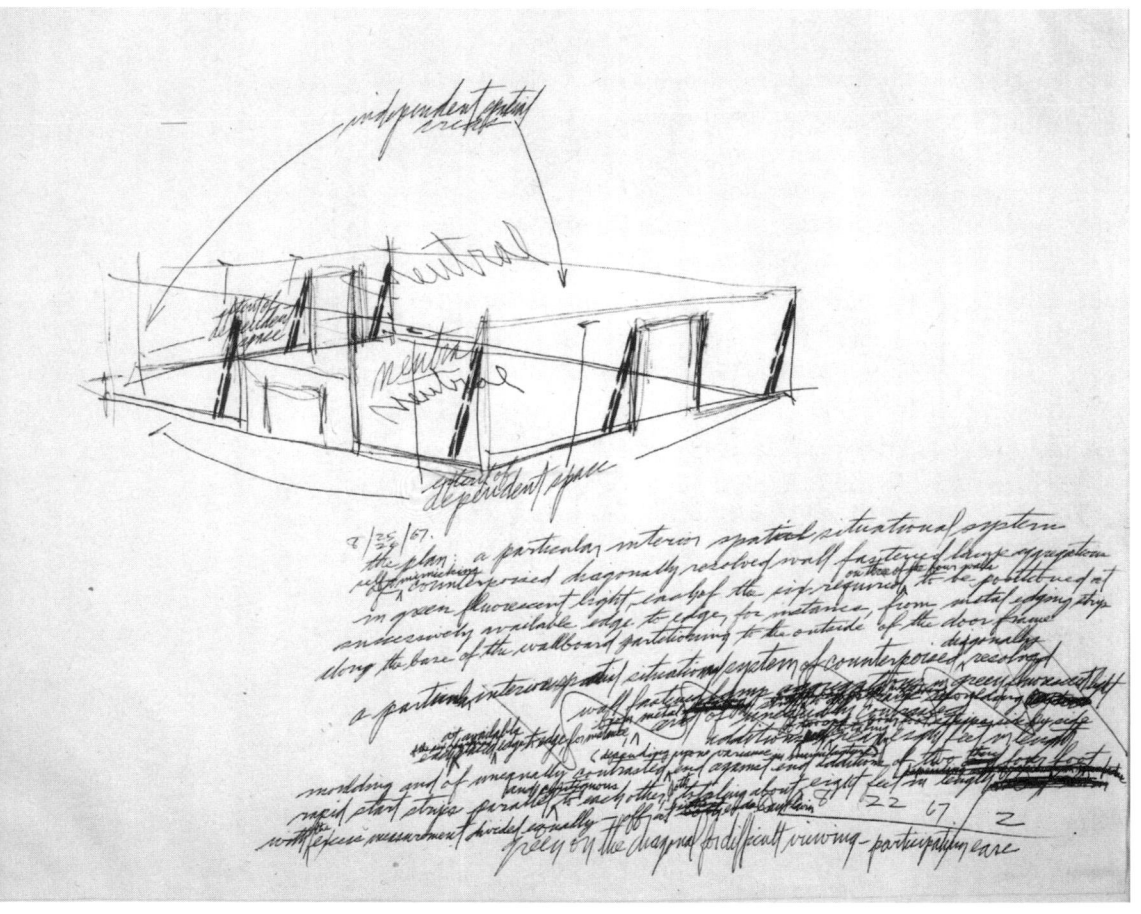

zontally along the skirting around the edge of the floor. The note suggests that this alternative would not work because the measurements were not properly estimated.

The second diagram confirmed his first idea but made the progression less straightforward, creating what he called "independent spatial areas"—that is, the areas without lights (although of course, they are filled with light). The new arrangement left one corner by the window and one whole wall empty, with two lights each on the remaining walls. This can be seen in a remarkable photograph of Flavin taken by Arnold Newman that was published in *Look Magazine*, which invited readers to simulate the effect by cutting it out and folding up the four walls to make a paper model. This was not Flavin's idea—but from my point of view, it nicely turns the installation back into paper. You can see the spread of diffuse light and the way the green lights end up looking white after a short while. The notes on the diagrams show how Flavin wanted to disrupt an even or regular progression of the lights, to switch direction, to scramble it all a little, not in a dramatic way—in the least noticeable way perhaps, but with more variable and unpredictable results. What is important is that the results were unpredictable to Flavin himself. It was he who first noted that the "participatory phenomenal effect . . . not mentioned in 'the plan,' was discovered after but a few moments in the gallery. Since the room was pervaded by green light the light providing tubes appeared to empty of almost all color. When the onlooker then turned toward daylight or another artificial source outside the greened gallery, he could see only a complementary rose color." Donald Judd made a point of this in his review of the show.[13]

The word *diagram* was used as the title of an exhibition of Flavin's and Judd's working drawings held at the Center Gallery in Washington, D.C., in January and February 1966. I think it is significant that Flavin exhibited his drawings throughout his career, not only because it says something about his view of them but also because it shows that the drawings were always a part of the staging of the lights. In the catalogues of the early shows of Flavin's work, most notably the 1969 Ottawa show, it is striking how much space was given over to the drawings. It is equally striking how little notice, on the whole, critics took of the drawings—except to deride them either as uninteresting early work or as "negligible," or "jotty" or "inept." All these terms could apply to the diagrams of the Kornblee shows, which were among those included in the Ottawa catalogue. It is as though drawing is overwhelmed by the sheer affect of the lights. By comparison, the drawings seem deliberately underwhelming—either quickly penned or simply and mechanically drawn. There is nothing precious about them and not much attention given to their presentation. But my point is that this is at least partly the point. Brydon

Smith, who curated the Ottawa show, thought that they were essential to understanding Flavin's development and his working process.[14] This is undoubtedly true, but I would go further to say that they also play a part in staging the lights: they help to dramatize the disproportion between affect and effacement that Flavin's work depends on.

Flavin commented later that it was difficult to know how to show his drawings, which he described as "these so personal memos of mine."[15] So personal, it seems, that they did not take well to public exhibition. Little loose-leaf pages did not look well framed, he noted. Many of the drawings from the loose-leaf notebooks were hung, often in groups, for the Saint Louis show in 1973 when he made that comment. "'Personal': that's a word that does not sit neatly with the word 'diagram.'" So is he talking about his sketches of friends? His seascapes? The little sketches that he continued to make? Those were included in the Saint Louis show too, but I think he was referring to the notebook drawings—after all, these are the memos he made that look so throwaway but which he kept so assiduously. What can *personal* mean in this context? *Personal* seems to be what was abandoned in minimalism, in the effacement of the artist as maker. I think that what the term means in this context has to be fairly complex—it may not be the word I would choose, but it points to an intimate relation in excess of the apparent neutrality of the style of drawing.

But neutrality was never Flavin's aim. There may be very little there; in a room of fluorescents the room may seem almost empty. There may be no single object to look at. The diffuse light might dissolve the elements of the room to nothing. The compilation of quotations that Mel Bochner selected and published in *Art and Artists* at the end of 1966—which was enlarged when it was republished in the Ottawa catalogue—includes a telling quotation from Flaubert that gets to something of Flavin's affective tone: "I feel nothing but immense and insatiable desires, an atrocious ennui and continuous yawns."[16] Translated to Flavin, this would read, "I feel nothing . . . but everything." Heightened indifference tips over into pure affect. The misanthropic, spleenish Flaubert is not a bad model for Flavin. Flaubert alternated between meticulous material description of routines and habits in his most famous novels to a less-well-known but remarkable visionary excess in novels like Salammbo and St. Antoine. Flaubert once wrote a letter in which he described the violent pleasure that he felt, wondering whether he could produce that effect in a book—that sense of inexorable reality. There is a similar kind of disproportion in Flavin between the inexorable materiality of a literal thing like a fluorescent light fixture and sheer, all-enveloping affect. Flaubert and Flavin could be seen to represent two key historical moments in the experience of the technologized subject.

"These so personal memos of mine": they record the process of becoming. And as a record, they are always carefully annotated and dated, so they also become his archive. There is a link to be made here with his writing, which Robert Smithson rightly called autobiographical.[17] Flavin's remarks in *Artforum* in 1966 were subtitled "excerpts from a spleenish journal." This was the editor Phil Leider's addition, in response to the bile they characteristically contained. But it also draws attention to their diaristic structure. Flavin writes his thoughts as one would make entries in a diary. He writes them in the form of letters or elaborate aphorisms. But like the carefully dated drawings, this structures the autobiographical in a particular way, by marking time. The date he includes on the drawings may be the date the work was drawn or the date it was conceived—drawings could be backdated by as much as twenty years. This makes them, too, seem diaristic—a kind of graphic "record of thought," as he called it.

By stressing the autobiographical dimension I do not mean to return Flavin to a retrogressive notion of the artist as creator. After all, it is precisely that idea of the artist that his work radically undermined. I don't want to bring it back through the back door of his drawings. And although Flavin, with all his notekeeping, undoubtedly had an eye to posterity, it was part of a new way of thinking and looking rather than an old one of an artist's linear development. His whole method of diagramming was designed to be applied "again and continually," to use the same material over and over. The rolodex cardfile he kept was fittingly organized on a circular rotation rather than a linear model.[18] Drawing played a strategic role in this radical redefinition of the role of the artist. A paper world seemed to go hand in hand with *both* a more bodily sense of the encounter *and* a more conceptual emphasis on dematerialization—which could empty the room of art objects entirely.

If the critics were not enamored of Flavin's drawings, then many artists were taken by the possibilities of diagramming, notably, Mel Bochner, whose 1966 exhibition *Working Drawings and Other Visible Things Not Usually Thought of as Art* has been called the first conceptual art show. Flavin's *the nominal three* was central to Bochner's elaboration of a serial method, but Flavin had also redefined the value of the working drawing. The images were always more than just working drawings for Flavin. Bochner collated xeroxes of drawings by a range of artists, including Flavin, in four identical ring-binder files shown on four pedestals. In addition he had anonymous diagrams, including a diagram of the workings of the Xerox machine used to photocopy the drawings. Bochner makes a move here that goes beyond minimalism but is also rooted in it. Bochner saw in Flavin a logic that took him in a different direction from Flavin and the other minimalists. From the process of becoming that was drawing, Bochner imagined new ways of understanding how drawing works not only as a means of destroying what had gone under the name "art object" but also as a means of generating art in a new set of relations.

The art critic Rosalind Krauss once said that the fluorescent tube acted like a graphic device because "it possesses both the figurative density of a line and the inherent ambiguity of its position in space." When asked whether he had thought of this connection to a graphic device, predictably enough Flavin hated the idea and insisted, "It is not drawing in space." Nor was it sculpture. Nor was it "painting on the wall."[19] He answered by insisting on the paradox between the uncontrollable, contingent spread of light and the look of the fixture, the literal thing that a fluorescent tube was. Well, it's not drawing in space, but that is not quite what Krauss was suggesting. While I would not want to call the tubes graphic, drawing occupies a strategic place in imagining that new set of relations. On the one hand, they are too diffuse to add up to drawing; on the other, we can see Flavin's method as diagrammatic in a way that exceeds the literal thing that a drawing is.

When the art critic Phyllis Tuchman asked Flavin, "What's the relationship of diagrams to dedications to installations?" he began his answer by saying, "The diagrams are a minimal, graphic rendering of the equipment in locale. The simplest, easiest form is laying this out on graph paper." He claimed that the dedications were sentimental and should not be fretted over: "It's the kind of trifling that makes life easier to take from time to time." In the context of what I have said so far about Flavin's sense of paradox, these claims fit together quite happily—what started out feeling like contradictions are not contradictions in Flavin's world. Even the certificates produced to authenticate works—again, schematic drawings on graph paper that accompanied the works—seem to operate in this extended sense of a network that Flavin creates. It is not just the installation itself that constitutes the system but also this wider network of dedications, notes, memos, plans, certificates, and so on.[20]

When we call Flavin's approach diagrammatic, the word has to extend, I think, to take in all these coordinates. To some extent this means reading the diagram against what a diagram is conventionally thought to be (as a purely rational and technical tool). Flavin's diagramming spreads outward to plot the coordinates of a body within an architectural space. And of course there is always at least one body at stake in Flavin's situations that will exceed a pre-given system: the viewer's body, our own, as soon as we enter the room. Fluorescent light is remarkable precisely because of the way it casts light in a diffuse way over walls and floors but also over spectators—yet it is also remarkable because it seems to drain the body of substance, of flesh. The organic world of bodies, under these conditions, becomes more or less featureless and inorganic. Although mobile (people move through these installations rather than stop still for long), bodies become colorless and fleshless in a room of green fluorescent light. In Flavin's progression of green lights at the Kornblee did he not work through various possibilities in order to scramble the givens of the architectural space? The lights set in a corner destroy the corner and flatten it. A given structure is destroyed by light, but another structure has come into being. The thunderstorm drawings do not seem so far away any more.

I would like to end by looking at one final cluster of drawings and lights from the early seventies. From about 1970 Flavin produced drawings on graph paper—not as plans for works not yet completed but after the works that had already been built and, often, sold. He did not physically make them himself. Sonja Flavin made them, just as she had early on in his career installed the lights; after the two were separated some drawings were made by his partner Helene and some by his son Stephen. One set was made after his corridor piece *untitled (to Jan and Ron Greenberg)* (fig. 8). This was one of two corridors that Flavin created between two galleries of the Saint Louis Art Museum in 1972–73. The other was *untitled (to Emily),* which consisted of four kinds of white fluorescent tube. These two corridors were the first works for which

Fig. 8. Dan Flavin, *untitled (to Jan and Ron Greenberg)*, 1972–73, yellow and green fluorescent light, 8 ft. (244 cm) high, in a corridor measuring 8 ft. (244 cm) high and 8 ft. (244 cm) wide, length variable. Dia Art Foundation.

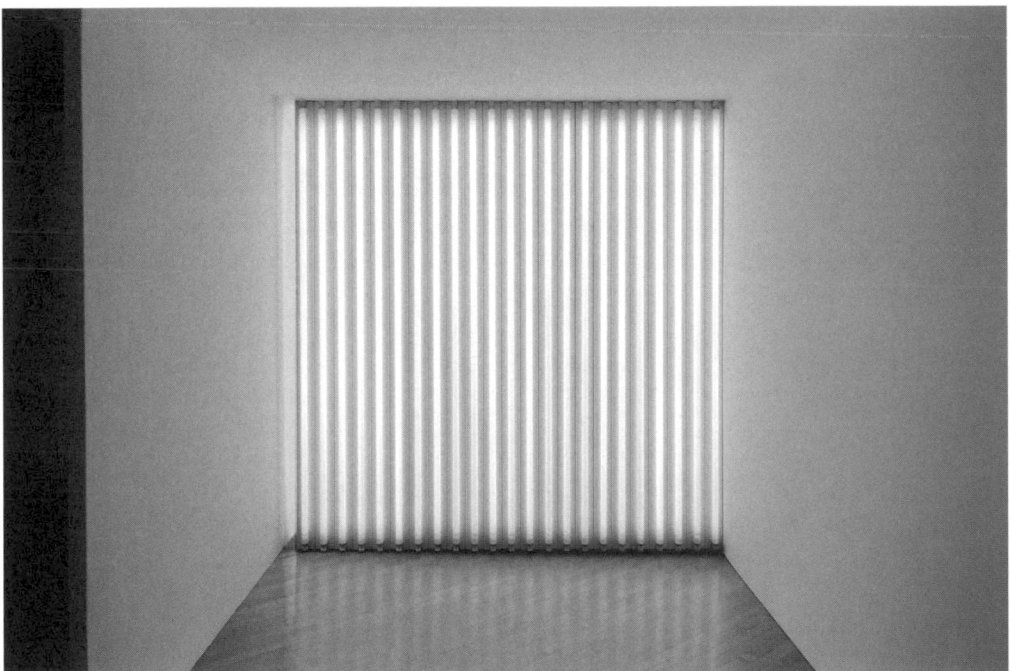

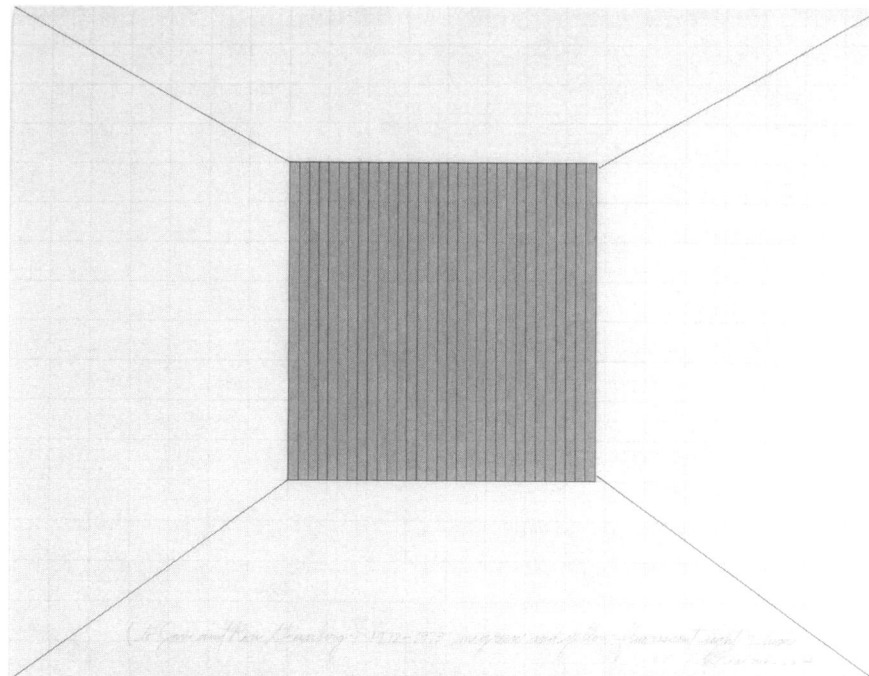

Fig. 9. Dan Flavin, *(to Jan and Ron Greenberg) 1972–1973 in green and yellow fluorescent light 8' high (green on front, yellow to the rear)*, 1974, colored pencil and ink on graph paper, 17 × 22 in. (43.2 × 55.9 cm). Collection Stephen Flavin.

Flavin had constructed an architectural space rather than simply using a given one. His diagrams show how the two works were to be placed side by side in the Saint Louis installation, and in a final diagram he has written the colors of the lights over their placement. They are much larger than his own rougher, provisional drawings, and they use the graph paper as a ready-made template to fill in the colors at the dead center of the page (fig. 9). Younger artists like Mel Bochner or Eva Hesse had been using graph paper since the mid-sixties, but Flavin, while capitalizing on its currency among conceptualists and process artists, also used it distinctively, not to say a little idiosyncratically.

The graph-paper diagrams were executed by Sonja and were created for a show at Leo Castelli's, Flavin's gallery in New York, in 1974. What Flavin made was a rough drawing for the graph-paper diagrams, listing in sequence the different color combinations (fig. 10). Strictly speaking, this is a diagram of a diagram of a situation. But in the space between diagram and situation erupts a fairly dramatic disturbance of what one might expect of such a well-lit place. This constellation brings together the various components I have discussed in this essay. When the two corridors were again shown next to each

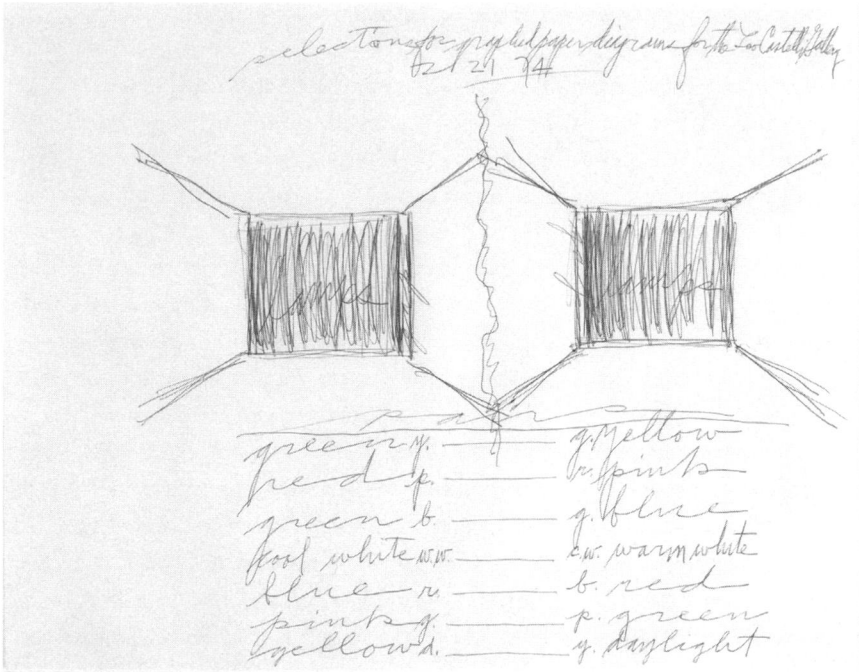

Fig. 10. Dan Flavin, *selections for graphed paper diagrams for the Leo Castelli Gallery*, 1974, ballpoint ink on paper, 8½ × 11 in. (21.6 × 27.9 cm). Collection Stephen Flavin.

other at the 2004 Washington retrospective, replicating the Saint Louis installation, the interaction between them was striking. First you saw the dazzling yellow lights of *untitled (to Jan and Ron Greenberg),* but the work was so bright that it was hard to look at. On the right side you looked through a slat of green light to the other end of the corridor. To reach it you walked through the white lights: warm white, cool white, daylight, soft white. The other side, when you came to it, was just as bright green, with a vertical strip of yellow. As you looked back at the white corridor, its walls turned a dramatic pink. Despite the ready-made elements, these effects are made entirely in experience. This is one situation made out of two. As such it demonstrates how much a mobile spectator is the connective tissue within a network of effects which spreads out not just across walls but between rooms and spaces. Flavin's fluorescents may not exist as art unless they are switched on, but neither do they exist as art without the spectator to link and plot the various coordinates. If we think of this in terms of a method that might be called diagrammatic, it marks out time as well as the spatial points of a room and destroys the usual temporal markers just as the light compresses and so destroys the length of the corridor by blocking it off in one and elongates and expands the space of the other.

The graph-paper drawings add to the network of spreading connections. They both are a product of and reflect back on the method. They document a temporary installation but as drawings they belong to a paper world that is ephemeral. Keeping paper is keeping a record of thought. They are hardly monuments to permanence (just as Flavin's monuments to Tatlin were, as he insisted all art was, temporary). In theory at least, these drawings are like the lights: always, as Dan Graham stressed, replaceable.[21] But just as Flavin's diagrammatic method was not confined to his drawing, so too a network of connectives could annihilate the distance between the understated spareness of a working drawing and the overwhelming affect of the situations.

A temporal diagram: how then do we plot its coordinates? Drawing—and the graph-paper drawings only dramatize this—involves a different model of making art, one which does not depend on the author's hand. Drawings invoke new ways of thinking and looking, and to this end necessarily depend on a history of drawing as a means to renegotiate the idea of what it is that an artist does. In that respect they invoke the moment of constructivism and the historic avant-garde's attempt to redefine what art could be for a technologized subject. Flavin's response transforms that problematic for a minimalist generation and a consumer culture. Drawing is a means of projecting, imagining, planning situations, but it is also a way of archiving those projects and plans. It is both time future and time past. The drawings take on the look of technical drawings, and certainly when they use graph paper this effect is enhanced. They deploy the light systems of a spectacular technologized culture.

But the drawings also leave a paper trail that classifies, indexes, makes notes. There is something archaic about this, just as Flavin could point to something a little archaic when he called his 1964 exhibition of fluorescents at the Green Gallery a "cavern of muted light."[22] Rather than machine-age, the drawings are artisanal in the end: a little cottage industry *chez Flavin*, reflecting his interest in and collecting of crafts. A paper world can be throwaway or it can accumulate—it can look to the future but it can also be a throwback. Of course, there is another side to this. The paperless world that technology promised never did, or has never yet, come to be—computers tend instead to proliferate more paper than ever before. It is significant in this context that toward the end of Flavin's life, some of the graph-paper drawings, made by his son Stephen, were digitalized and made on a computer as if to intensify—rather than resolve—this set of connections.

Notes

1. W. G. Sebald, *Austerlitz* (London: Hamish Hamilton, 2001), 3, 4.

2. Elaine de Kooning, "Two Americans in Action: Franz Kline and Mark Rothko," *Art News Annual* 27 (1958), cited in James Breslin, *Mark Rothko, A Biography* (Chicago: University of Chicago Press, 1993), 388; Mel Bochner, audiotape, Barnett Newman Symposium, Harvard University, 1992, cited by Richard Shiff in "Whiteout: The Not-Influence Newman Effect," in *Barnett Newman*, ed. Ann Temkin, exh. cat. (Philadelphia: Philadelphia Museum of Art, 2002).

3. In "some more information . . . (to Sabine)," in *Neue Anwendungen fluoreszieren-den Lichts mit Diagrammen, Zeichnungen und Drucken von Dan Flavin/new uses for fluorescent light with diagrams, drawings and prints from Dan Flavin* (Stuttgart: Edition Cantz,1989), 45–49. For essays dealing with aspects of Flavin's graphic output see *Dan Flavin: Drawings, Diagrams and Prints* (Fort Worth, Tex.: 1977). As Judd described their differences, "I want a particular, definite object. I think Flavin wants, at least first or primarily, a particular phenomenon," Judd, "Aspects of Flavin's Work," in Dan Flavin, *fluorescent light, etc. from Dan Flavin/ lumière fluorescente, etc. par Dan Flavin*, exh. cat. (Ottawa: National Gallery of Canada, 1969); Peter Ballantyne, conversation with the author; "Dan Flavin Interviewed by Tiffany Bell," in Michael Govan and Tiffany Bell, *Dan Flavin: A Retrospective*, exh. cat. (Washington, D.C.: National Gallery of Art, 2004), 198.

4. Tiffany Bell, "Fluorescent Light as Art," in Govan and Bell, *Flavin: A Retrospective*.

5. This is *Vincent at Auvers* (1960). Flavin made the foldout washes into a series, carefully numbering each one. One has a fingerprint in the lower right-hand corner, and parts of it look like they were drawn with his bare finger furrowed through the liquid paint; but it is also carefully numbered seventeen.

6. Flavin's interest in Kline was mentioned by his friend Michael Venezia at the symposium on the occasion of the Dan Flavin retrospective, National Gallery of Art, Washington, D.C., October 2004.

7. Dan Flavin, "'. . . in daylight or cool white.' an autobiographical sketch," *Artforum* (December 1965): 21–24, reprinted in Govan and Bell, *Flavin: A Retrospective*, 191, 190; on artists' search for debris, see my discussion of Agnes Martin in *The Infinite Line* (New Haven: Yale University Press, 2004); Flavin, "'. . . in daylight or cool white,'" 191.

8. Tiffany Bell discussed Flavin's interest in collecting drawings at the 2004 Flavin symposium. In later years Flavin used an ever greater degree of shorthand by "diagramming" the arrangement of tubes in a work: he would write out the names of the colors and stretch the words out so that they took the shape of an elongated tube. Franz Meyer discusses the role of handwriting in Flavin's drawing in his essay in *Flavin: Drawings, Diagrams and Prints*.

9. Flavin, "'. . . in daylight or cool white,'" 190.

10. Camilla Gray, *The Russian Experiment in Art, 1863–1922* (London: Thames and Hudson, 1971), 171 (a later edition of the large-format *Great Experiment*).

11. Dan Flavin, "The Artists Say," *Art Voices* 4 no.3 (summer 1965): 72, reprinted in Dan Flavin, *three installations in fluorescent light/drei Installationen in fluoreszierendem Licht* (Cologne: Kölnische-Verlagsdruckerei, 1973), 84.

12. Flavin, "'. . . in daylight or cool white,'" 191.

13. Flavin, *three installations*, 24; Judd, "Aspects of Flavin's Work," cited in Donald Judd, *Complete Writings, 1959–1975* (Halifax: Press of the Nova Scotia School of Art and Design, 1975), 200.

14. The Center Gallery exhibition was called *Diagrams: Dan Flavin/Don Judd*. For some of the criticisms of the drawings, see, for example, Peter Plagens: "Flavin's merits as a draughtsman are negligible," in Paula Feldman and Karsten Schubert, eds., *it is what it is: writings on Dan Flavin since 1964* (London: Thames and Hudson, 2004),136. Brydon Smith in *fluorescent light . . . from Dan Flavin*.

15. *drawings and diagrams from Dan Flavin, 1963–1972* (Saint Louis: Saint Louis Art Museum, 1973).

16. Mel Bochner, "Less Is Less (for Dan Flavin)," in *Art and Artists*, 24–27, republished in Bochner, *Speculations écrits, 1965–1973* (Geneva: Fondation Mamco, 2003), 86–90. A longer version was published in *fluorescent light . . . from Dan Flavin*.

17. Robert Smithson, "A Museum of Language in the Vicinity of Thought," in *Robert Smithson: The Collected Writings* (Berkeley: University of California Press, 1996), 78.

18. Flavin's words, "All my diagrams, even the oldest, seem applicable again and continually," appear in *Dan Flavin: The Architecture of Light*, exh. cat. (Berlin: Deutsche Guggenheim, 2000), 74; according to Tiffany Bell, Flavin's rolodex has been lost, but the photocopy she made in the 1980s is at the Dia Foundation.

19. Rosalind Krauss, "New York," *Artforum* (January 1969): reprinted in Feldman and Schubert, *it is what it is*, 52; "Dan Flavin Interviewed by Phyllis Tuchman" (1972), in Govan and Bell, *Flavin: A Retrospective*, 192.

20. Flavin, interview with Tuchman, 194. Flavin started making certificates in 1970. These consisted of a colored drawing on graph paper, with a description and a signature, marked, "a certificate only." Like the diagrams they were made by Sonja, Helene, or, later, Stephen Flavin. Tiffany Bell has clarified that the certificates were usually made after the works were bought and that Flavin would only agree to remake or repair a damaged work if the certificate was still in existence (which is still the case for the Flavin Studio today). For a discussion of the certificates, see Tiffany Bell, "Fluorescent Light as Art," in Govan and Bell, *Flavin: A Retrospective*, 123–24.

21. Dan Graham, "My Works for Magazine Pages: A History of Conceptual Art, 1965–1969," in *Dan Graham*, ed. Gloria Moure (Barcelona: Ediciones poligrafa, 1998), 62.

22. Flavin "'. . . in daylight or cool white.'"

Jeffrey Weiss **Blunt in Bright Repose**

Painting, noun. The art of protecting flat surfaces
from the weather and exposing them to the critic.
—Ambrose Bierce

A picture ought to be looked at the
same way you look at a radiator.
—Jasper Johns

Everything made since Duchamp has been
a readymade, even when hand-painted.
—Gerhard Richter

Flavin's art implicates ambient space in a fashion that has come to seem id-
iomatic to the art of the sixties. But Flavin's medium, fluorescent light, occupies a peculiar place at the origination of that history. The very nature of the
fluorescent lamp as fixture, prefabricated hardware straight off the stockroom
shelf, is unique among the materials of art during this period. Its identity is
also ready-made and thoroughly undisguised, something it came to share only
with Carl Andre's bricks (which the lamps, as medium, predate by several
years), although the fluorescent lamp was a relatively recent technological device, having been perfected during the late 1930s. "Phenomenal" this art of
light may be, as Donald Judd would claim in his often-quoted text for Flavin's
retrospective exhibition in Ottawa in 1969.[1] Yet the lamp does remain baldly

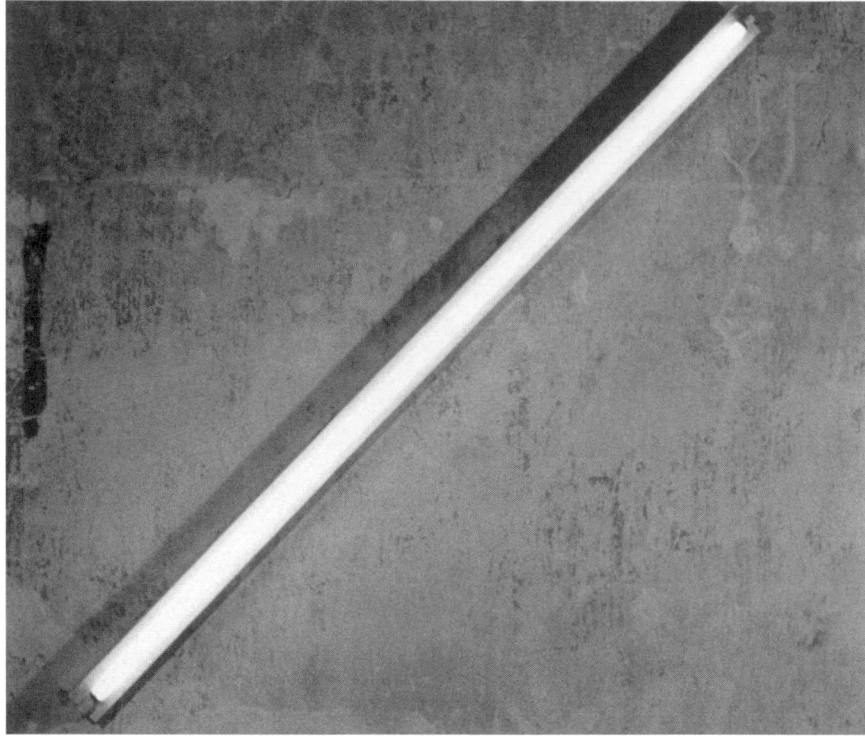

Fig. 1. Dan Flavin, *the diagonal of May 25, 1963*, 1963, yellow fluorescent light, 8 ft. (244 cm) long on the diagonal, on Flavin's studio wall. Photo courtesy of Dia Art Foundation, Ira Licht donation.

exposed, and the work therefore holds the banal object at the center of its ambient being.

That Flavin's ambition for his work was complex might be said to begin with this duality. That it was possibly ambivalent is evinced by the multiple metaphors and other references he chose to heap onto it from the start, addressing it in terms that were alternately lofty and plain: the icon and the monument, for example, are two exalted categories from the history of devotional and public art that are primary referents for Flavin, although he deploys both genres with pointed irony, the ephemerality of the fluorescent tube—its limited life expectancy was something he often spoke of—undermining the presumed commemorative, transhistorical, or sacred values such categories mean to represent. Ironic "pseudo-monuments," he later said of the *"monument" for V. Tatlin* series. Especially during the 1960s and 1970s, Flavin's work is often serial or permutational, drawn from a standardized system of component parts—the lamps—available in four lengths and ten colors, and in this respect nonreferential. Yet while there are untitled works by Flavin, more are dedicated—to people, sometimes to events or ideas—than not, and the word *untitled* was itself used by him as a kind of name, spelled out, along with the dedications, in lowercase: *untitled (to the "innovator" of Wheeling Peachblow)*.

The prime example of ambivalence fittingly occurs with Flavin's initial work solely composed of fluorescent light, the lone eight-foot yellow tube ("gold" in the parlance of commercial lighting) first directly mounted at a 45-degree angle on the artist's peeling and abraded studio wall in 1963 (fig. 1). Originally christened *the diagonal of May 25, 1963* (commemorating the epiphanic day the lamp was discovered and designated a self-sufficient work), in the space of a year it was exhibited—in "daylight" white, not gold—and renamed: lowered from the center of the wall and made to touch the floor, it was "dedicated" to Constantin Brancusi in 1964; and in Flavin's autobiographical statement of 1965, ". . . in daylight or cool white," it was further declared *the diagonal of personal ecstasy*. In the same text, the fixture as object was subverted by Flavin's own claims for its opticality; there he described the naked lamp—the *diagonal*—as "a buoyant and insistent gaseous image which, through brilliance, betrayed its physical presence into approximate invisibility."[2]

We are close again to the rhetoric of the sacred, even as Flavin's mannered language alerts us to an ironic voice, much the way the phrase "personal ecstasy" itself remains a grown-up Catholic schoolboy's profaning pun. But the pictorial is also at stake: mounted on the wall, the lamp is characterized as an "image." As low-tech object, it is understood to occupy two different states, its concrete "physical presence" (as hardware) dematerialized not only by vibratory brightness—literal luminosity, another ironic, even sarcastic, turn on the metaphorical light of painting—but by the material nature of the tube's own contents, which, Flavin reminds us, consist, in part, of gas—more precisely, a medium composed of mercury vapor and argon gas.[3] (A secondary place might also be made for sound, the low, incessant buzz that is sometimes emitted by a fixture's electrical ballasts.) Quantifying the real limits of this object is further frustrated by the act of beholding: "Regard the light and you are fascinated—practically inhibited from grasping its limits at each end." So we have come full circle back to Judd: the lamp as object was never solely Flavin's medium. Since it produces real light, it is primarily an optical instrument (when the electricity is switched off or the lamp expires, the art stops). Solid physical presence dissolves into "approximate invisibility."

Yet, "blunt in bright repose," the lamp will hold its own. Flavin would soon claim to favor "the composite term 'image-object,'" which "best describes my use of the medium." There is no personal ecstasy, after all, without the object-presence of the diagonal phallic tube, a point made less delicately clear by Bruce Nauman alone on the floor of his empty storefront studio in 1965 (fig. 2), in a representation that is surely a riff on the appearance of Flavin's diagonal in *Artforum* that year, where it illustrated ". . . in daylight or cool white." Soon the language of Flavin's work would be often additive or

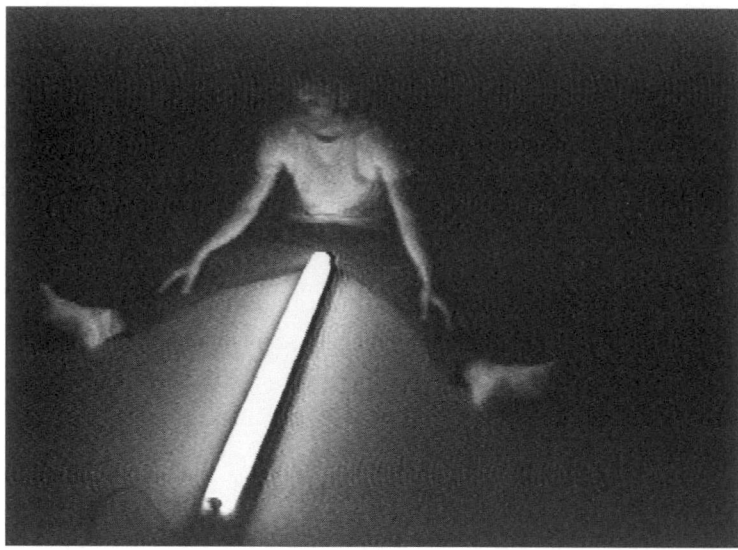

Fig. 2. Bruce Nauman, *Manipulating a Fluorescent Tube*, 1969, videotape, black and white, sound, 60 min., to be repeated continuously. Distributed by Electronic Arts Intermix, New York. Courtesy Sperone Westwater, New York.

modular by nature, something that is wholly dependent on the tube as a clearly defined compositional element. In a 1964 interview he flatly referred to his work as "an arrangement of sticks, of color sticks that are luminous, if that. The thing is more and more an object for me." After the mid-sixties, Flavin generally planned his work in relation to the perceptual effect of light on the overall space of the room and even the influence of one work on another when installed in the same space; but when he came to compose on the sheet, he generally thought in terms of the lamp as line, as the many drawings and notebook sketches for the Tatlin series attest, each "monument" the reconfiguration of an identical or nearly identical number of fixtures represented on the sheet with single straight strokes of the pencil. "The light is almost secondary in an awareness of the objects," Mel Bochner wrote in 1966. "Any attempt to posit the objects with a transcendent nature is disarmed by the immediacy of their presence."[4]

"I like everything about Dan's work except the lights." Sol LeWitt's remark to Bochner brings us closer still to the lamp as integer. Speaking of the Kornblee Gallery installation in his seminal account "Serial Art Systems" the following year, Bochner seems to shift his perception: now, "the fixtures are obliterated by their own light." Even so, photographs of Kornblee show that the fluorescent tubes are jarringly alien within the historicized interior. And with reference to *the nominal three,* Bochner credits Flavin's work with virtually introducing the use of "a basically progressional procedure"—that is, lamps deployed across the wall according to the arithmetical series [1 + (1 + 1) + (1 + 1 + 1)]. Written this way (rather than 1, 2, 3), it is not just the series, as Bochner observes, but the shape and physical disposition of the straight tubes that can be "graphically visualized." Flavin concurs: in a published letter from 1963, he said the work comprised "basic counting marks (primitive abstractions) restated long in the daylight glow of common fluorescent tubes."[5]

The ambivalence of Flavin's work is expressed by the objects and installations and narrated, so to speak, by the rhetoric of his letters and statements, which immediately found its way into the critical exchange. Most important, with its dependence on the wall (as support and as reflecting surface), Flavin's "limited light" is thoroughly grounded in his work's relation to painting. And while Flavin sometimes rejected the association with painting, he also engaged it often enough, even in the balance of artists—Henri Matisse, Piet Mondrian, Barnett Newman, Ad Reinhardt, Cy Twombly, Robert Ryman, and others—whom he named as dedicatees for his work. Only Flavin, among the community of antipainters in New York, could be dismissed—as he was by Lucy Lippard in a review of the Green Gallery show—as a sort of painter after all, one whose work (even worse) is compromised by the decorative.[6] That is, only Flavin among them was a flagrant colorist, this during the chromophobic sixties, when a certain kind of avant-gardism was ethically opposed to color, especially mixed color and pictorial light. Flavin's *a primary picture,* shown at the Green Gallery, makes a succinct point: named for painting, the work describes the rectangular shape of a canvas through an arrangement of two- and four-foot fluorescent lamps—an empty frame—mounted flush with the edge of the wall; the vacant center receives reflected light, but so does the wall beyond the frame.

While we want to address Flavin's work in electric light as a complete oeuvre, there are two parts: an early and a late career, with virtually no middle. As the work becomes expansive in its physical reach, colonizing increasingly larger interior spaces and occasionally even leaving the wall for the center of the room—something that Flavin claimed brought "the lamp as image back in balance with the lamp as object"—its pictorialism also mounts (albeit in terms which are now technological).[7] Specifically, the immaterial light openly engages the history of painting as a metaphorical practice, the representation of light-filled space in nature. This aspect of the work was developed shortly after Flavin recognized the space-filling, "situational" properties of real luminosity, and it lasted for close to three decades, until his death. Yet three years of early and breakthrough work represented by the contents of the Kaymar and Green Gallery exhibitions and the studio installation of the gold *diagonal* specifically address very different terms, terms pertaining to the material fate of paint itself (noun as well as verb)—to paint as hardware—as a condition for the optical pictorialism of light and space per se. The operative conceptual device is the readymade.

It is commonplace to invoke the Duchampian readymade in accounting for Flavin's fluorescent lamp, but doing so usually serves the hardware half of an oppositional dyad: lamp versus light/color. Lippard herself illustrates this in the Green Gallery review: "By the act of arranging the 'readymade' fluorescent tubes in their shiny white metal fixtures on the walls in simple groups or forms, Flavin makes them into reliefs or 'paintings in light,' leaving behind the found object esthetic, and accepting the responsibility of creating fine art. But having made this decision, he has not yet succeeded in coming to terms with or adequately exploring the nature of fluorescent light and color."[8] Notwithstanding her careless elision of the readymade and the found object, two distinct categories, Lippard's judgment is useful in its quasi-moralizing way—that phrase, "fine art"—and the line she draws is clear; it is the "coming to terms" with light and color that will permanently occupy Flavin after the Green Gallery show. But the judgment is also conventional in its dualism, just as Judd's argument is—in its identification of painting with light or "illusionistic space" as *distinct* from the object per se. We are distracted from a separate identity for the radiating lamp in its relation to the medium of paint, a separate fulfillment: the lamp's proximity to the industrial life of paint within a system of standardization, prefabrication, and choice, a system in which, further, the metaphorical role of color in painting is replaced by a concrete autonomy for color that belongs as much to the realm of language and inventory as it does to the precincts of the brush.

"There's still magic in the idea," Marcel Duchamp demurred in an interview with Katherine Kuh, when asked to demystify the significance of the readymade. "But there are small explanations and even certain general traits we can discuss. Let's say you use a tube of paint: you didn't make it. You bought it and used it as a ready-made. Even if you mix two vermilions together, it's still a mixing of two ready-mades." Not the paint tube as personalized found object, which is what it was when Robert Rauschenberg affixed a crusty, squeezed, and depleted tube of oil paint onto a small red combine in 1954,[9] but the readymade: fresh from the stockroom or the window display and filled with color, an estranged, prefabricated, "utilitarian" object, wayward and reoriented, unimprinted by personalized use or personal desire. Not finding, but selecting. The point for Duchamp is not that painting had now become a function of the principle of the readymade but that it had long been such a thing. Yet these remarks were published in 1962, just months before the epiphany of the gold *diagonal* emerged from within the "blank magic" of the icons and liberated the standardized eight-foot lamp—the tube of color-light, the "tube" of "pigment."

More, as Thierry de Duve has discussed, Duchamp repeated the premise of the paint tube as readymade in multiple interviews and statements between 1961 and 1963, including his remarks at a symposium on the occasion of the *Art of Assemblage* exhibition at The Museum of Modern Art in 1961. Doesn't the prefabricated standardization of fluorescent color pointedly correspond to this principle? And Flavin's isolation of the yellow lamp, mounted on the wall in a manner that reifies its functionality while defeating its function—like a bicycle wheel on a stool? "A common eight-foot strip with fluorescent light," Flavin wrote of the *diagonal,* "of any commercially available color" (the choice of yellow is, in this observation, implicitly quasi-arbitrary, the larger point being that any selection will be limited by the prefabricated inventory of available options). Recall Duchamp: "You *bought* it and used it as a ready-made" (emphasis mine); and elsewhere, in 1963: "A tube of paint that an artist uses is not made by the artist; it is made by the manufacturer that makes paints. So the painter really is making a readymade when he paints with a manufactured object that is called paints."[10]

De Duve's argument, which is relevant to the ideological and aesthetic functioning of Flavin's work, concerns the readymade as a manifestation of "pictorial nominalism" (the phrase comes from Duchamp's own notes in 1914): Duchamp's readymades, which directly follow his own abandonment of painting proper, specifically, if paradoxically, reference the emerging condition of modernist painting—especially with the rise of abstraction—as itself a series of abandonments of the "degraded" conventions of painting as craft. This culminated in the work of Kasimir Malevich and Piet Mondrian, among others, around that time. But handicraft was, in de Duve's reading, "already dead," in fact "assassinated," not by painters but by the complex historical conditions of industrialization. The readymade can, in this way, further be said to belong to painting—to invoke the name of painting—in that it internalizes the cause of the death of painting by "being an industrial object"; conversely, this cause is identified by Malevich through his introduction of a "mechanical, clumsy technique," such that his work remains painting even as it repudiates old notions of "grand painting" and artisanal practice. As de Duve argues, this notion of a "mechanization" of painting pertains, as well, to the role of color in abstraction, specifically the work of Vassily Kandinsky in Munich (where Duchamp spent time in 1912) and—in Duchamp's Parisian milieu—Franticek Kupka and Robert Delaunay. The industrial manufacture of pigment packaged in portable tubes had permitted (through convenience) the pursuit of plein-air painting, culminating in impressionism, for which the act of painting is organized as "a series of choices within a standardized logic of colors." This rationalization was developed by painters such as Georges Seurat and Paul Signac, who formalized a pointillist or divisionist technique for the application of "pure" color as individual, unmixed points or units, "explicitly turning the hand of the painter into a clumsy machine that operated in steps and rejected the blending continuity of handicraft." It is not only the paint itself that is industrialized but the artist's hand. Delaunay and Kupka implemented divisionism in their own work (and pursued the scientizing theories of simultaneous contrast derived from the scientist and philosopher Michel-Eugène Chevreul, who was an important source for Signac) before the leap of pure painting; this, in turn, coincided with (and partly motivated) Duchamp's renunciation of "retinal" painting and the subsequent emergence of the readymade.[11]

The notion of "mechanical" technique begs the question of a redirected rather than an abandoned practice of craft, but it is irrefutable that the technique of early abstract painting represents a radical shift of process, one that diminishes values associated with the complexities of touch in the application of paint to canvas, just as the rationalization of color represents the prevailing influence of industrial means. The implications of these circumstances can be further refined, for the development of the flexible, portable tin tube both industrialized (and thereby commodified) the object-nature of artist's paint: together the container and the pigment represent a new compound entity. Duchamp's readymade internalizes painting through the operation of pictorial nominalism, while the readymade status of all painting is established— at least as a conceit—by the invention of the tube. The consequences for the readymade as an internal critique of avant-garde practice are, as de Duve shows, vast. But it should be observed that Duchamp's formulation historically belongs to a second period of crisis in painting practice, one to which Duchamp referred when he told Kuh that abstract expressionism represents the "apex" of retinal painting: "I doubt whether this is the art of the future. One hundred years of the retinal approach is enough."[12] And within that setting, the tube of paint posits a handful of coordinates for a deadpan utilitarian principle for paint as a commercial system of predetermined or self-limiting options (the regimentation of "choice"), a principle which, in fact, occupied studio practice in New York among various artists whom Flavin, in his autobiographical statement, would shortly name.

The tube as tube. Flavin has recently been claimed as a Joycean; surely as much as "epiphany," then, the *diagonal*—his key move—can be said to turn on a pun. Between 1954 and 1963 (Rauschenberg's paint tube and Flavin's fluorescent one) lies the great divide: the combine oozes paint, abstract-expressionist materiality—spillage and trace (similarly, Flavin's pre-icon assemblages, such as *mira mira*, from 1960, with its tin can "found flattened in the gutter," are generically *trouvés*); the lamp, instead (through the mechanized elements of color and radiated and reflected light, all contained within the tube and dispersed, rather than dispensed, from it), *signifies* "paint," specifically paint as system, the predetermined palette. "There was," Flavin explained, in contemplating the *diagonal* and referencing the standardization—lengths and colors —of the lamps, "literally no need to compose the system definitively." Duchamp himself, in 1962, is clear: "My Ready-Mades have nothing to do with the *objet trouvé* because the so-called 'found-object' is completely directed by personal taste. Personal taste decides that this is a beautiful object and is unique. That most of my Ready-Mades were mass-produced and could be duplicated is another important difference." (Odd to see *readymade* switch to the upper case, for painting through the readymade is decidedly a lowercase operation.) The rhetoric of Flavin's autobiographical account is Duchamp's own: "any commercially available color." Banality—of the object itself and its standardized color—is one source of the *diagonal* as a leveling device; another is the act of informal rotation: the 45-degree placement of the gold *diagonal* was satisfying, and striking enough to slightly defamiliarize it as a lighting fixture, "but any other positioning could have been just as engaging," Flavin wrote. Elsewhere, in 1964: "It is an industrial object; it's just a reiteration of it or disorientation of it."[13]

"Somewhat in my mind at this time, were quietly rebellious thoughts about proposing a plain factual painting of firm plasticity in opposition to the loose, vacuous and overwrought tactile fantasies spread about yards of cotton duck . . . which inevitably overwhelmed and stifled the invention of their practitioner—victims—a declining generation of artists whom I could easily locate [at] prosperous commercial galleries." In 1965, in the autobiographical statement from which I have been quoting, Flavin identifies three painters whose work, toward the end of the period of the icons, "was somewhat new to my attention": Jasper Johns, Barnett Newman, and Frank Stella. It is a meaningful list, the very three painters whose individual relationships to the medium together describe a problematic of plain factual painting. These artists "did not hold an appropriate clue for me about this beginning," Flavin wrote, referring to the jump from the icon to the bare tube; but the fact that they are named at all is, of course, our appropriate clue, for it betrays their relevance during the moment of truth.

To begin with Stella: "the restrained multi-striped consecutive bare primed canvas-pencil-paint frontal expanse play from Frank Stella." In 1960 Stella abandoned the so-called Black paintings and, as told to William Rubin, turned to metallic paint (fig. 3). "During his first months in New York, Stella became intrigued with the metallic paints he saw on sample cards of commercial paint dealers, but 'didn't know what to do with them' at the time. It was while first sketching the designs for what would become the Aluminum series that he began to think about the possibilities of metallic paint." Commercial

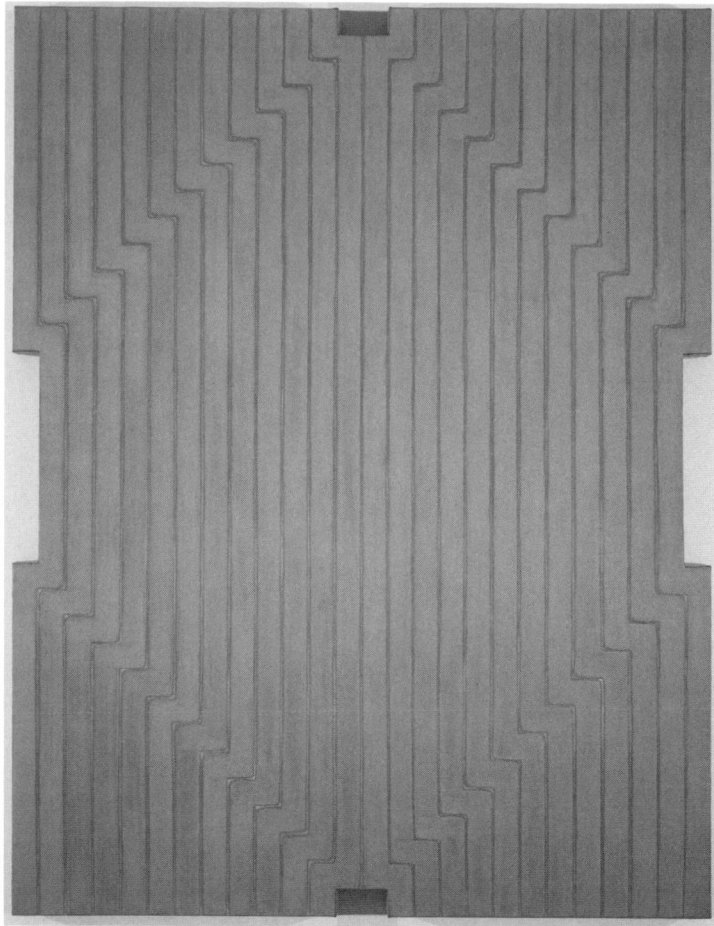

Fig. 3. Frank Stella, *Marquis de Portago* (Version I), 1960, aluminum oil paint on canvas, 93½ × 71½ in. (237.5 × 181.6 cm). The Robert and Jane Meyerhoff Collection, Phoenix, Maryland.

house paint had been Stella's medium since the mid-fifties (and in this, it was Pollock's house paint that is the sanctioned precursor), but metallic paint finally expunged the fine-art quality that had lingered with the Black paintings: "The aluminum surface," Stella told Rubin, "had a quality of repelling the eye in the sense that you couldn't penetrate it very well. It was a kind of surface that wouldn't give in, and would have less soft, landscape-like or naturalistic space in it."[14]

In other words, the metallic paint projected its own light—reflected light—rather than a metaphorical representation of light and space in nature, eliminating even the vestige of naturalism. As color, Rubin rightly adds, the aluminum paint references the industrial and the manmade; by extension, while paint in the Black series "had involved somewhat uneven densities in the layering and a soft irregular edge" and even bore a certain relation to the convention of chiaroscuro, the bands or stripes in the Aluminum series were sharply defined and applied along ruled pencil lines, although there remained a "slight bleeding of the oily binding agent." Executed with more precise edges, the bands—only as wide as the brush used to apply them—belong to the domain of predetermined dimensionality. The paint was drawn from the ready-made sample card, like the fluorescent lamp, and like the lamp it was not without its double life: "There was also a lot of ambiguity in it," Stella remarked of the metallic paint. "It identifies its own surface yet it does have a mysterious quality in one sense. . . . That shimmering surface has very much its own kind of surface illusionism, its own self-contained space." "Sienna, umber, ochre, black and white": these pigments drawn from nature, which Flavin itemizes with reference to the kind of painting he abandoned when he turned to the electrical "shimmer" of the icons, remind us that the space of illusion that hovers before the metallic surface of the Aluminum paintings (Stella's pre-Flavin space of "brilliance" and "approximate invisibility") is the denatured and immaterial space of the technological.

One irony of the paintings is that they were described at the time in opposing terms. The heavy surface of a metallic painting encouraged Judd to think of it as a "notched slab"; "something of an object, it is a single thing, not a field with something in it, and it has almost no space." But Michael Fried claimed that the reflected light of metallic paint "dissolves one's awareness of the picture-surface as a tactile entity in a more purely visual mode of apprehension" and, "despite its implications of materiality," renders the paintings "curiously disembodied." No space or the space of illusion. It is not enough to say that these are the responses we would expect from Judd and Fried given the opposed positions of the two critics concerning the state of painting at the time and the separate properties of the medium they were determined to preserve. In fact, the opposition is impossible to resolve, as both writers knew, because the Aluminum paintings hold both claims even if—like rabbit/duck—they cannot be perceived at the same time. It is useful to recall that Stella himself was apt to deny painting-as-object as a premise for his work, claiming instead that the unconventional three-inch depth of his stretchers (which was partly credited with heightening object quality) *emphasized* the surface by holding it away from the wall. Further, unlike Rothko, Stella explained, he does not paint the tacking margins of his canvases (another element in the objectification of painting).[15] Yet, again, for Stella the material nature of the surface itself was intensified by the metallic paint.

The hard fluorescent lamp, which repels the eye, wants to dematerialize, to become, through its literality, the surrogate for painting as a metaphorical language of color and space; optically disembodied by reflected light, the canvas covered with metallic paint wants to "identify" the heavy materiality of its own surface. Flavin's icons, colored blocky wooden constructions faced with Masonite and appended with incandescent and fluorescent lights, were already ambiguous in this regard. Judd said they are objects only: "They are put together bluntly; the materials are considered bluntly. . . . The blocks are not paintings; they have none of painting's scheme of something framed; they are not composed in the ordinary sense; they don't involve illusionistic space."[16] But they explicitly derive from the object-construction of a stretched canvas, something Judd himself was working through at the time in his own studio; they were, as Flavin described, "based on a hierarchical relationship of electric light over, under, against and with a square-fronted structure full of paint 'light.'" Finally, for all the titles that reference kitsch and street culture as well as sentiments of grief and loss—sacred, in the case of *icon VII (via crucis)*—the icons also introduce the ready-made lamp itself as object, mechanizing the element of luminosity.

The icons series was named for the Byzantine icon, and the deeply relevant role of the icon as an objective and symbolic model for the Russian avant-garde would have been known to Flavin through the recent publication of Camilla Gray's *The Great Experiment: Russian Art, 1863–1922* (1962), which he owned, although the initiation of the series predates Gray.[17] Above all, the gold-ground icon, as Flavin demonstrates in his appreciation of the "Novgorod icon" at The Metropolitan Museum in 1962, was valued equally for its reflected light and for its presence (its warped condition emphasizes this) as a heavy object. It might be useful to add, however, that in the world of Byzantine studies, *icon* describes not only sacred gold-ground panel painting but also wall mosaics, which in turn incorporate the full space of the church—both the walls and the ambient space of the beholder. This extended definition of the icon and its relation to space was already theorized in 1947 in a book on Byzantine decoration by Otto Demus, whose language—regarding the presence of the pictorial in real space—is stunningly pertinent to the rhetoric of the literal and the pictorial circa 1961, the year of Flavin's first icon.

Demus writes, of Byzantine mosaics representing single individual holy figures on the walls of a single church, "Their relation to each other, to their architectural framework and to the beholder must have been a principal concern of their creators." The author attempts to establish a "theory of the icon," describing a classical-period "system" in which iconography and form are "but different aspects of a single underlying principle which might be defined, crudely perhaps, as the establishment of an intimate relationship between the world of the beholder and the world of the image." He speculates that strict frontality or semi-frontality in the pictorial disposition of figures motivated a formal solution through which a nonnarrative relationship among them could be established, allowing them to maintain the decorum of frontality yet achieve a separate coherence overall. This solution came with the implication of "real space" through the introduction, architecturally, of curved niches ("excrescences of the general space") within which flat frontal mosaic figures could be made to turn: "They move and gesticulate across the physical space which opens up in front of the golden walls." Demus posits an infusion of the pictorial into the space of the beholder: "The Byzantine church itself is the 'picture-space' of the icons," a space which was "common to the holy persons [the figures represented in the mosaics] and to the beholder"; there the picture "opens up into the real space in front, where the beholder lives and moves." The element of light is indispensable: "To this spatial *ambiente* also belongs the actual light. Just as the Byzantine decorator did not represent space but made use of it by including it in his icons, just as he took into account the intervening space between the icon and the beholder, so he never represented or depicted light as coming from a distinct source, but used real light in the icons and allowed for its effects in the space between the picture and the beholder's eye in order to counteract its disturbing influences. The first resource is illustrated by the inclusion of shining and radiating material in the picture, especially gold."[18]

The very idea of radiating gold asks us to position Andy Warhol inside the reflective matrix of the early sixties; Warhol's eighty-four-inch metallic *Gold Marilyn Monroe,* which was exhibited at the Stable Gallery in 1962, is surely the archetype for a ready-made technological "icon." But, conceptually, "picture space" can also be enlisted to describe the domain of Flavin's lamp, from the icon series to the gold *diagonal* and on into the situational nature of the more complex installations (even if these were preceded by the campy ambient shimmer of Warhol's Factory studio on East 47th Street, which was lined with aluminum foil in late 1963); it accommodates the condition of the pictorial as a phenomenon not of representation but of frontality ("frontal expanse play") and of actual space charged through the agency of reflected light. It is, then, useful as a nonsculptural and nonliteralist model for a phenomenon that somewhat defeats characterization in those terms, specifying gold pigment as the source of light which materially activates the space between the image and the "eye" of an ambulant beholder.

But the fact that such a formal operation was described some fifteen years before the emergence of a related problematic in contemporary art debates, and that it is theorized with language that is virtually identical to the rhetoric of those debates, also brings us back to the peculiarity of Flavin's work. While it is, of course, true that the significance of 1960s formalism belongs to its own world of shifting critical imperatives, and further true that the mysticism inherent in the deeply complex experiential ambitions of Byzantine church space has no genuine cultural relevance to the late mid-century avant-garde in New York, picture space (as a critical construct of the 1940s) predates minimal art. As an incarnation of the play of pictorialism in actual space, it possesses no ambiguity. In Flavin's hands, the icon is positioned at the center not of an opposition but of a modernist tautology (one for which Stella's metallic paintings are an antecedent): beginning with the icon series but culminating with the independent lamp, Flavin's exposed fixtures manage to be both the medium and—almost unmanipulated—the work itself, even as they maintain their identity as common functional things, which function (unaltered, despite the strategic disorienting rotation of the lamp as object) is inseparable from the production of something like picture space.

Flavin's icons are also quasi-serial in nature. (The Byzantine icon is itself premised on standardization and repetition in relation to an imagined archetype, but I am in danger of leaning too hard on the icon as a specific precedent.) It is perhaps not surprising that some of Flavin's sheets of sketches of

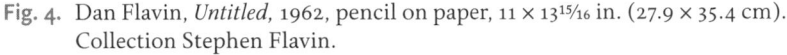

Fig. 4. Dan Flavin, *Untitled*, 1962, pencil on paper, 11 × 13¹⁵⁄₁₆ in. (27.9 × 35.4 cm). Collection Stephen Flavin.

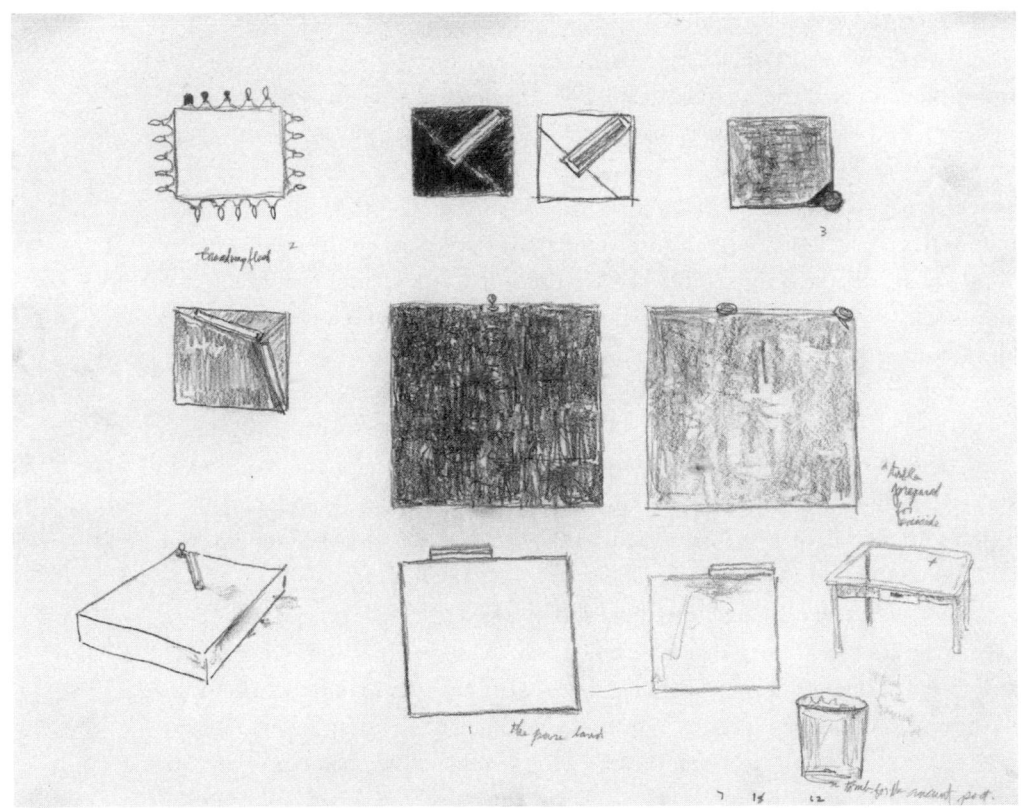

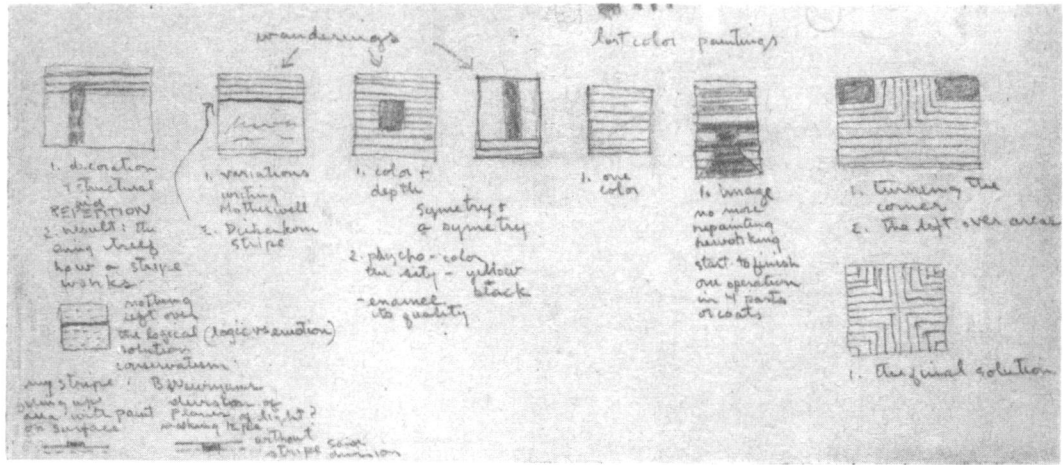

Fig. 5. Frank Stella, sketches on page 82 of Carl Andre, *Passport*, 1960, pencil on wove paper mounted on wove paper, 3¹¹⁄₁₆ × 8⁹⁄₁₆ in. (9.37 × 21.75 cm). Addison Gallery of American Art, gift of the artist.

multiple square-format icons (fig. 4)—which both record existing objects and anticipate future ones— closely recall the similarly tiny sketches that were integral to Stella's process a year or two before (fig. 5), just as he was advancing toward a true serial method, "converting the process of painting into a system of picture making," as Robert Morris would later write of Stella, "in which the arbitrary and incremental are abolished in favor of compulsory development." In the sketches, we might compare the migration of the tube (along with incandescent bulbs) around the perimeter and across the surface of Flavin's icon panel to the shifting configurations of Stella's stripes ("how a stripe works," in the words of one of his notations on an early sheet, and "REPETITION"). For Morris, Stella's move lay at the origin of the development of systems during the 1960s from minimal to conceptual art; it represents the closing of a "circle initiated by the Readymade, which had employed the ultimate method of the *a priori:* choice alone."[19]

"Plain factual painting." The original commercial function of metallic paint was to dress the surfaces of hot pipes, radiators, and the like. It derives its appearance from ground metallic powder and therefore is, so to speak, a literalist's pigment, being largely composed of that which—in its intended realm of use—it is meant to represent.[20] The perceptual heaviness it imparts to surface (to paint film on canvas) bears both a physical and a metaphorical relation to its material origin as an impenetrable industrial shell. Physical impenetrability is, in turn, displaced in Stella's Aluminum paintings as reflectivity, which makes them optically impenetrable, allowing for no sense of internal depth (as opposed to the shadowy depths Rubin claimed for the Black paintings). Further, reflectivity, which is derived from the pigment's material relation to actual light, locates the perceptual space of the painting between the surface and the beholder rather than behind the picture plane ("repelling the eye" while producing "its own self-contained space"). Even more than paint produced from natural pigments, or from synthetic pigments intended to conjure natural ones, aluminum paint is, then, a true industrial readymade, as close to a standardized manufactured object as paint can possibly be ("as good as it was in the can," Stella would say in 1964 concerning his ambition to apply commercial house paint to canvas in a manner that is more direct than the "drawing with the brush" that had characterized de Kooning's and even Pollock's use of house paint—and, indeed, "almost all twentieth-century painting").[21] Stella would subsequently fulfill the identification of paint with readymade through the agency of "system," in Morris's use of the term, by producing the Benjamin Moore series, which was exhibited in its entirety in Paris during fall 1961: thirty-six square canvases (six of them large format) representing six configurations in each of six primary and secondary colors of Benjamin Moore alkyd paint on raw cotton duck.

Stella's commercial or industrial media and his predetermined systems of nonrelational design and quasi-mechanical or rote application can be traced to his repeated recourse in statements and interviews of the period beginning in 1960, to the model of the house painter: to painting as a utilitarian practice of numbing repetition, an operation that qualifies as painting (literally, applying paint) yet keeps its distance from the kind of technique associated with the presumably exhausted artisanal practices of "fine art" (fig. 6). The house painter example is extrapolated from the materials and tools of abstract expressionism (the shift from the palette to the can, as Stella has described), but radical in its new implications for practice and technique. Again, abandoning what Stella referred to as "drawing with the brush," the new ambition is to *make* a painting, now connoting a direct act of construction or fabrication.[22] By extension, Stella's moves together constitute a state of painting that is attenuated by Flavin's fluorescent lamps: just as standardized dimensions make the lamp an element in arrangements of preset dimensionality, these fixtures also represent the first artificial light medium manufactured in a standardized range of colors—colors which were largely unnecessary to the function of the fixture as a cheap, convenient, lasting source of utilitarian illumination.

Anti-artisanal, Flavin's fixtures—in their application as functional objects and as art—require selection and labor only. The conditions for painting as fabrication and for the appearance of color as an industrial readymade are a historical recapitulation: Seurat, Duchamp said, "made his big paintings like

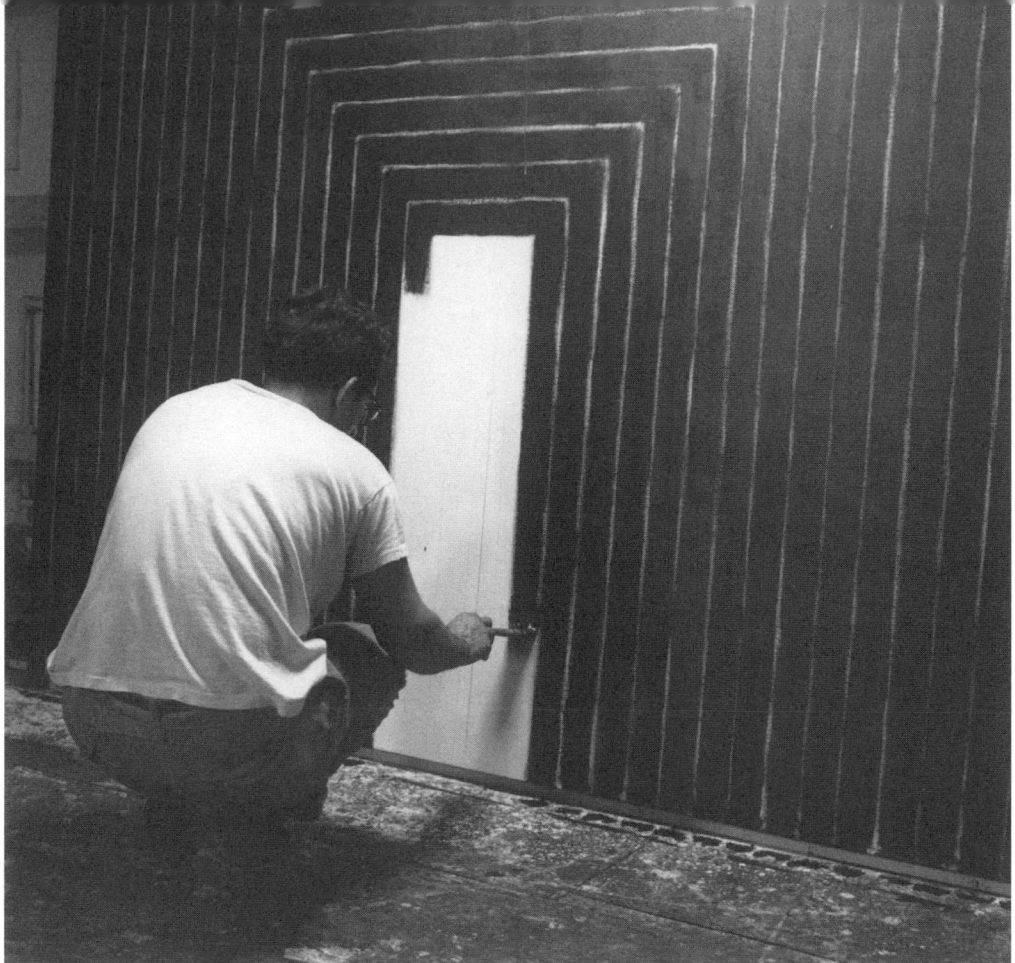

Fig. 6. Hollis Frampton, *Untitled* (028 painting Getty Tomb) [unpublished print], neg. 1958–62, print 1991, gelatin silver print, 7⅜ × 7⁷⁄₁₆ in. (18.73 × 18.89 cm). Addison Gallery of American Art, gift of Marion Faller, Addison Art Drive.

a carpenter, like an artisan. He didn't let his hand interfere with his mind." And in 1912, during the very moment Duchamp himself was struggling with his "passage" from cubist painting, on the eve of the invention of the readymade, Picasso introduced red, yellow, and blue Ripolin-brand non-fine-art enamel paint into the shadowy ocher and gray province of analytic cubism. There, applied in isolated patches of hard, shiny color, Ripolin floats against the dark, shallow relief space with the high-key presence of a commercial signboard. (It was, in fact, a tin advertising plaque for Sapolin paint—a similar product—showing a child painting the rails of a bedstead red, yellow, and pink that Duchamp altered when he created *Apolinère Enameled* [fig. 7], an assisted readymade, in 1917.) "Constructing" a painting would, in Picasso's work, take the form of the small *papier collé;* Stella's stripes and Flavin's lamps

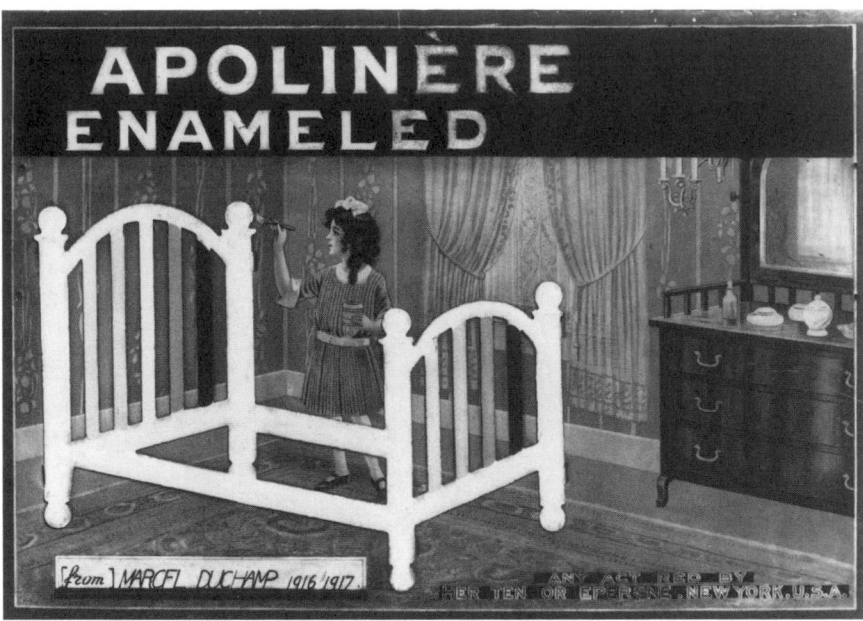

Fig. 7. Marcel Duchamp, *Apolinère Enameled*, 1916–17, rectified readymade: painted tin advertisement, 9¼ × 13¼ in. (23.5 × 33.65 cm). Philadelphia Museum of Art, The Louise and Walter Arensberg Collection.

occupy larger dimensions. In Flavin's case, these dimensions belong to the mundane realm of construction or habitation: the eight-foot measurement of the longest available fluorescent lamp precisely represents the standardized size of other commercial building materials, such as the precut four-by-eight-foot sheets of plywood and Masonite that Robert Mangold used to fabricate the works for his Wall series in 1964.

This eight-foot measure is conditioned by the scale of the human body in relation to the realm—and the economy—of utilitarian work space. It also happens to be the median height of a large number of canvases by Barnett Newman, although the distinction is as meaningful as the correspondence: the eight-foot unit is exact in Flavin and Mangold, while it is approximate in Newman, whose appeal to corporeal scale is, of course, intuitive rather than predetermined by industrial standards. The difference is generational. The element of scale in Newman's work derives from the realm of abstract expressionist ambition, in which the size of the canvas roughly circumscribes the compass of the artist's reach, a principle that physically implicates the close proximity of the body—and the perceiving eye—of the beholder. Ultimately, in this context, transcendence was also in play: scale was often further intended to serve metaphorical ends (perceptually, pictorial space remains ambiguously flat and deep), often touching the realm of the "sublime," while dimensions from painting to painting would change with the varying demands of "relational" composition. The industrial standards that support the work of the younger artists are, instead, strictly modular. Interestingly, Stella did not adhere to this form of modularity; the Black and Aluminum paintings are odd sizes, instead, which is to say—as Stella sometimes did—that while his mechanical technique was premised on a functional application of paint, the large dimensions of his canvases (especially the Black paintings, which were mostly horizontal) were not predetermined but loosely intended to challenge the physical ambition of painters from the previous generation, Newman above all. Stella's modularity occurs, instead, inside the margins of the canvas with the banded repetition of the design, which replicates the shape of the stretcher and indexes the banal application of paint—the stripes conform to the standardized dimension of a housepainter's brush.

Scale, then, has a bearing on the metaphysical reach of Newman's work, and despite Newman's role for artists of the generation of Stella, Flavin, and Judd, for whom the relation between the physical and the perceptual in his painting was already quasi-literalist, it is revealing to read Flavin—given his personal relationship with Newman, who spoke on the occasion of the opening of Flavin's retrospective exhibition in Ottawa—as saving the sacred in Newman's work. In an obituary written on Newman's death in 1970 for *Newsweek* magazine, Newman was described as believing that "painting had to be about its own physical properties—color, form and texture," a claim Flavin declared "chronologically absurd." He continued, "Why I believe that [Newman] could have easily and assuredly concocted his own *on the spiritual in art*." What lies behind this remark must be Flavin's anxiety for his own work, on behalf of which he often disavowed the sacred associations of light, but which, after all, is filled (by way of dedications) with references to mortality and loss. Flavin's works dedicated to Newman from 1971 would be explicitly commemorative; he later referred to one sequence exhibited at the Dwan Gallery in New York, as "the Newman memorial lighting,"[23] although he was careful in the dedication specifically to honor Newman's late red-yellow-blue paintings, which were among the artist's least openly symbolic—and, flatly painted in acrylic, his most openly indebted to developments in new art at the time.

Newman exhibited perhaps his most peculiar painting, *The Wild* (fig. 8), at the Allan Stone Gallery in 1962, in a two-man exhibition with de Kooning. The work was painted in 1950 and shown at the Betty Parsons Gallery the following year. But its appearance in 1962 (less than six months before Flavin discovered that the solitary lamp would "sustain itself directly, dynamically, dramatically in my workroom wall") is striking, and it would be remembered two

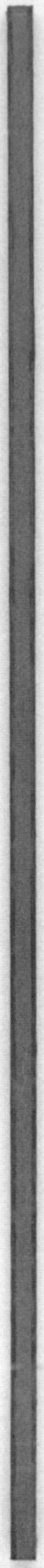

Fig. 8. Barnett Newman, *The Wild*, 1950, oil on canvas, 7 ft. 11⅜ in. × 1⅝ in. (242.3 × 4.1 cm). The Museum of Modern Art, New York. Gift of The Kulicke Family.

years later in Judd's important text on Newman. *The Wild* measures an astonishing 95⅜ by 1⅝ inches; in other words, it is almost exactly the same dimension as an eight-foot fluorescent tube. Painted red over gray, it was produced—as were all of Newman's "zip" paintings—with the aid of commercial masking tape, which was laid down the middle of the extremely narrow canvas during a first application of gray paint, and then taken up; the reserved area of bare canvas (the zip) was painted over with cadmium red, which extends from top to bottom but is irregularly brushed from side to side. By one critic, at least, *The Wild* was understood to represent a singular achievement for Newman in that, while most of his work had "expanded aggressively out of all proportion to the incident involved," this painting succeeds in "making act and form-symbol simultaneous." The critic is Sidney Tillim, no fan of Newman's, and it is the eccentricity of *The Wild* that allows Tillim to position it somewhat apart, not only from Newman's oeuvre, but from the overall ambitions of Newman's generation, the subject with which he begins his review of the Allan Stone exhibition: "Abstract expressionism . . . can be partly defined by its failure to live up to the intellectual content of its inspiration" (that being the various tendencies of the prewar European avant-garde, which were subjected by the Americans to gross "rhetorical simplifications"). Tillim believed that Newman never developed an adequate substitute for the overt and discarded symbolism of his early work, managing to endow his paintings of the fifties with "presence only in the physical sense." It is *The Wild* which Tillim reluctantly acknowledges to be one kind of solution; the way Newman reached it was to "limit the dimensions of his canvas to the size of his gesture."[24]

The radical reductivism of Newman's work permits this crucial juncture between image and "act." In *The Wild*, the two things are uniquely coequivalent. This is accomplished through the predetermined dimension of the strip of masking tape, the device that Newman used throughout his work but which, in this painting, establishes—and almost literalizes—dimension and scale (the tape is one inch wide for utilitarian and commercial reasons, and therefore "actual size"). *The Wild* is no wider than it needs to be, allowing enough margin to give the taped reserve its place in pictorial space, while its height is the mean eight-foot extension of a typical Newman canvas. It thereby remains painting even as it represents a compression, not just of "act and form symbol," but of gesture, medium, device, and scale. *The Wild* does not just satisfy the minimum means required to achieve a viable work; it is, in its way, the fullest expression of the viability of the oeuvre.

In his autobiographical account, Flavin specifies Newman's technique, his "'easy' separative brushed on vertical bar play in relatively grand scale." The quotation marks around *easy* signal vague skepticism regarding a quality that, depending on one's vantage, suits or plagues Newman: his "clumsy" application of paint. This is Stella's term, and he certainly valued Newman's technique around 1960 as a model for the direct execution of "good" paintings.[25] It is important to remember that it was not possible to address Newman's technical capacity using conventional standards of quality or finesse.[26] Stella, of course, took the so-called clumsiness to be an advantage; we have to assume that Flavin did as well. The role of masking tape in governing the dimensions and character of Newman's primary "form-symbol" is unthinkable as a tool for the conventionally nuanced manipulation of paint; certainly the trace of such a tool—such as the reserved zip—has no place apart from the predetermined, standardized parameters for a pictorial operation that adheres to the concrete, measurable surface of the stretched canvas (this is also true for Mondrian's use of colored tape), despite the range of feathered and scraped variants of the one-inch zip that Newman developed throughout his mature career. (Significantly, Stella produced a small group of diminutive stripe "paintings" in 1959 in which the stripes are formed solely with half-inch wide shiny silver burglar-alarm tape, works that are transitional between the Black and Aluminum series.) Attempting to account for *The Wild* provoked Tillim to contradict the rhetorical clichés of abstract expressionist space—narrowness, not breadth, is his criterion. The zip, the measure of irreducibility in Newman's work, is Newman's "gesture"; yet the condition of the irreducibility of that gesture is the industrial origin of the readymade—the zip as strip.

Between the constriction of *The Wild* and the expansiveness of *Vir Heroicus Sublimis* (painted the same year), both cadmium red, which painting more bluntly inhabits actual space? Do we determine this with reference to the plane of the wall, or to the fullness of the room—to the pictorial (to color and light), or to the situation of the object? In this case, can pictorial space, which is metaphorical, even be distinguished from the "real" space of painting? These are the questions posed by the irreducible fluorescent lamp, a "common eight-foot strip of light," with its illumination of the full planar surface of the wall (not to speak of *the nominal three,* the first—and wholly New-manesque—work by Flavin to spread itself structurally across the full expanse of the wall, from one edge to the other), where scale is a standardized function of room space and actual size, and "act and form-symbol"—the placement of the ready-made lamp and its significance as an inscrutable entity—"are simultaneous."[27]

When Bochner first saw the photograph of the gold *diagonal* in *Artforum,* he thought it was an assemblage: he mistook the grainy image of Flavin's studio wall for the surface of a Johnsian gray painting produced by a young imitator and mounted with a fluorescent tube. It is a meaningful mistake. Johns had already been producing paintings with attached objects. In his autobiographical statement, Flavin characterized Johns's work as "homely objective paint play about objects," and the description should not be taken for granted: *homely* modifies Johns's technique, even if we know it can also reference Johns's choice of the flat image, such as the target or flag, which (a point made by critics from the start) also counts as an object. "Paint . . . about objects" describes the thick, deliberate application of paint used to "represent" those images and to sustain the other appended objects. Johns's entire project during this period is conditioned by the objectification of paint: the object-image is ready-made; mixed with encaustic (which preserves the autonomy of each stroke) and often limited to a deadened gray, paint is matter; the brushstroke, now antimetaphorical, is largely an index of labor; surface, often built up with newsprint beneath the paint, is an entity in itself. "The canvas is object, the paint is object, and object is object."[28] Johns had been one obvious model for Flavin's icons; perhaps Flavin's studio wall *should* be taken as a Johnsian surface. The photograph, after all, is a representation, not a record; it flattens and above all pictorializes the gold *diagonal* as line and plane, emitting and inflected by actual light.

Not homely, but "homeless" is how Clement Greenberg characterized Johns's work in 1962, ascribing it to the category of "homeless representation," which Greenberg invented in order to diagnose a tendency—"after abstract-expressionism"—of "painterliness that is applied to abstract ends, but which continues to suggest representational ones."[29] De Kooning and Richard Diebenkorn are cited as prime examples of the tendency, but Greenberg explains that Johns is a special case: his work is poised between abstraction and representation, between the paint surface and the motif. "Everything which usually serves representation and illusion," by which Greenberg means a painterly play of light and dark, "is left to serve nothing but itself, that is, abstraction; while everything that usually serves the abstract or decorative—flatness, bare outlines, all-over or symmetrical design—is put to the service of representation." Stella (who does not appear in Greenberg's narrative) is relevant, for he claimed to derive his own motif—the pattern of stripes—from Johns's targets and flags. In this sense, the stripe was already available in ready-made images appropriated by Johns; as a motif in painting, it is, then, twice ready-made. Stella might be said to have returned flatness, bare outlines, and all-over design to the service of the abstract.

The reverse is true of Flavin. A problematic of abstraction and representation would at first seem far from the center of Flavin's work, yet homelessness is thoroughly endemic to the readymade—the disoriented utilitarian object that retains its plastic identity but is no longer its functional self. Flavin's displaced lamp occupies this state through its proximity to painting. It is, in Flavin's own words, an *image*, "a buoyant and insistent gaseous image," even as it remains (a few sentences later) the "distended luminous line of a standard industrial device"—that is, both mundane and abstract. The homelessness of the lamp, the post-painterly pictorialism of a utilitarian light, is established by this reciprocity of abstraction and functionality (press it into a corner and "it can completely eliminate the definite juncture by physical structure, glare and doubled shadow"). In other words, that which makes the lamp useful—its light and shape—also renders it, when rotated or reoriented, antifunctional and therefore abstract; yet the procedure that makes it abstract transforms it into an "image"—that is, an image of itself, a "fetish" (again, Flavin's term). As an industrial thing—both as object and as system—the ready-made lamp is close to being styleless, and from one work (or "proposal," as Flavin says) to another there is no progress, no residue of taste: "I sense no stylistic or structural development of any significance within my proposal—only shifts in partitive emphasis—modifying and addable without intrinsic change." In this way, because its pictorialism and its utility draw from the same source, it is unique as a readymade in its capacity for negative apotheosis: the readymade returned to its original functional setting. "Electric light is just another instrument," Flavin wrote in 1966. "The lamps will go out (as they should, no doubt). Somehow I believe the changing standard lighting system should support my idea within it. I will try to maintain myself this way. It may work out."[30]

Greenberg's homelessness depends on the flatness of Johns's motif, which marries it—as object that is image—to the surface of the painting. The work succeeds, Greenberg concludes, when the "contradiction" is explicit (when the image and the manipulation of the medium are held in tension). The fluorescent lamp belongs to the realms of the pictorial and of the objective, so its contradiction—let us say its ambivalence—is heightened. What of Johns's own sculpture? For Greenberg, these works "amount to nothing more than what they really are: cast reproductions of manmade objects." It is not

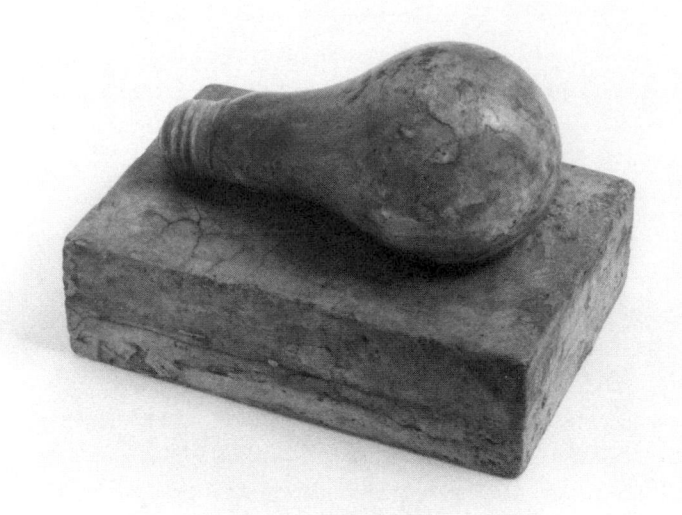

Fig. 9. Jasper Johns, *Light Bulb*, 1960, plaster, 4⅛ × 5⅞ × 4 in. (10.5 × 14.9 × 10.2 cm). Collection of the artist.

without meaning that between 1958 and 1961, these "objects" are flashlights and lightbulbs, actual hardware (some shown with sockets and wires) coated or cast with opaque, heavy materials: plaster, "sculp-metal," and bronze (fig. 9). The bulb and the flashlight are now our industrial signifiers of the pictorial—of light. The logic of irony here pertains to the way Johns reproduces the identity of the original yet negates many of its properties (transparency, fragility, hollowness, and, of course, the functional emission of electric light); this is Johns's homeless lamp. Object sculpture is a legacy of the readymade, and, like painting after Duchamp, it largely eschews craft. But plaster and sculpt-metal, like encaustic, are laid on and, as surfaces, formed almost like paint; when they harden and dry, they preserve the signs of their manipulation, turning a generic thing into a unique one. Both Johns's choice of objects and the materiality of his treatment of them are specific to separate properties of the paint medium, which remains his primary subject. Still, in a manner of speaking, Johns's sculptures turn the readymade—the electric light fixture—into a found object, even an archaic one; in 1965 he told David Sylvester that he had in mind exactly the kind of "generic" flashlight he wanted to use, but styles had changed, and for a "common object" it turned out to be hard to find.[31]

Johns's pictorial nominalism also takes a another form, in works that name color—literally, with the words "RED YELLOW BLUE" stenciled onto

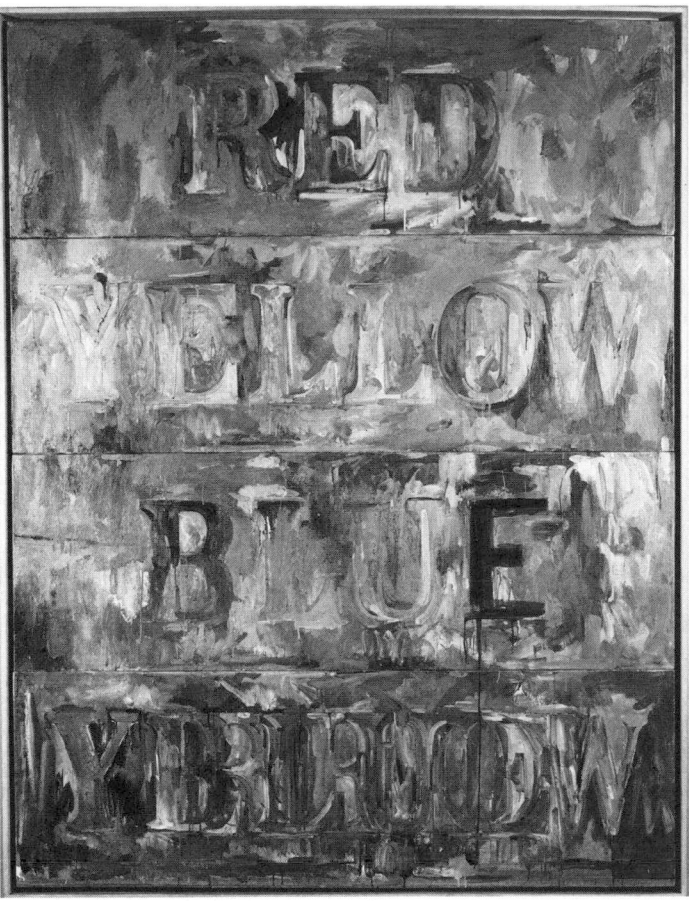

Fig. 10. Jasper Johns, *By the Sea*, 1961, encaustic on canvas (four panels), 72 × 54½ in. (182.9 × 138.4 cm). Private collection.

paintings (as well as drawings) from 1959 through the early sixties and beyond (fig. 10). The colors themselves are also used in some of the works, but to no obvious programmatic advantage. They are cut loose from symbolic associations and clear formal purpose. Johns almost manages to make the two operations—deploying a color and naming it—function as one. While the works are hand painted with enormous focus and care, the paint is applied with quasimechanical repetition—the strokes serve no conventional purpose, but might be said to exist (tautologically) to materialize the paint. The paintings are effigies both of the ready-made image they represent and of painting itself as an act. The colors—the three primaries—are not industrial readymades per se, although the stencils used to represent their names are. The three colors form a list. Newman applies color "mechanically," his "gesture" laid in with a painter's standardized commercial tool; motivated by Newman, Stella's application of color—one painting/one color—is derived from a strictly utilitarian practice; Johns's colors are named with standardized stencils. In the stockroom, each ready-made fluorescent color is contained by a single tube; each one is selected from the catalogue of designated options, a commercial naming procedure (and each is identified by name in the medium line of the work, even in their "titles"); each color remains independent of the others—they mix only as reflected light, although (see Rubin on Stella's Aluminum paintings) their sharply defined edges "bleed" into one another and into perceptual space. At last, color and, now, pictorial light, are purely a function of inventory. And inventory, a condition of the readymade, is color's redemption "after abstract-expressionism" (Greenberg). Sensation is processed through system in the literalist's era of doubt. Yet from within the confines of the hardware there remains a separate phenomenon.

Reviewing Flavin at the Green Gallery in 1964, David Bourdon already got most of it right. He takes the trouble to explain that the tubes "are commercially available in red, pink, yellow, green, two shades of blues and several shades of white" (inventory). He spies the pictorial: "A single eight-foot cool-white tube includes the wall as a work of art by casting light on it." He captures the life of the lamp in commercial culture, including religious kitsch: "These tubes probably owe as much to electrified marquees as they do to tiers of votive lights." He identifies the model of the readymade in a specifically meaningful way: "The tubes derive, ultimately, from Duchamp's first purchase in a hardware store" (and his train of thought seems to ascribe the simplicity of the art to Duchampian lassitude: "It would be hard to do less"). He digresses, describing the coincidence of a window display at the Semicraft Lighting Company on West 47th Street (the "Semicraft" name is too apt to have been invented), which he strolled past after leaving the Green Gallery; in the window, a clutter of "colored and fluorescent tubes . . . look[s] like the Flavin show being dismantled"; yet he slyly cautions that, although "anyone can put an eight-foot pink fluorescent tube in the corner of his living room and claim to have an artwork" (anti-artisanal technique), if it's not selected and placed by Flavin, it's a "forgery" (authorship as Duchampian aesthetic conundrum). But Bourdon also describes Flavin's work, which he likes, as "eerie"; he tries to capture that impression: "This art takes on a kind of biological luminescence. The works literally radiate energy. . . . The light has an intangible fluidity that contrasts sharply with the rigid contours of the tubes themselves."[32]

The "biological" allusion is close, but not quite satisfying. A better metaphor can be lifted instead from John Ashbery, who wrote in 1966 that looking at an early Johns painting—a dense and enigmatic work from which the viewer seems excluded—is like watching a battery being charged.[33] This is a perfect image because it is not quite organic and not quite mechanical, but, being chemical, possesses associations with both. In the context of advanced art, it introduces us to a realm of properties which obtain but which seem to escape the categories—specific object, inherent color, primary structure—that are typically said to inform the language and the values of the period. The practice of emerging abstraction was, around 1913, conditioned by the challenge of the readymade; painting around 1960—the period of painting's second ontological crisis—is viable (knowingly or not) only as an operation that internalizes or, at least, acknowledges the Duchamp gambit. In the time of plain factual painting, the coexistence of the industrial and the pictorial was not a contradiction or a rupture; it was a necessary construction. It may be the opticality of fluorescent light that attaches Flavin's work to the conventions of painting. But while color-light expresses picture space, the fluorescent lamp —the tube—is itself a space, and that space is filled with gas.

"A buoyant and insistent gaseous image which, through brilliance, somewhat betrayed its physical presence into approximate invisibility." The fixture is hardware; the light is pictorial; between them is lodged the glass tube, which contains color—pigment—in the form of a fluorescing element, vapor and gas. The chemical gaseousness of the fluorescent light medium, which was picked up by Bochner (was he drawing his language from Flavin's autobiographical statement in *Artforum*?), stands out, being wholly anomalous during the period. Something like it is evoked by other critics who specified the duality of the lamp: its solid form and its unquantifiable diffusion of light. The tube alone bore the dual identity: Bourdon used the words "intangible fluidity" to describe the way the luminous tube looks as a vessel of vaporous color which can be observed through the glass to vibrate and flow; Dore Ashton called it "pulsating light, producing a strange and . . . compelling effect." But the gaseousness exists both inside and outside the tube—"the incorporeal radiation that can't be measured," in the words of another critic.[34] On both sides, a literalizing of the pictorial occurs: in ambient space, the perceptual diffusion of color through light and atmosphere; within the tube, diffusion in the form of a chemical reaction. Or, put differently, the metaphorical operation can be reversed: the expansiveness of radiating light in actual and perceptual space is prepared inside the tube, where the trapped gas enacts a separate formless filling of empty space.

The readymade negotiates the relation between Flavin's work and painting, but the final, ontological turn is prepared by *The Large Glass* (fig. 11). In 1960 Duchamp's notes for the work (which had been on view at the Philadelphia Museum of Art since 1954) were published for the first time in a full typographic translation. The book was greeted by Johns himself in the art press

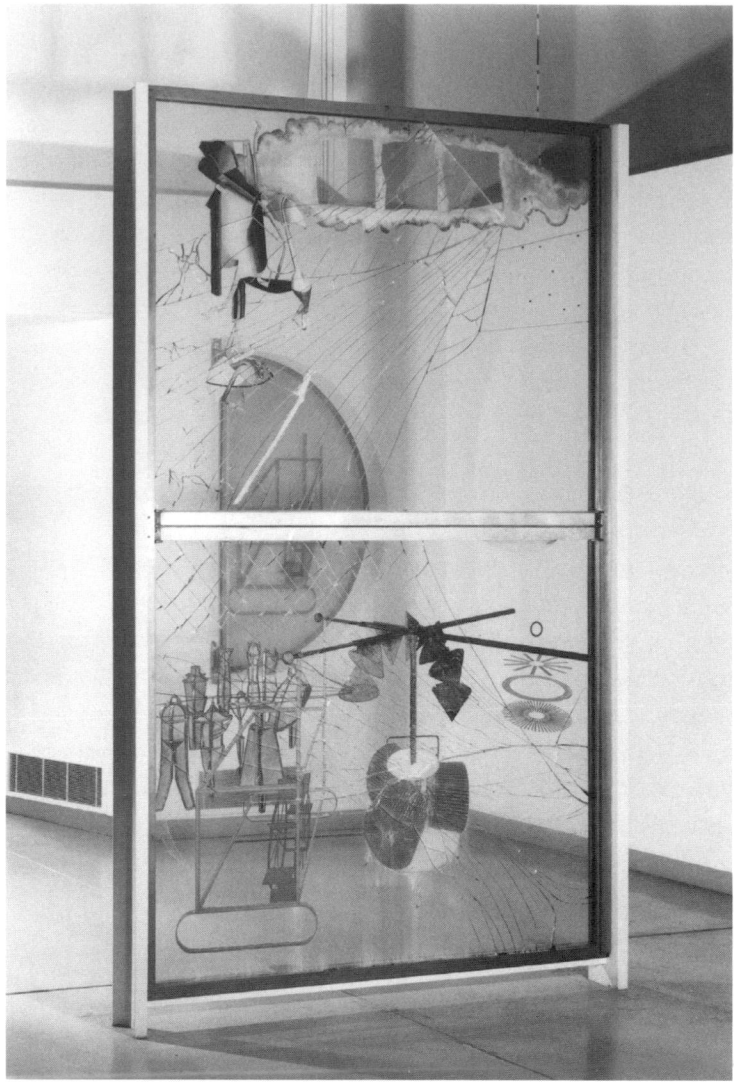

Fig. 11. Marcel Duchamp, *The Bride Stripped Bare by Her Bachelors, Even (The Large Glass)*, 1915–23, oil, varnish, lead foil, lead wire, and dust on two glass panels, 109¼ × 69¼ in. (277.5 × 175.9 cm). Philadelphia Museum of Art, Bequest of Katherine S. Dreier, 1952.

that year: "Finally, all the notes from the *Green Box* are published in English."[35] Produced between 1915 and 1923, *The Bride Stripped Bare by Her Bachelors, Even (The Large Glass)* was, of course, repeatedly referred to by Duchamp as a "painting" (eventually, a "delay") and, as de Duve has discussed, it can be addressed in the context of Duchamp's renunciation of painting practice; indeed, de Duve describes the "bachelor" and the "chocolate grinder" as figures for the painter who grinds his own colors. But more, Duchamp's complex notes for the design of the *Glass* (a large, colorless, mechanical image in oil paint, lead foil, lead wire, and dust sandwiched between glass panes) are filled with propositions concerning color and light. Specifically, in a lengthy note, Duchamp calls for the *Glass* to possess "*Interior lighting*": "that each substance in its chemical composition / is endowed with a "*phosphorescence*" and lights up like luminous advertisements / not quite?" Most important, he means to reconcile color as property, color as light, and color as substance: "Its *light* is not / independent of its color.—In short / the color-effect of the whole / will be the appearance of / matter having a source of light / in its molecular construction." Duchamp is speaking of "native" versus "applied" color in a reality made possible by "slightly distending the laws of physics and chemistry." He posits an aesthetic dimension in which substance, color, and light are confluent: "The substance of each part is / both a *source of light* and a *color.* / (in other words *the apparent / color of each part is the source / of visibility in color of that* / part." The section following "*Interior lighting*" explains the process of what Duchamp referred to as "illuminating gas."

The Large Glass, as we know, is, among many other things, a both comic and melancholic biomechanical allegory of erotic desire and frustration— "bachelors" below, "Bride" above. What of the illuminating gas? It rises, seeking to attain the Bride, through twenty-four "capillary tubes," in the course of which it is transformed, occupying solid and liquid states and, eventually, "congealed in the form of elemental rods." The rods are dispensed from "8 horizontal tubes," each breaking "through fragility into unequal *spangles lighter than air.* (retail fog)." Passing through sieves, the spangles come to occupy a state of "liquid elemental scattering"—"a *scattered Suspension*" or "Vapor of inertia" which retains its "liquid character through instinct for cohesion." This is "the only manifestation of the individuality of the illuminating gas in its habitual games with conventional surroundings."

Duchamp's precise satirical account is startling in the context of the *Glass* as a species of "painting" now transmogrified into a narrow chamber of electrochemical activity. In 1960 the *Glass* was delivered in English through the transcription of the *Green Box,* in time for the "tube of paint" and the gold *diagonal.* The *diagonal* is a commercial appliance; its contents are space and illuminating gas, the substance of the immaterial; it emits a scattering suspension which fills the room and repels the eye—retail fog. The state and identity of the exposed glass tube is fluctuant: it contains and dispenses; it is radiant and vaporous; modular; memorializing, ephemeral, banal. Capillary tube; elemental rod; form-symbol; name. Luminous advertisement (but not quite). Bearer of molecular color. Votive light. Priapic object of personal ecstasy. "It is the essentially optical, immaterial, noncontainable, nontactile nature of color that is inconsistent with the physical nature of sculpture," wrote Morris in 1966.[36] But the *pictorial* required a new allegory, a new physics (a Duchampian erotics?) of color and light. Trapped and ready-made yet effulgent and almost alive, the gaseous color-light is painting's altered state.

Notes

Epigraphs: From *The Devil's Dictionary* (1911), as quoted by Dan Flavin in his remarks on the occasion of the opening of the Donald Judd retrospective at the National Gallery of Canada in Ottawa, 1975, reprinted in *Chinati Foundation Newsletter* (2001): 25. Johns, interview in *Time* magazine, reprinted in Kirk Varnedoe, ed., *Jasper Johns: Writings, Sketchbook Notes, Interviews* (New York: Museum of Modern Art and Harry N. Abrams, 1996), 82. Hans Ulrich Obrist, ed., *Gerhard Richter, The Daily Practice of Painting: Writings, 1962–1993,* trans. David Britt (Cambridge: MIT Press 1993), 101.

1. Steve Morse, "Technical Aspects and Some Sited Works of Dan Flavin," in *Light in Architecture and Art: The Work of Dan Flavin* (Marfa, Tex.: Chinati Foundation, 2002): 130; Donald Judd, "Aspects of Flavin's Work," in *fluorescent light, etc. from Dan Flavin/ lumière fluorescente, etc. par Dan Flavin,* exh. cat. (Ottawa: National Gallery of Canada, 1969), reprinted in Donald Judd, *Complete Writings, 1959–1975* (Halifax: Press of the Nova Scotia School of Art and Design, 1975), 199–200.
2. Dan Flavin, "'. . . in daylight or cool white.' an autobiographical sketch," *Artforum* (December 1965): 21–24, reprinted in Dan Flavin, *three installations in fluorescent light/drei Installationen in fluoreszierendem Licht,* exh. cat. (Cologne: Kölnische-Verlagsdruckerei, 1973): 84–88, and Michael Govan and Tiffany Bell, *Dan Flavin: A Retrospective,* exh. cat. (Washington, D.C.: National Gallery of Art, 2004), 189–92. Unless otherwise noted, all citations by Flavin are to this autobiographical statement.
3. Morse, "Technical Aspects," 128.
4. Flavin, "some remarks . . . excerpts from a spleenish journal," *Artforum* (December 1966): reprinted in Flavin, *three installations,* 91; a video from 1969, *Manipulating a Fluorescent Tube,* records an activity that Nauman first performed in 1965. Bruce Glaser, "New Nihilism or New Art? Interview with Stella, Judd and Flavin," transcript of an interview originally broadcast on WBAI FM, New York, in February 1964. Later revised and published in *Art News* and elsewhere, Flavin's participation was, at his request, edited out. For the full interview, see James Meyer, ed. *Minimalism: Themes and Movements* (London: Phaidon, 2000), 197– 201. Bochner, in *Arts Magazine* (September–October 1966), reprinted in Paula Feldman and Karsten Schubert, eds., *it is what it is: writings on Dan Flavin since 1964* (London: Thames and Hudson), 29.
5. Sol LeWitt, quoted in Mel Bochner, "Less Is Less (For Dan Flavin)," *Art and Artists* (December 1966): 27; Mel Bochner, "Serial Art Systems: Solipsism," *Arts Magazine* (Summer 1967): 40, 42; Dan Flavin, letter to Seymour H. Knox, reprinted in *three installations,* 83.

6. Lucy R. Lippard, "New York Letter," *Art International* (February 1965): 37.

7. For the supplanting of the pictorial sublime by the space-filling character of technological mediums ("the knowledge that invisibility itself—the air—is filled with electronic signals"), see Jeremy Gilbert-Rolfe, *Beauty and the Contemporary Sublime* (New York: Allsworth, 1999), 54. It is the medium of video, however, that is Gilbert-Rolfe's primary concern.

8. Lippard, "New York Letter," 37.

9. Katherine Kuh, *The Artist's Voice* (New York: Da Capo, 1962), 90; Robert Rauschenberg, *Untitled*, 1952 (Ebsworth Collection).

10. Thierry de Duve, *Kant After Duchamp* (Cambridge: MIT Press, 1996), 161–63; Marcel Duchamp, "I Propose to Strain the Laws of Physics," interview with Francis Roberts, *Art News* (December 1968): 47; the interview was conducted in Pasadena, California, in 1963.

11. See de Duve, *Pictorial Nominalism: On Marcel Duchamp's Passage from Painting to the Readymade* (Minneapolis: University of Minnesota Press, 1991), esp. 154–58, and de Duve, *Kant After Duchamp*, chap. 3, "The Readymade and the Tube of Paint." I have obviously presented an extremely abbreviated summary of certain aspects of a long, complex argument concerning Duchamp's relation to and significance for modernist art practice, avant-gardism and a philosophy of the audience for art. In his writing on the work of Gerhard Richter, Benjamin Buchloh has also described terms for painting after Duchamp. His consideration of the "detachment" of metaphysical meaning from the monochrome in relation to Richter's Color Chart series (initiated in 1966) is obviously relevant to my discussion. See Buchloh, "Readymade, Photography, and Painting in the Painting of Richter" (1977), in Buchloh, *Neo-Avantgarde and Culture Industry* (Cambridge: MIT Press, 2000): 365–403. For Duchamp and de Duve's "nominalism" in the work of Ellsworth Kelly, see Yve-Alain Bois, "Ellsworth Kelly in France: Anti-Composition and Its Many Guises," in *Ellsworth Kelly: The Years in France, 1948–1954*, exh. cat. (Washington, D.C.: National Gallery of Art, 1992), 28. See also Philip Armstrong and Laura Lisbon, "As Painting: Problematics," in *As Painting: Division and Displacement*, exh. cat. (Columbus: Wexner Center for the Arts, The Ohio State University, 2001): 40–44.

12. Kuh, *Artist's Voice*, 85.

13. For the Joyce comparison, see Michael Govan, "Irony and Light," in Govan and Bell, *Flavin: A Retrospective*, 31–34, 37; Glaser, "New Nihilism or New Art?" 198.

14. William S. Rubin, *Frank Stella*, exh. cat (New York: The Museum of Modern Art, 1970), 60.

15. The Judd-Fried opposition is made by James Meyer, in *Minimalism*, 123. See two reviews of Stella by Judd from 1962 and 1963, respectively: "Frank Stella" and "Toward a New Abstraction," reprinted in *Donald Judd: Complete Writings*, 58, 91. Michael Fried, *Three American Painters*, exh. cat (Cambridge: Garland, 1965), 44. Glaser, "New Nihilism or New Art?" 198.

16. Donald Judd, "In the Galleries," *Arts Magazine* (April 1964), reprinted in Judd, *Complete Writings*, 124.

17. For Gray, the icon, and the Russian avant-garde, see Hal Foster's essay in this volume.

18. Otto Demus, *Byzantine Mosaic Decoration: Aspects of Monumental Art in Byzantium* (London: Kegan, Paul, Trench, Trubner, 1947), 3–4, 9–10, 13–14, 35.

19. On the Byzantine icon see Hans Belting, *Likeness and Presence: A History of the Image Before the Era of Art* (Chicago: University of Chicago Press, 1994); Robert Morris, "Some Splashes in the Ebb Tide," *Artforum* (February 1973), reprinted in Morris, *Continuous Project Altered Daily: The Writings of Robert Morris* (Cambridge: MIT Press, 1993): 127–29; Stella wrote this on one of the notebook drawings that he made in conjunction with his now-celebrated Pratt lecture in 1960; the drawings were salvaged by Carl Andre and incorporated into Andre's handmade book *Passport*. Morris, "Some Splashes in the Ebb Tide." Morris is referring to choice in the sense of mere choice—an act of designation not of taste, which is "the greatest enemy of art," Duchamp said to Kuh.

20. It must be said that preindustrial earth-color pigments were also partly composed of the natural materials that are represented in landscape painting. My argument supplements that of Gilbert-Rolfe, who traces the antecedents of the disembodied light of color video to the emergence of modern artists' colors first produced in Germany by the nineteenth-century petrochemical industry, which, taken up by impressionist painters, mark "the passage from what a color is as part of the world to what it can do in approximating a perceptual condition" (Gilbert-Rolfe, *Beauty and the Contemporary Sublime*, 31). With Stella's Aluminum paintings, industrial colors are applied to a kind of painting that, in its practice, its materiality, and even its "abstract" properties relating to pictorial space, negotiates between the handmade and the industrial, or readymade.

21. Glaser, "New Nihilism or New Art?" 199.

22. Stella, "The Pratt Lecture," reprinted in Meyer, *Minimalism*. For a different, lengthy discussion of Stella's claims for the technique of the house painter and other issues of standardization in his work in relation to American commercial and corporate culture in the context of the reinvention of the artist's studio, see Caroline A. Jones, *Machine in the Studio: Constructing the Postwar American Artist* (Chicago: University of Chicago Press, 1996), chap. 3, "Frank Stella, Executive Artist."

23. Dan Flavin, unmailed letter to Douglas Davis, July 21–August 22, 1970, reprinted in Flavin, *three installations*, 114; *"on the spiritual in art"* refers to a book by Wassily Kandinsky, first published in English in 1946. See Flavin's letter to Virginia Dwan dated December 10, 1970, reprinted in Flavin, *three installations*, 115.

24. Judd, "On Barnett Newman," written in November 1964 but not published until February 1970, in *Studio International;* reprinted in Judd, *Complete Writings*, 200–202; Sidney Tillim, "Month in Review," *Arts Magazine* (December 1962): 39. Flavin included Tillim in a list of three critics—with Clement Greenberg and Michael Fried—whose reputations as the "three finest minds of contemporary art" were undeserved: "None of these preposterously praised, presumptuous, self-appointed, self-indulgent, self-inflicting appraisers and moderators on art is known as an artist first" (letter to Phil Leider, November 15, 1968, reprinted in Flavin, *three installations*, 108).

25. See Jones, *Machine in the Studio*, 155–56. De Duve includes Newman, with Pollock and Stella, in his lineage of modernist and postwar practitioners who—painting in the age of the readymade—dispense with the artisanal.

26. Our appreciation of Newman's technique—or, at least, the language we use to describe it—has changed in recent years, although it would be wrong (falsely deradicalizing) to conflate Newman's technique with conventions of pictorial "craft."

27. To younger artists, the zip belonged to real space, not to the metaphysical; yet that was its own dilemma. "[Newman's] work doesn't suggest a great scheme of knowledge," Judd wrote. "It doesn't claim more than anyone can know" (Judd, "On Barnett Newman," 202). We might say that Judd's Newman invites interrogation: What *can* anyone know? Mel Bochner would soon produce various installations—with masking tape—that measure actual space, demonstrating that measurement is a representation; the vagaries of pictorial space have been eliminated and the strip of tape alone is left behind.

28. Mel Bochner, conversation with the author, July 2005. Bochner specifically had in mind Johns's painting *Water Freezes* (1961), in which two gray-painted panels are separated vertically by a thermometer. Jasper Johns, interview with David Sylvester, 1965, reprinted in David Sylvester, *Interviews with American Artists* (New Haven: Yale University Press, 2001), 167.

29. See Clement Greenberg, "After Abstract Expressionism," *Art International* (December 1962): 25–26, for the discussion of Johns.

30. Flavin, *three installations*, 90.

31. Sylvester, *Interviews with American Artists*, 152–53.

32. David Bourdon, reprinted in Feldman and Schubert, *it is what it is*, 22–23.

33. John Ashbery, "Brooms and Prisms," *Art News* (March 1966): 58.

34. Dore Ashton, "Excavating the Recent Past," *Studio International* (August 1966): 102, reprinted in Feldman and Schubert, *it is what it is*, 28; Jill Johnston, "Reviews and Previews: New Names This Month," *Art News* (January 1965): 13, reprinted in Feldman and Schubert, *it is what it is*, 26.

35. George Heard Hamilton, trans., *The Bride Stripped Bare by Her Bachelors, Even, a typographical version by Richard Hamilton of Marcel Duchamp's Green Box* (New York: Wittenborn 1960). All Duchamp quotes are from this edition. Jasper Johns, "Duchamp," *Scrap* (December 23, 1960), reprinted in Varnedoe, *Johns: Writings*, 20–21.

36. Robert Morris, "Notes on Sculpture, Part 1," *Artforum* (February 1966), reprinted in Morris, *Continuous Project Altered Daily*, 4.

Jeremy Gilbert-Rolfe   **Space and Speed in Flavin**
Minimalism, Pop Art, and
Mondrian

Fluorescent lighting was first theorized about by the French physicist Alexandre Becquerel in 1857 and was introduced into everyday life by General Electric in 1938. By 1961, when Dan Flavin showed his first fluorescent tube works, the fluorescent tube was, like the Campbell's soup cans, whose image Andy Warhol would begin to use in 1962, a familiar object. If the tube's familiarity encourages me to want to see Flavin's work as illustrating an interdependence between pop and minimalism—the tendency with which he is most often associated—the complexity of his works' visual affect suggests that that something may be gained from comparing his work with Mondrian's. But, unlike Mondrian's, Flavin's work continues to recall a nineteenth-century concern with natural light and its simulation. It cannot avoid doing so, because unlike oil paint, fluorescent light is automatically reminiscent of impressionist color.

Fluorescent light is produced by running an electrical charge through a gas containing mercury, which in its turn releases light photons. Mostly ultraviolet and therefore invisible, the photons are converted into visible and more intense light by phosphors, which line the tube's interior and give off white light when exposed to light themselves. When the phosphors are adjusted to produce colored light, it is a color filled with white, like the palette invented by the impressionists to depict daylight. I think this sets Flavin's work apart from that of his contemporaries. The gas running through the tube causes a perceptible movement that is neither quite pulse nor flow, and too continuous to be described as a vibration.[1] Moreover, when looking at a Flavin we know that the visible movement of the gas is dependent on an invisible current traveling at a speed beyond the perceptible. This sense of the instantaneous delayed—electricity slowed down by gas, an invisible force made visible by a tangible one—is both very contemporary and another factor that links Flavin to impressionism, a movement that was anathema to minimalism and pop.

The impressionists used colors with a lot of white in them—traditionally called "tints" as opposed to "tones"—colors with black in them ("hues"), and colors without either black or white added to approximate the intensity and brightness of daylight. Possibly because of the influence of the scientist and philosopher Michel-Eugène Chevreul, the impressionists determined that the light of the brightest part of the day could be most closely approximated by a white light which contained equal amounts of the primary colors.[2] The phosphors in white fluorescent simulate the brightness of daylight in exactly this way. Instead of starting with a colored ground that would establish a midtone from which to go up or down the scale, the impressionists used a white ground and added colors mixed with white. Impressionist paintings appear to be filled with light because impressionist color is filled with and supported by white. I have elsewhere described impressionist color as the antecedent of video color, which like fluorescent can't not be filled with white light.[3]

Electric light entered the everyday at the same time that the impressionists were trying to make painting simulate the brightness of the brightest part of the day, and its intensity and potential equivalence with bright daylight—or for competing with it—is part of the content of Manet's *A Bar at the Folies-Bergère* (1883). The electric lights in *A Bar at the Folies-Bergère* are painted with much thicker paint than the dimmer gaslights, and this and their whiteness —when one would expect them to have been in reality much more yellow— suggest that Manet is comparing electric light to daylight when he makes the electric lights not only the thickest but the brightest things in the painting.

Flavin never referred to Manet or to any of the impressionists, probably because he felt he had little to do with them. But he dedicated a work to Matisse—whose work is certainly continuous with impressionism—in which white similarly stands for daylight and its effects. But where the impressionists' paint is quite thick and replaces the smooth white ground with another surface, Matisse's color is thin and depends on the white ground to intensify its luminescence. The brushmarks are (usually) distinct from one another but they lie *in* the ground as much as *on* it because the paint is more like a glaze than whipped cream, the consistency recommended by the impressionists. Matisse leaves the ground exposed in many places so that its whiteness adds intensity to the colors by surrounding them as well as being seen through them. The effect is of color that seems to vibrate in a different way from the impressionists' equally colorful, but thicker, marks, surfaces, and spaces.

In Matisse color seems to be inseparable from its ground, thin fluid instead of impasto crust, and in this respect his painting creates an effect closer to fluorescent light than do impressionist works. Perhaps it is for this reason that Flavin could see a connection between his own work and Matisse's. Flavin's *untitled (to Henri Matisse)* (1964) relates to the white wall behind the installation in a way straightforwardly comparable with that in which the vertical colors on either side of the door in Matisse's *Seated Woman with a Book* (1920) dissolve into a white ground intensified in turn by what's been inserted into it (figs. 1, 2). *Seated Woman with a Book* hung in the Philadelphia Museum of Art, and Flavin almost certainly knew it. In *untitled (to Henri Matisse)* and the bit of *Seated Woman with a Book* with which I've compared it, color undermines any sense of solidity and certainty in the relationship between doorframe and wall in the one and tubes and wall in the other. This use of fluorescent's brightness to undermine a relationship between two things, substituting perceptual, or retinal, uncertainty and ambiguity for empirical verifiability, distances Flavin's practice from that of the minimalists. Inasmuch as the minimalists' aspirations were set out by Donald Judd, Flavin's colleague and champion, Flavin's use of color that is both naturalist in reference and also bright enough to dissolve forms causes his work to exceed in some respects and in others to hinder Judd's reading of it. Flavin's ambiguous, intense, naturalistic even though electrical color is the antithesis of Judd's minimalist aesthetic of determinedly synthetic colors that are always subordinate to constructed form.

Oddly, if only at first sight, what separates Flavin from minimalism connects his work to contemporary life as a whole even as it underscores his continuity with ideas originating in the nineteenth century. Flavin's fluorescents activated an environment of spatial-temporal affect that depends on our taking technology into account, if not for granted. (The impressionists could not take technology for granted but they were quick to take into account.) The impressionists' interest in making paint seem to match the brightness of a sunny day, an intensification of painting's ability to simulate the natural world, coin-

Fig. 1. Dan Flavin, *untitled (to Henri Matisse)*, 1964, pink, yellow, blue, and green fluorescent light, 8 ft. (244 cm) high. Dia Art Foundation.

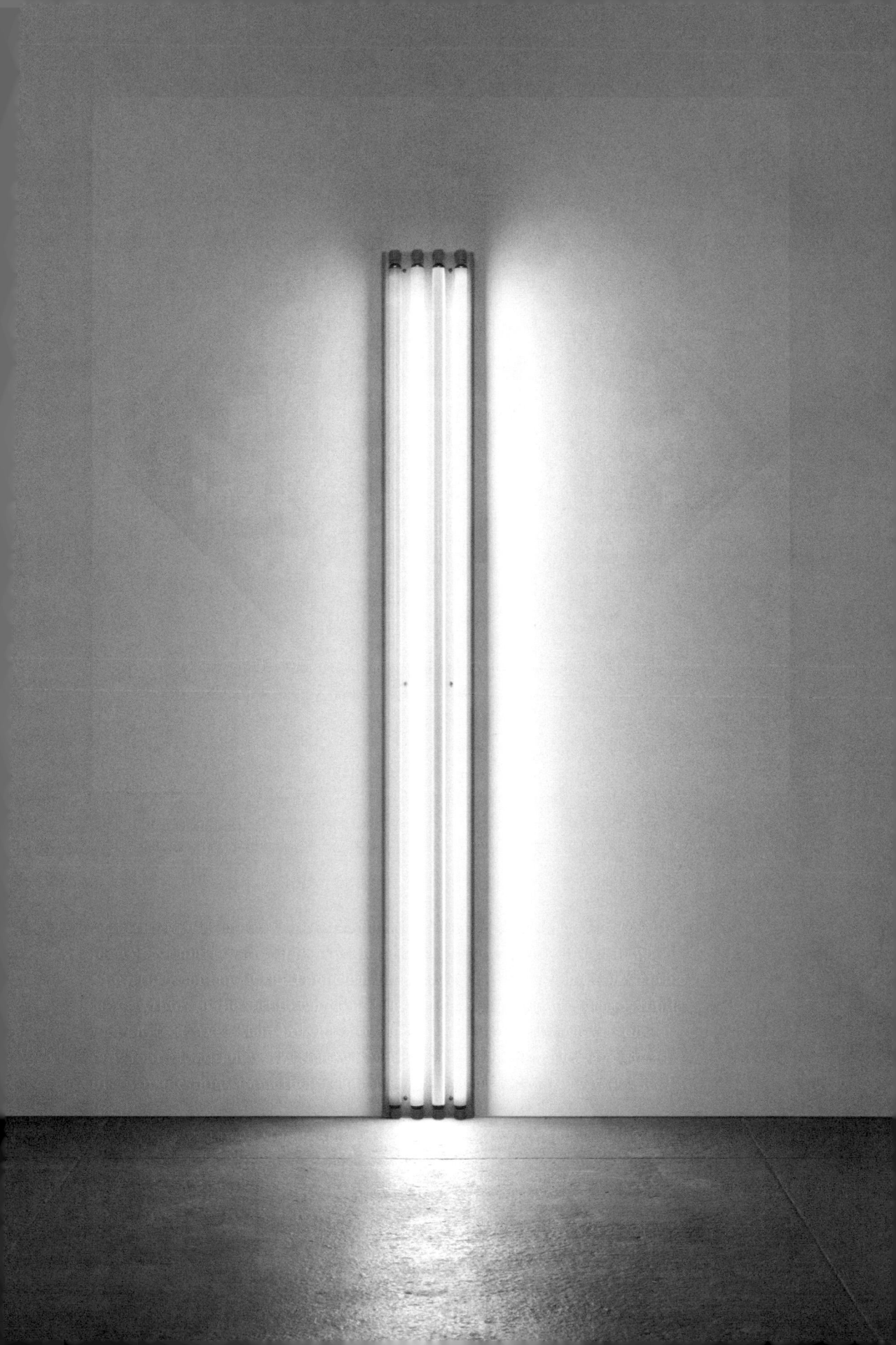

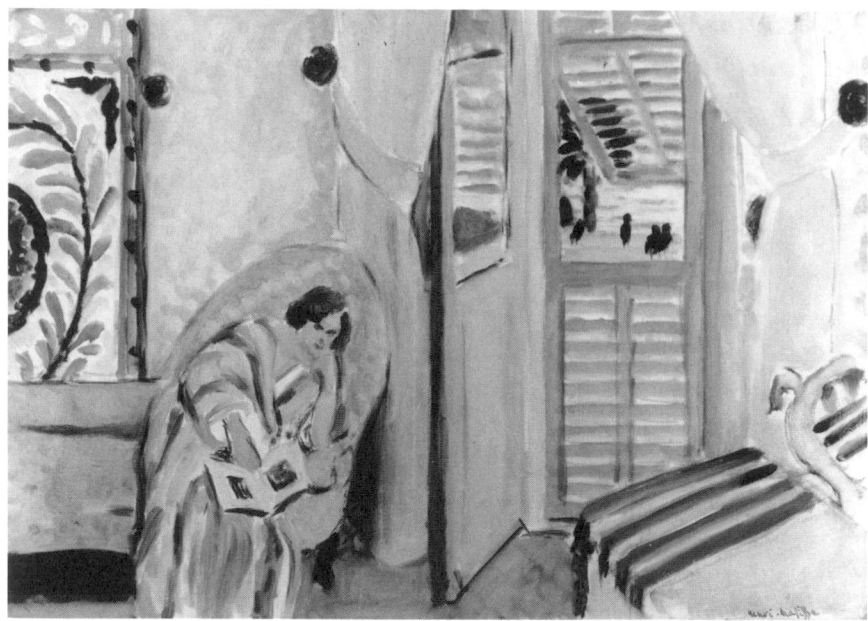

Fig. 2. Henri Matisse, *Interior, Nice, Seated Woman with a Book*, 1920, oil on canvas, 18½ × 26 in. (47 × 66 cm). Private collection, photo courtesy Acquavella Galleries, Inc., New York.

cided with a technology that not only made this possible but caused the acceleration of the pace of everyday life and changed perceptions of that world. Jules Verne's *Around the World in Eighty Days,* published in 1872, described a circumnavigation of the globe that took a quarter of the time it would have taken in 1848. (An American travel agent offered such a package tour shortly after the book came out.) As Verne's story made clear, the railway was at the heart of the transformation. Thanks to the railway the world shrank not only at the international but also at the local level. It now took hours by train instead of days by stagecoach to travel from Lyon to Paris, and impressionism reflected the less contemplative, more mechanically inflected view of the world that came with exchanging ten miles an hour behind a horse for twenty-five or more on iron rails. Impressionism belonged to a world in which the city dweller could invade the country, make use of it for recreation, and then go home, all in the space of a day.[4]

Nature had been contained by technology, or was on the way to being so, to a degree we have now come to regret, but which in the third quarter of the nineteenth century seemed simply exciting. The impressionists' interest in daylight—both depicting it and working in it— reflected a "naturalism" that drew its inspiration or volition from technology. It had to do with an intensity and speed that came from industry rather than the countryside, which now became a place of clear color that one could visit—and it was from advanced technology too that the impressionists got the materials with which to realize a nature as intense or bright as the real thing, or as close to it as oil paint could get. The impressionists' unprecedented approximation of daylight was made possible by the mineral colors which had been developed during the first half of the century and continued with the creation of viridian in 1859, alizarin crimson (1868), and a few other colors from the German petrochemical industry that enabled Monet and other impressionists to take plein-air painting to a new level of naturalism.[5]

Bright colors induce rapid eye movements, and in this sense an impressionist painting imposes the accelerated pace of contemporary life on its viewers. This effect is, if anything, even more true of Flavin's work. Light is much brighter than paint, which can only depend on it, and works made of light can't be looked at in the same way as those made of paint. Impressionist painting competes with sunlight by supplementing bright colors with rapid movements, not only of the eye, but of many slightly different-colored brushmarks, which vibrate among themselves all the more because they are made out of colors that already maximally vibrate in a gestureless gesture which perhaps not-so-distantly invokes the mechanical. But where even the brightest impressionist painting can unfold relatively slowly before our gaze, a Flavin can't: fluorescent is too bright to stare at for long. Our eyes can't move rapidly enough to keep up with the intensity of the electric light. Our relationship to the work has to be of a different kind from the one we might have with a painting (let alone a colored sculpture) and the difference has to do with the speed as well as the intensity—in practice they are inseparable—of electricity.

Impressionism belonged to the age of steam, the passage from horse to iron horse; Matisse's life encompassed the ascent of the combustion engine from horseless carriage to fighter jet, outer limit of the engine that needs air. From the middle of the nineteenth century to that of the twentieth our experience of space was progressively altered as communication became faster and faster. But the contemporary world has realized a potential apparent fifty years ago and since then become a world in which the idea of going ever faster has become old-fashioned, because we can go as fast as we like, and been replaced by another, the idea of electronic as opposed to mechanical speed—not constant acceleration but consistent instantaneity, not that which could get even faster but that which is immeasurably fast all the time. What we look at when looking at a Flavin is what fluorescent light is doing to the space. It is the light it casts—in which we are likely to be standing—that defines, or, more precisely, blurs, the work's relationship to wall, room, and viewer. If the naturalism of fluorescent light makes it hard to reconcile Flavin's practice with minimalism because it blurs a distinction that minimalist artists generally sought to maintain—between that which could be read as a construction and everything else—while linking him to things they mostly rejected, such as illusion and, implicitly, prettiness, so does its artificiality, in that its electric brightness makes it impossible to see the work wholly as an object. We see it instead in terms of a sense of time and intensity conditioned by the speed of the electronic.

Jean-François Lyotard compared time in Barnett Newman's paintings to the imperceptibly delayed instantaneity of satellite transmission (direct descendent of the railway's electric telegraph), which could mean that Newman anticipated a technology he didn't live to see become ubiquitous (he died in 1970) and exactly describes the movement that runs through his paintings. (In my view, the comparison speaks to the possibility that painting reaches out to a technological sublime it cannot inhabit because it is handmade, which could have some bearing on Flavin's choice of materials.)[6] Barnett Newman had a more thoroughly documented influence on Flavin than Matisse or the impressionists, and, following Lyotard, one could say that Flavin's work is neither handmade nor a reembodying of a technological condition it does not inhabit, but instead begins by incorporating what Newman and other predecessors point toward: the speed of electricity and the otherwise unattainable —because made by electricity—colors that come with it. Impressionist paintings dissolve form through a staccato regularity that belongs to the steam engine; Flavin's work does so through a delayed but regular electrical movement that is neither mechanical nor animal but can be compared to both.

In addition, electricity makes the work independent of the daylight to which it otherwise implicitly appeals and in whose simulation it is founded. In Matisse form is subverted by the transparency of the paint and the white surrounding the colors, allowing for a rhetoric of dissolution caused by several movements (in and across and around) that depend on our perceiving what is actually reflected light as light coming from within. A Flavin work is in fact light coming from just below a surface that is imperceptible when lit; the object is dissolved by the light it generates. This is another reason why his work can't be accommodated by the terms within which he seems to have meant to work. The minimalists wanted their work to be about real space as opposed to the space of illusion, but this distinction is less easily made with works that illuminate and color themselves and the space they occupy than it is with sculpture. It is true that when we look at a Flavin we are seeing something and that it is real; but the perception that an object is being dissolved by and into the light it is itself does not comfortably fit any definition of the real except in an extremely metaphorical sense.

Flavin and the minimalists didn't want to be metaphorical, however;

they wanted to be empirical. Judd is as clear about this as he is indifferent to the ways in which empiricism doesn't work for Flavin. The first among these follows from empiricism's requirement that the object of attention be isolated from the subject regarding it. This is hard to achieve when subject and object (viewer and art) are both bathed in light of the object's making, the characteristic of Flavin's work which more than any other makes me think it better to approach it through models of indeterminacy such as those offered by impressionism, Newman, and Matisse. Impressionist painting is made of, and about, indeterminacy. The colors describe not things but responses to things, atmosphere as a subjective condition. The impressionists sought to frustrate the overdetermination of traditional composition by cropping the scenes they depicted as a camera would, with plenty of attention to the space on either side of the picture, which contained action continuous with it but which one could only imagine. Newman, a New Yorker who wanted to go to the tundra because there one can turn around 360 degrees and the horizon would be flat throughout, uses lateral extension in a manner directly derived from impressionism—which he regarded as the most revolutionary nineteenth-century art movement because of the anonymity of the impressionist brushmark—in the interests of the indeterminacy which is, as Lyotard reminds us, a condition of the sublime. Matisse, by confusing image and ground, can perhaps be said to present an indeterminacy of intension rather than extension. And I could also return here to the indeterminacy presented by a doorframe melting into a wall. Indeterminacy in Flavin's work is—like its automatic invocation of impressionist color—another quality that comes with its being made out of fluorescent tubes. It is indeterminate in two ways which also suggest why it's hard to think of making a Flavin the object of an empirical inquiry: it is a kind of light and thus not perceived in the way a tangible object such as a box is but rather as that which robs things of their tangibility; and for the opposite reason, at the same time it is a familiar object—and in its familiarity as much a sign as a thing—and therefore, too, much less specific than a box.

If Flavin's dedication of works to Matisse and Newman can be taken to support my connecting him to a tradition of the indeterminate, however, there are plenty of dedications which underscore his own commitment to the position with which he's usually identified. *Pink out of a corner (to Jasper Johns)* (1963) recalls Frank Stella's remark that he owed it all to Jasper (fig. 3). Johns is important to this discussion because he is the pop artist whose work shows most clearly that though pop is minimalism's polar opposite or exact complement they share a common attitude to the work of art considered as an object. It might even be possible to make the case that Johns is as much the source of the minimalists' preoccupation with objectness as anything else. Like Stella,

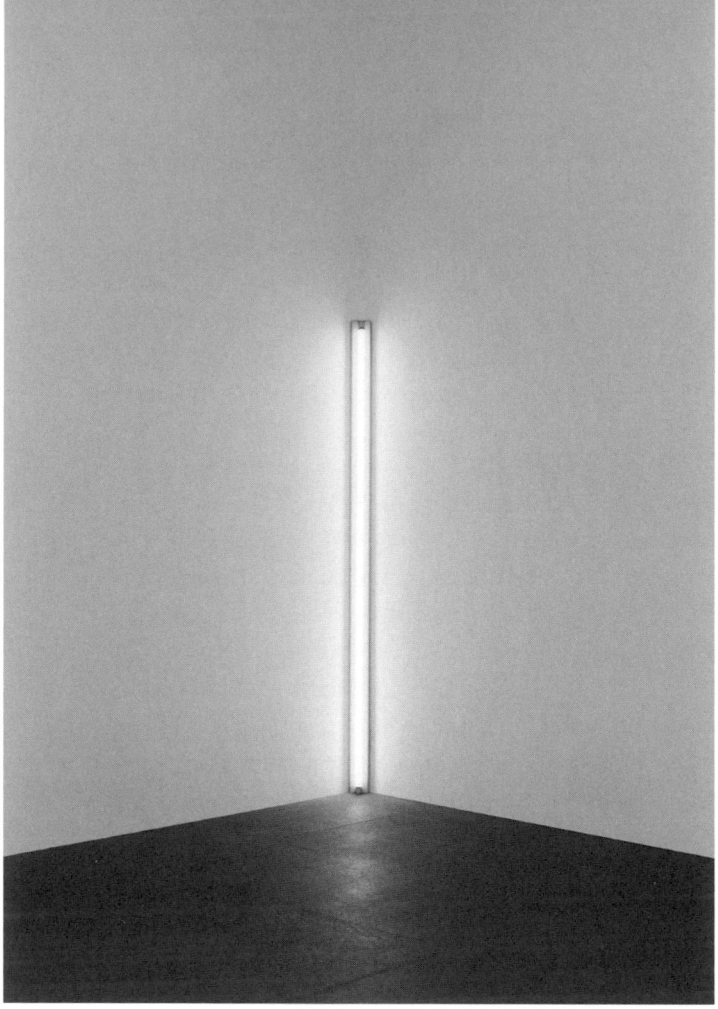

Fig. 3. Dan Flavin, *pink out of a corner (to Jasper Johns)*, 1963, pink fluorescent light, 8 ft. (244 cm) high. Photo courtesy of Dia Art Foundation.

Flavin began his career with the equivalence between scale and size of the New York School painters, Newman in particular, in mind, but it was Johns's *American Flag* (1954) that made painting into an object as well as and as much as either space or surface. That Johns did it by way of Marcel Duchamp, while the minimalists would, after the publication of Camilla Gray's book on the subject in the early sixties, prefer to invoke Russian constructivism as precedent, tends to enhance the thought that minimalist art is pop with the image eliminated.[7] While inadequate, there is something to such a description. Flavin's dedication to Johns is a reminder of his (and Stella's and Judd's) relationship to pop as an art of the recognizable, of objects which are signs as much as things—like Andy Warhol's Campbell's soup can images or, more pertinent still to an artist associated with minimalism, his *Brillo Soap Pads Box* (1964; see fig. 5).

As with his using color which immediately—at the level of recognition and association—and implicitly connects him to impressionism, Flavin's use of fluorescent tubes and fluorescent light similarly implicates him in pop art's exploitation of the recognizable and familiar. It seems to me that we can't overlook this side of Flavin's work when accounting for our experience of it. Similarly, while Flavin's work is made of, in an important sense is about, light, a phenomenon rather than a thing or a sign—and is in that about a kind of visual experience which pop art's fundamental predilection for reading over seeing precludes—we see it as electric at the same moment that we see it as light. The tube may have become so familiar that it is usually invisible unless an artist draws our attention to it; Flavin placed a work in Pennsylvania Station in New York which had people looking up at a bank of lights most would rarely notice. And we may have become so used to fluorescent light that it is possible to say that its familiarity has naturalized the force that runs through it.

But looking at a Flavin reminds us of the historicity of electricity as much as phenomenally engaging us with light. The idea of the instantaneous which comes with electricity is as much a historical feature of the work as the fact that we associate fluorescent light with certain spaces—institutional and mercantile rather than domestic, for example. We cannot be told not to notice any of these properties of the work, which define it and are what it presents, but that is what a minimalist reading of the work requires. It is not as flippant as it may sound to say that suppressing rather than emphasizing the familiar associations of familiar objects was a large part of what distinguished minimalism from pop. Judd wanted to designify the recognizable as much as possible not because he was an abstract artist in the fullest sense, which, however, for him meant the most traditional sense: while he wanted to insist on the materiality of his work he would discuss it only in terms of structure and, to a lesser extent, affect. He rarely if ever acknowledged the common associations of Plexiglas and stainless steel—the stuff elevators are made of—and plywood, usually a temporary material or one which is covered but in Judd's work is neither, insisting instead, by implication, that "empirical" specifics such as height, width, depth, and materials could be presented in such a way as to displace more or less absolutely the familiar associations of those same proportions and materials. The minimalist work was distinguished from pop by being immediately recognizable as art.

Flavin's work is certainly immediately recognizable as art, but still it seems to me that his position could never be as secure as Judd's. His work slips away from the specificity minimalism demands precisely because the fluorescent tube is already more specific than, say, stainless steel or plywood. Steel and wood may remind us of this and that, but Flavin's tubes are just like any other tubes; they are not cut to size or specially made. Designification is much harder when the sign retains its original form, and because of this it was much harder for Flavin to limit the work's field of reference. Judd sought to designify common building materials in order to be in charge of the signification that remained; his materials continued to refer to industrial practices, but he had a critical use for their impersonality: it could embody minimalism's anti-gesturalism. Flavin is wholly minimalist in his anti-gesturalism, but his ability to similarly de- and then re-signify the tube is in comparison limited: the tube is just like the ones at the hardware store and continues to have strong associations which are reinforced by its still functioning as a light. And some of these are associations on which the work relies, making it impossible for Flavin to have much to say about how they are received. His works, like Matisse's, rely on colors that dissolve and are not discordant, and have associations with fashion and luxury whose uncontrollability are what Matisse is about and which remain comparably uncontrollable when Flavin uses them. One difference between the two artists is that in Flavin these properties are themselves anchored in a banal object which never becomes a neutral vehicle for light, even as it disappears into its own luminosity, because of its specific ubiquity in the world at large.

Both Matisse and pop lead to the not unrelated question, which I have discussed elsewhere, of how, in the discourse of the art world (nor is the larger world immune) serious—in the sense of dreary—consequences have flowed from the fact that the words *gravity* and *light* both commonly refer to a phenomenon and a conventional connotation derived from it. Leo Steinberg once told me that when the first pop art show was held at The Museum of Modern Art in New York in 1962, the critic Hilton Kramer was on a discussion panel held in connection with it and trashed the show with all the conservative fervor for which he'd subsequently become even more well known. Duchamp was in the audience and said to Leo afterward that he felt that Kramer had been "insufficiently lighthearted," and while sharing nothing else with Kramer's worldview I think it fair to say that minimalism was also seldom lighthearted. On the contrary it was and remains a movement dependent on bringing together the two connotations of the word *gravity,* and I think that this is another important sense in which Flavin's use of fluorescent color makes his work incompatible with the critical assertions of a tendency with which he would otherwise be wholly identified. Minimalism implicitly had a problem with the word *light.*

Minimalism's defining text is Judd's 1966 essay "Specific Objects," which repeats in what are meant to be empirical rather than metaphysical terms the argument advanced by Newman in 1947 in an essay called "The Sublime Is Now." Both Newman's and Judd's essays or manifestos invent fantasy art histories which make American art more immediate and direct than its European antecedents. In an interview a couple of years earlier Judd had declared, "I'm totally uninterested in European art and I think it's over with. It's not so much the elements we use as their context." He didn't explain what he meant by context, but he implied that it was intellectual and ideological, as he went on to say, "For example, they might have used a diagonal, but no one there ever used as direct a diagonal as Morris Louis." The reference to Louis is suggestive. Louis's colors are very bright and their edges imprecise because the paint is stained into the canvas. Given Judd's insistence that he saw only gravity in Jackson Pollock's drip paintings, I think it probable that in Louis too he saw gravity and specificity where others might see color that refused to be held in place by materiality.[8]

Michael Govan, in his essay for the Flavin retrospective's catalogue, sees Judd echoing the constructivist Vladimir Tatlin when, in "Specific Objects," he calls for "riddance of the problem of illusionism and of literal space, space in and around marks and colors." Judd—for whom, as for Newman, "European'" actually meant "French"—concurs with Tatlin in regarding these as "the most salient and most objectionable relics of European art."[9] Judd must have seen Louis fending off illusion and European degeneracy with gravity. It was the fact that Louis stained and poured his paint onto unprimed canvas that appealed to him, not the fact that the colors have an uncontrollable perceptual relationship to the white cotton that surrounds them. But if Flavin represented an advance on Louis, not because Louis was comparably degenerate but because Flavin's work was not circumscribed by anything resembling pictorial space or the limits of the stretcher, I don't think that any greater directness for his diagonal could be said to accrue from that. Rather, if Flavin's *diagonal of May 25, 1963 (to Constantin Brancusi)* (1963; fig. 4) is a more "direct" diagonal than anything found, for example, in either Brancusi or Tatlin, its greater or more intense diagonality derives not from its freedom from pictorial space but from its being a very bright fluorescent tube. Johns's *Flag* is not a picture of a flag because it doesn't show it "in" a depicted space but instead juxtaposes the flag (an object which is first an image) onto painting (an object which is first a surface), and Flavin's tube is likewise a tube rather than a representation of a tube, just as it is very bright rather than an attempt to simulate brightness. The elements that distinguish this diagonal from diagonals in earlier kinds of art derive from pop art, which used the sign that was always already an object, as was pointed out at the time by John Perrault, but I think with little response from anyone else.[10]

By the time Judd published "Specific Objects" Flavin had made the work

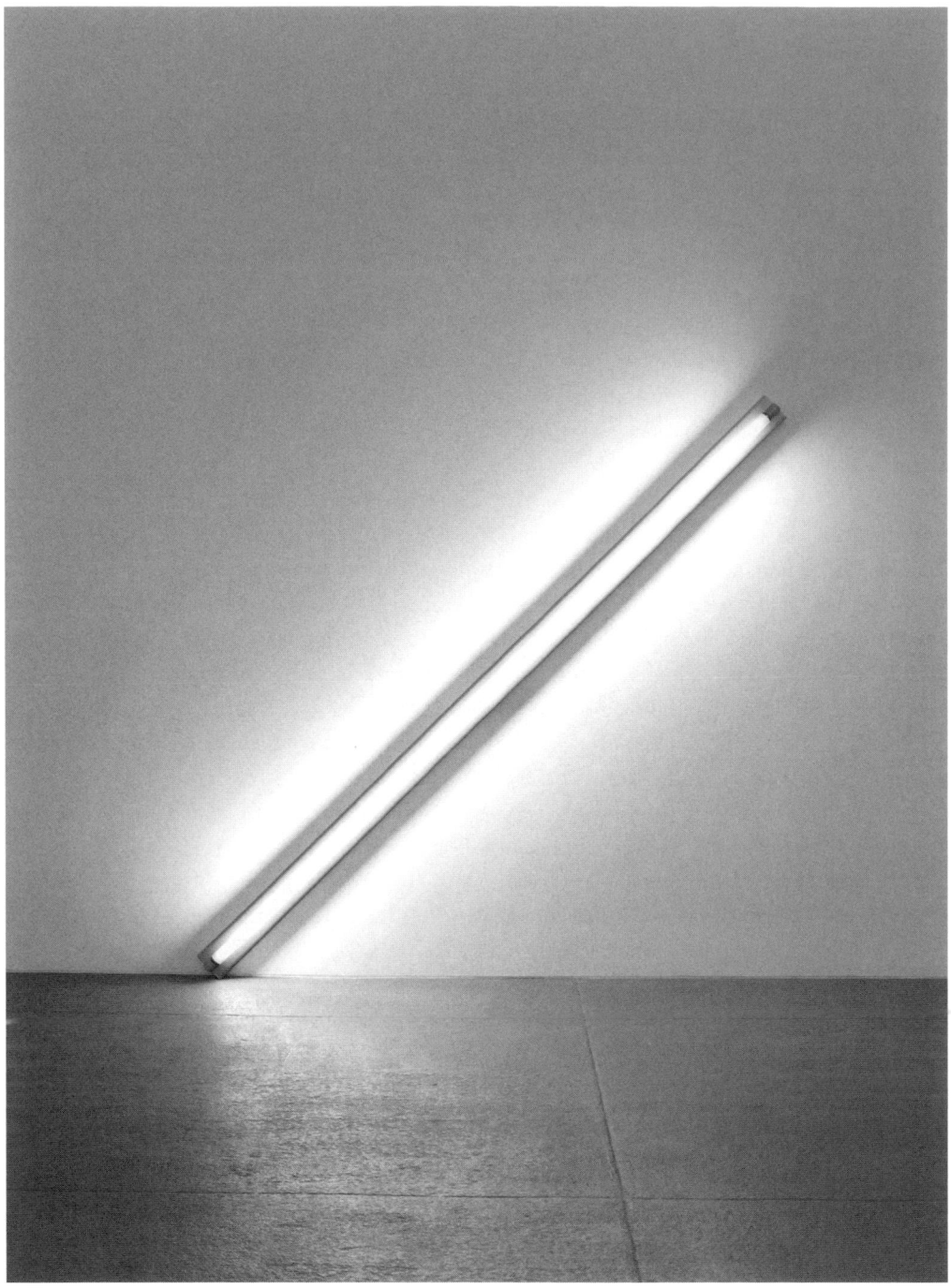

Fig. 4. Dan Flavin, *the diagonal of May 25, 1963 (to Constantin Brancusi)*, 1963, yellow fluorescent light, 8 ft. (244 cm) long on the diagonal. Dia Art Foundation.

dedicated to Matisse with which I began, which uses exactly those colors most likely to create the kind of spatial illusion deplored by Tatlin and Judd because, as in Matisse's painting, they dissolve form rather than specifying planes, creating not only a space but one that is not bound to measurement and specificity. Although Tatlin liked to use perspective to complicate the space in the corners of rooms, he otherwise, like Alexander Rodchenko, wanted to abolish illusion because it was bourgeois; Judd wanted to abolish it because it was European and therefore insufficiently lighthearted. Flavin's and Matisse's colors are above all easy to associate with lightheartedness. Matisse always does associate them with it, and in doing so sees them as fundamental to the kind of spatial illusion he wants to produce: "I have a great love for bright, clear, pure color, and am always surprised to see lovely colors unnecessarily modified and dimmed. . . . [I]f I am not mistaken, only plastic form has true value."[11] I would argue that the association is automatic, that light and color induce different sensations and suggest different logics than do things and gravity, and that this is why they lead Flavin's work away from the ideas he is otherwise eager to embrace. "Space in and around marks and colors" robs the support of its role as the provider or location of specificity because it replaces "real" three-dimensionality with an "illusory" one. Likewise, in Flavin, but not in Judd (or Sol LeWitt), color undermines or parallels structure and to that extent automatically subverts any idea of the specific, leading (seducing) the viewer of Flavin's work away from the stern world of the minimal regardless of Flavin's own conscious allegiance to the minimalist faith in the empirically real.

Flavin's *the diagonal of May 25, 1963 (to Constantin Brancusi)* undermines Judd's use of the word *direct* because it contradicts Rodchenko. Color, being a phenomenon as opposed to a proposition, is always and can only be direct—which is also true of diagonals, one might think. It is for that reason that color and light, unlike drawing, cannot comfortably be made part of a regime of specificity. Especially not when the color and light are intense. Rodchenko sought a solution to color's automatic production of spatial illusion—an unreal three-dimensionality—in the idea of monochrome, which ties one color to one plane, and Judd used color pretty much as Rodchenko recommended. But monochrome cannot identify a color with a plane when the plane is the surface of a fluorescent tube. Whether monochrome or polychrome, the brightness and electric movement of the colors Flavin uses undermine the minimalist definition of specificity precisely because it was derived from equating the real with the verifiably three-dimensional.

The difficulty that Flavin poses for Judd's (and Rodchenko's) idea of the real as that which is measurable and tangible lies in light's not being a thing, least of all an object like a chair or even a sculpture. Light is a phenomenon, and diagonals are signs, and the former will not behave like a material any more than one diagonal is capable of being more "direct" than another. And this difficulty is further complicated by Judd's, and Flavin's, attempts to specify what material differences themselves may or may not mean—a complication compounded in Judd's case by his distressing habit of being most vague when he is most specific. His assertion in defense of Flavin that "materials vary greatly and are simply materials," begs the question of how responses to that variety vary greatly as well, and include the issue of aesthetic affect, as that has to do with sensation and its conceptualization, as well as correlative questions about the materials' similarities or parallels with other things in the world.[12]

Andy Warhol's Brillo boxes recycle an object which is also a sign, and in their case the specificity of the object depends on its acting as both iconic and indexical sign. Their reality lies well outside of the demonstrably three-dimensional. Judd's work may be a triumph of designification compared to that, but his assertion that materials can be just materials is nonetheless no more than an example of his trying to control whatever signification remains once most of the familiar has been removed or otherwise obviated (figs. 5, 6). His attitude is reminiscent of Stella's famous—and roughly contemporaneous —remark that in his paintings "what you see is what you see." As Arthur Danto has said, Stella's formulation cannot be true. Without a theory of art— and one doesn't see theories with one's eyes—black paint would be just black paint. To make art one has to have an idea about it, a theory of what it is.[13] Judd's and Stella's attempts to preclude talk of the spiritual or metaphysical only draw attention to their preoccupation with what they don't want to discuss. As usual, Judd should have read his Heidegger: materials are only just materials when you're trying to ignore what they have to say. Heidegger also notes that we cannot look at anything without bringing associations into play: we do not actually see a book but colors connected to sensations that are largely about touch rather than sight. The fluorescent tube and its colors are never *just* seen, or, rather, seeing them is never a matter of the purely visual because nothing is. Illusion always requires us to ignore a great deal, but it's a bit of a stretch to insist on such repression as a precondition for the anti-illusionist, implying as it does that we must suppress the real in order to experience it. Moreover, if something isn't "really" there, it is also "only" there (and nowhere else).

To summarize, materials are not simply materials in Flavin for a number of reasons. A fluorescent tube is already a thing toward which—like a Brillo box—the viewer brings a preconception. So is the light that comes out of it. Light as such is manifest only via a material condition which is not light itself (this is also true of primary structures like the diagonal, which are ideas be-

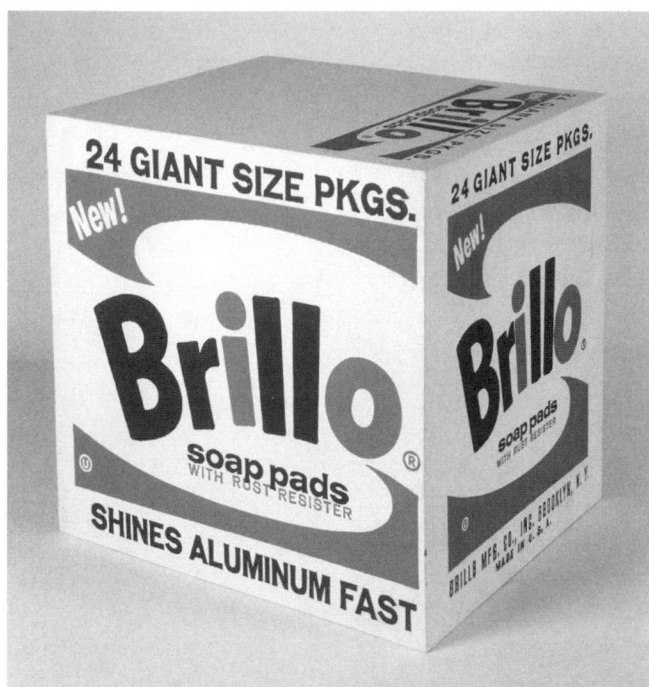

Fig. 5. Andy Warhol, *Brillo Soap Pads Box*, 1964, silkscreen ink and house paint on plywood, 17 × 17 × 14 in. (43.2 × 43.2 × 35.6 cm). Founding Collection, The Andy Warhol Museum, Pittsburgh.

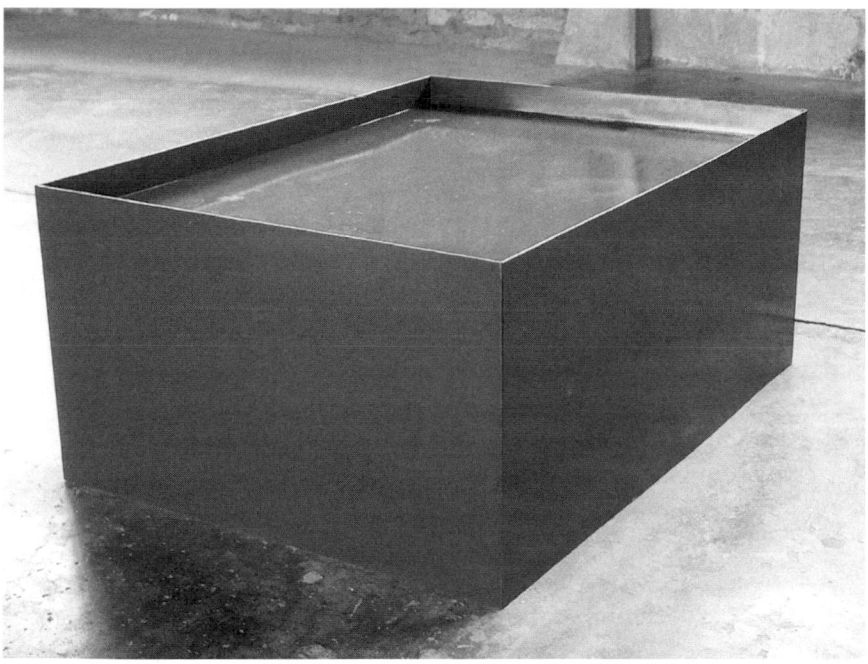

Fig. 6. Donald Judd, *Untitled*, 1965, brown enamel on hot-rolled steel, 22 × 50 × 37 in. (56 × 127 × 94 cm). Collection of Judd Foundation.

fore they are things, let alone specific materials). In addition, in Flavin's work, as in that of all artists, colors have art historical as well as cultural associations. The work dedicated to Matisse uses colors we've seen in painting, *the diagonal of May 25* uses a yellow you can have only in a fluorescent tube. In both the materiality of the fluorescent tube is by definition undermined by the light that emanates from it. The fluorescent light makes the specifics of the work considered as a three-dimensional, or in Judd's terms "real," object hard to see; the tubes' outline becomes uncertainly located just within or without the surface of the tube, which is itself an illuminated thickness. The only thing specific about Flavin's work is its ambiguity.

But Flavin didn't quarrel with Judd's assertion, and I think this may be because he agreed with it and with the assumptions behind it. He reacted testily to attempts to categorize his work, but his reactions were consistently sophistical and disingenuous. To a midwestern art fan who characterized him as a minimalist he retorted that his works were often polychrome, an evasive and unconvincing answer, in that *minimal* implies less or fewer not "one."[14] Flavin scattered one-liners around himself at the same time that he attacked what he called the "epithetical" in others; dedicated work to other artists while trying to avoid art historical associations; frequently took part in group shows with other artists and objected to being described as part of a movement. And I agree that his most important denial was his refusal to allow his work to be associated with the contemplative or the spiritual. It is implausible to think that the terms that come with light—intensity, disembodiment, luminosity itself—can be dissociated from the spiritual, but having said that I disqualify myself from further discussion on the grounds of incompetence. I began by saying that Flavin's work resists contemplation, which of course puts the contemplative at the center of our engagement with it.

But I think that Flavin, Judd, and Stella took an inherently silly position about meaning and interpretation because they were on to something concerning the expressive capacities of industrial materials. However, they were encumbered by a distinction between the real and the illusory which helped them make clear what their work was not but was not able to provide terms that could address what it was.

What was minimalist about their shared attitude was an idea of the primary. It was irrelevant whether Flavin used one or several tubes or colors. But minimalism was a movement whose members identified the minimal with the primary, intensified by association with the familiar. Geometric forms, legible and predictable order, reached a directness unprecedented in minimalism in Flavin's work in and through the recognizable and familiar dimensions of the fluorescent tube and, in Judd's, in and through materials found elsewhere, such as elevators and kitchens.

The fluorescent tube is not only an industrial object rather than a hand-made one; it is a familiar object with familiar dimensions. It has already been constructed according to architectural conventions which are themselves ultimately derived from generalizations about how tall the average person is. This blurs the distinction between real and ideal, between space as a precondition for being and space as an organized continuum that is largely the responsibility of architects and their ancillaries. The minimalists worked with industrial materials which were in that filled with signification and sought to turn those materials into objects that would be more direct than signs could ever be. That is what I mean by designification. Their idea of directness comes from Newman and the New York School, and so does their idea of designification, but it is what they all share with pop artists' sense of the object that distinguishes their work from Rodchenko's, Tatlin's, and Mondrian's ideas about real space. Their pursuit of specificity, partly a reinvention in contemporary American terms of Russian constructivist ideas, proceeded in conjunction with, and was informed by, pop artists' use of the recognizable and of the art object as something made from the same materials and, importantly, of the same size, as other familiar objects.

While seeking to pass beyond nineteenth-century naturalism, Tatlin, Rodchenko, and Mondrian had, like the impressionists and Matisse, worked with an idea of the real as a primary condition in which white paint meant white light; for them this was connected to the same discourse that saw light as not only spiritually but also physiologically good for you—which helps explain why there is so much fenestration in Mies van der Rohe. But in Flavin real space, which earlier artists had been able to imagine as a tripartite singularity —white paint, white light, transparency—can, as daylight gives way to fluorescent, be replaced by what one can only call illusion, or the truth about the real, which is that the latter is a construction, particularly for sensibilities as naturalized to electric light as to the light of the sun. This is why I want to end with Mondrian, to whom Flavin dedicated several works. I believe that the difference between Mondrian and Flavin is that in the latter's work distortion gives way to deferral and also that, in a manner comparable to the way bright lights and colors by definition undermine gravity and even seriousness, the fact that the room is flooded with electrically produced and transmitted color has the effect of qualifying whatever might once have been meant by real space.

Mondrian's last essay was called "A New Realism." His engagement with what he too called real space was straightforward in that he wanted his paintings to activate the space around them through what happened in or on them. Earlier in his career he had also been able to try out his ideas about activating real space in architectural collaborations, and one of the things he had com-

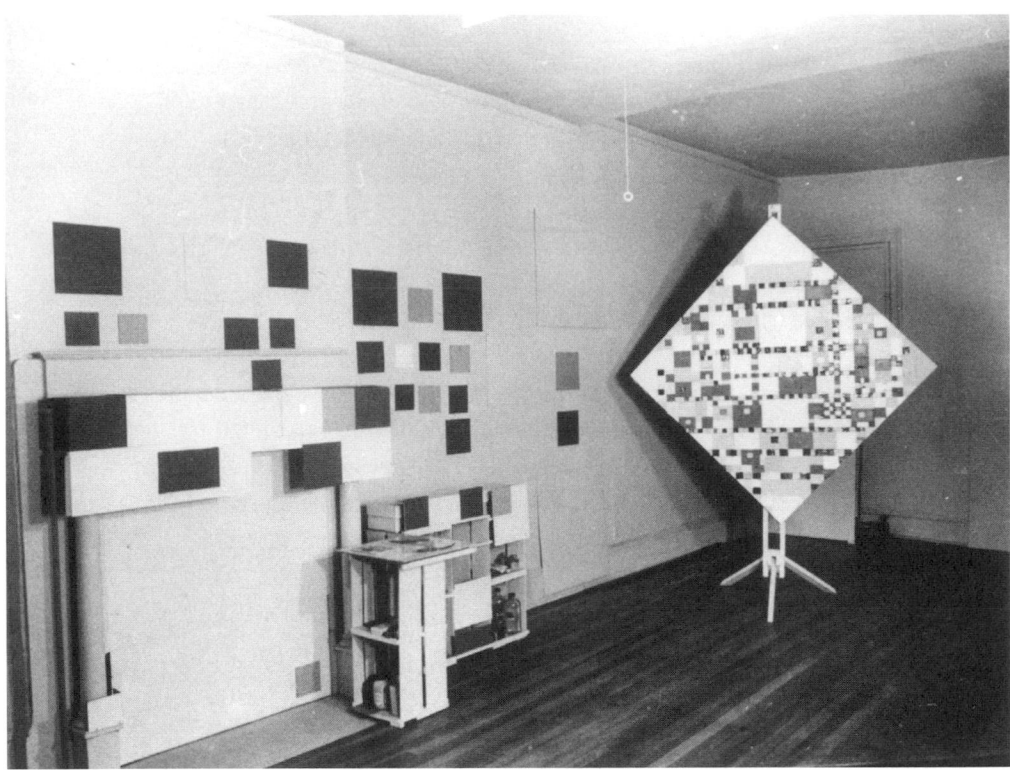

Fig. 7. Fritz Glarner, Piet Mondrian's 15 East 59th Street studio after his death showing *Victory Boogie-Woogie*, 1944, silver gelatin print, 7 × 9.5 in. (18 × 24 cm). Kunsthaus Zürich.

plained about at that time was that artists were making poor use of new materials. Later in life he had only his studio in which to work, and one of the last photographs of the studio, taken just after his death in 1944, shows *Victory Boogie-Woogie* (1942–44) at the back of the photograph and on the wall alongside it rectangles of color, which are also located around and in the fireplace. Mondrian, a recently arrived European, was in New York thinking about the possibilities of the wall years before Newman insisted that American painting alone had freed painting from pictorialism and activated the space beyond the frame (fig. 7).

Flavin was luckier and got to do what Mondrian had wanted to—make individual works like *Victory Boogie-Woogie* as well as works in which he could manipulate space using color, which Judd and Tatlin regarded as the enemy of the real. And so it is. Color robs surfaces of their specificity by making them more expansive or deeper or something else than they would be if they were unpainted or, especially, it they were painted white. The truth about color, its

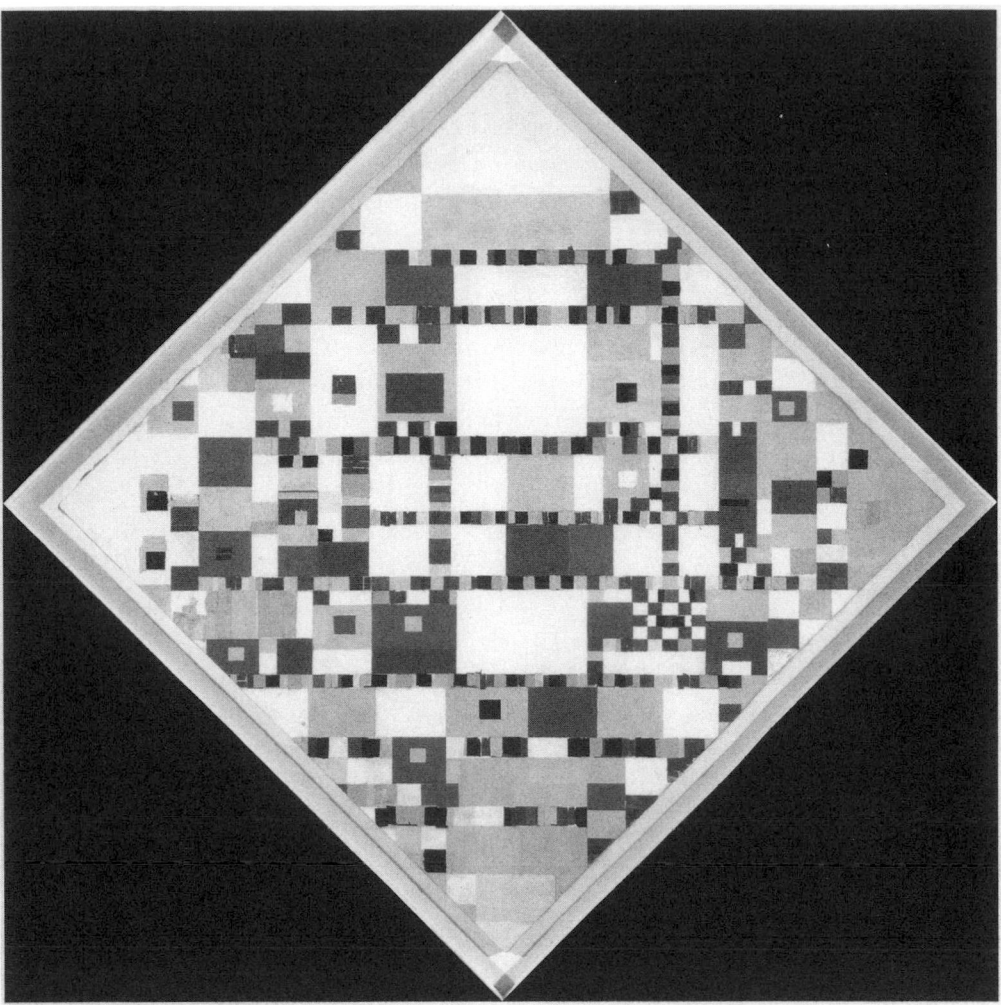

Fig. 8. Piet Mondrian, *Victory Boogie-Woogie* (unfinished), 1942–44, oil and paper on canvas, 50 × 50 in. (127 × 127 cm). Gemeentemuseum den Haguc.

reality, is that it can only create an illusion. *Victory Boogie-Woogie* (fig. 8) supplements rapid eye movements with rapid heart movements. It's all about sharp turns and modulated but clear breaks, which is why I want to insist that jazz rhythms of the sort to which its title allude are important, perhaps fundamental, to it. Yves-Alain Bois has noted that *Victory Boogie-Woogie* was one of only four Mondrian works that was wholly executed in America, and raised his own questions about their relation to the topography of New York City itself.[15]

Be that as it may, Mondrian's America was already the one we know: an advanced technological capitalism whose most popular music is of ultimately African origin—making quite a sharp break with Europe; it has since taken over the world—and in which the accelerated pace that was novel to the impressionists is both more accelerated and the only pace anyone knows. *Victory Boogie-Woogie* is already moving too fast to be looked at contemplatively; there are too many jumps and changes for the mind to wander over as it might over Monet's water lilies. If you get lost in it you'll find yourself caught up in a series of movements which you'll spend more time decoding than contemplating. Governed by a diagonality which is by no means direct, *Victory Boogie-Woogie* drives your attention out toward and on to the wall, a shift made easier by the painting's orientation as a lozenge rather than a rectangle.

If the speed with which details interact in *Victory Boogie-Woogie* anticipates the intensity of Flavin's lights, one big difference between the works of Mondrian and—especially—a work of Flavin's such as his 1996 Dia Foundation staircase is that in the Flavin daylight shares the space with but is not experienced as more intense or powerful than the colors of the work (fig. 9). On the contrary, it is marginalized. Previously it had set the standard; it was for the impressionists the brightest—white imitated sunlight, for Mondrian an ideal because white light is a combination of all the other colors—and therefore at once all the colors and none of them, the one and the many and the many as the one. Artificial white light is now as commonplace as natural white light, and natural light in the Dia staircase is adjunctive or supplementary rather than foundational. The distinction between real and illusory space with which Mondrian and Tatlin worked and with which Flavin thought he worked has been replaced by a distinction between natural and electric light and color, and one between interaction and deferral.

The difference is between the real as a property or quality still separable from its inflection by color and a real produced by and as an inflection and for that reason surely not best or usefully described as "real." This was always an implausible distinction, but it allowed an idea of form to cohabit with an exploration of phenomena, and as the shortcomings of Judd's thinking suggest it was only when phenomena were somehow thought to be irrelevant unless they were properties of form that it became self-debilitating. But whereas Mondrian worked with an interaction between white and other colors, in which white stood for an irreducible condition, Flavin created in the Dia staircase something in which the irreducible has been removed but in that deferred. It isn't there but our experience of the work will at some point lead us to consider the work as an inflection of a space we're never actually going to see uninflected. We are in the presence not of colors interacting with natural light to create a denaturalized space but of the natural playing a small part within the artificial. The role played by natural light in Matisse's or Mon-

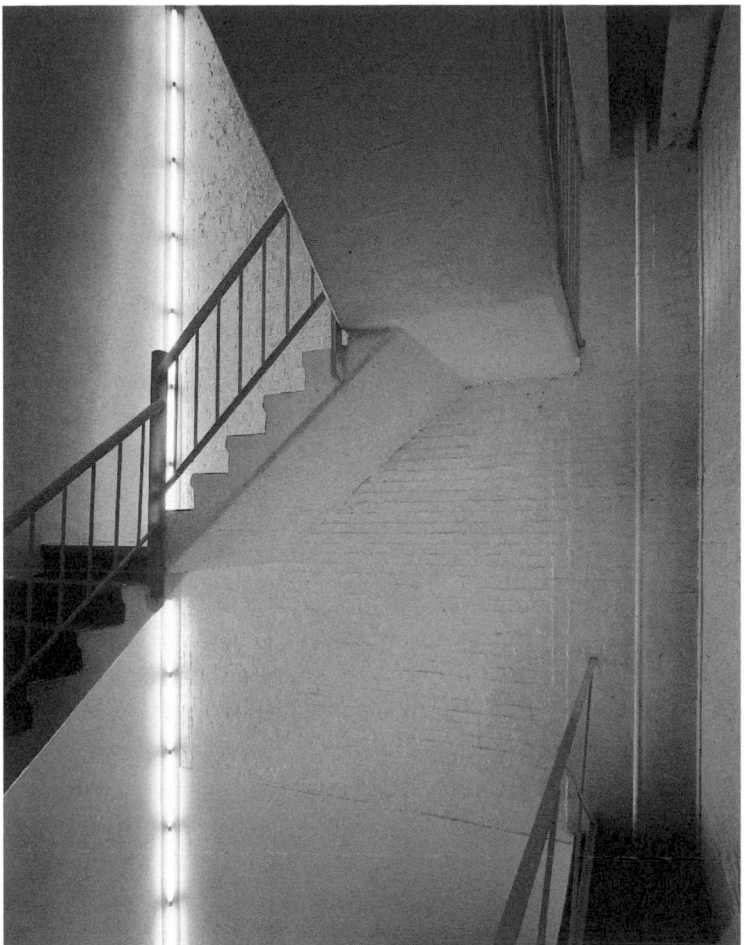

Fig. 9. Dan Flavin, *untitled*, 1996, blue and green fluorescent light, two
sections, each approximately 62 ft. (19 m) high; interior installation view, Dia Art Foundation, New York, long-term installation.
Dia Art Foundation.

drian's paintings (two directly comparable uses of whiteness as light) has been
transferred to an electric light and, as with whiteness in their paintings, it is
electric light that is the irreducible condition here. It isn't added to something
else, and turning it off will reveal nothing.

It is in this sense that the Dia staircase seems to me to be saturated with a
technological condition which the impressionists, Mondrian, and Newman
could only anticipate as an extreme condition of the one with which they were
familiar and which had produced them. It invokes or embodies no mechanical
movement or organic rhythm but is instead made out of the almost impercep-

tible vibrancy of electric current. We are surrounded by the work, so at any given moment there's a lot of it that we can't see, and it is impossible to fully separate surfaces from the effect light is having on them. These are kinds of indeterminacy for which we would use the word *sublime* had not Judd abolished aesthetic terminology in favor of the wholly evasive term *interesting*, his highest term of praise. It permits him to concentrate on an aspect of the work that is only incidentally interesting to anyone else and in the same breath to describe the indeterminate as specific. In a review of a Flavin exhibition in Ottawa, Judd describes the lit tubes as "intense" but also "very definite," and calls the works themselves "very much a particular visible state, a phenomenon," then goes on to say that "the singleness of isolation of phenomena is new to art and highly interesting."[16] I have suggested that Flavin's work is not about isolating phenomena—whether it be a unique isolation, as Judd seems to suggest, or not—except to the extent that every art form or medium privileges, and in that sense "isolates," certain phenomena, but even then only to resurrect or invoke what it can't embody.

I don't think Flavin's work is about isolating anything so much as it is about making electric light subsume natural light and in so doing infinitely deferring a return either to a "real" predicated on the natural, the irreducible, or to any category that could be isolated. There is no sense in which one is able to distinguish the tube as *a* light from *the* light in the room. The light is at once in one place and ubiquitous. While indeterminate the effect is no less specific, but it is by no means a property of color as color or light as light, were one to be able to talk about either of these in such terms. One does not go and see a Flavin and come away with the impression that one saw a particular colored light and that's that. His work is not about isolating phenomena but the reverse, and I think Judd's interpretation misses the point in much the same way that he did with Louis's diagonal. In both cases his desire to see things in terms of isolation—which is to say empirically—seems to oblige him to ignore the obvious. What is more "direct" or immediate in Louis's paintings than in those of Europeans is the color; its diagonal disposition is only one aspect of it and not one that anyone but Judd would be inclined to see as the main issue. Likewise, to be looking at a work which generates a color which (a) is specific to electricity and (b) saturates everything in the room including its viewer, and insisting on seeing an isolated phenomenon seems to me willfully obtuse.

The one thing one can't isolate is the real, and to discuss this I think one needs the specific language of the aesthetic. We didn't, as far as I can see, have much passion for real space until it started to disappear, in the late nineteenth century. If Flavin announces its disappearance or, alternatively, provides us with a contemporary example of its tendency to always be somewhere else—

since Oscar Wilde and others pointed it out in the nineteenth century, we have been aware that nature struggles to live up to the reality of its image— then just as I don't think *interesting* will do as a description of what that state might involve, I similarly doubt that a description of such a state could proceed from something other than the senses. It would therefore be aesthetic —*an*esthesia being what deadens the senses and *aesthesis,* one hopes, the opposite—as opposed to epistemological or a matter of empirical verification. The Dia stairway addresses the senses directly and makes color and illumination inseparable from that which is colored and illuminated. It deploys the terms of the sublime, particularly as these were defined in connection with painting—the unframed as the unbounded—as it replaces sunlight with electric light, which surrounds and envelops, replacing one specificity with another. In Flavin—as in the world at large—technology is seen or felt to replace the natural in the terms of a naturalist aesthetic. In saying this I am not resurrecting an eighteenth-century subject. I am on the contrary seeing the subject implied by Flavin's work as made possible by the degree to which the natural, and with it its subject, have changed not only since the eighteenth century but since—were it possible to date such a change—the transition from the mechanical to the electronic was completed at some point in the past fifty years.

If we have naturalized technology—if we can no more imagine life without the cell phone and email than medieval people could imagine life without angels—we have done so because it has technologized us. Nature has long since been adjunctive or subordinate to technology. The Caribbean Island is never as colorful as the poster in the travel agent's that led one to go there— which was David Hockney's example of the relation of pop art to nature, a sixties version of Wilde's comment about a sunset feebly attempting to impersonate a Turner and an example of how constant the relationship has been. And no natural catastrophe is as scary as nuclear war. (One might also think here of global warming, final and pathetic triumph of technology over that on which it depends.) Flavin was a great poet of the technologized subject, a person for whom electricity and daylight added up to a condition both uncertain and normal. Such a person would be likely to know that, like technocapitalism, the body is held together, naturally, by electricity. We share a need for oxygen with living beings and for electricity with computers and communication systems. The impressionist painting was made of a multitude of marks and could be seen to reflect a subject relating to the world through rapid eye movement. The theme is acceleration, a body living in a world where life is moving faster than ever before. Flavin's Dia staircase fills the space with electric light, displacing and contextualizing the natural light, which is also present and which could be seen to reflect a subject that knows itself to be driven by a comparably constant movement, as described by

Lyotard in his essay on Newman. The theme is instantaneity, a speed that cannot be exceeded and to which the idea of acceleration—of comparison—is in consequence irrelevant.

As for what is left of the—imaginary, symbolic—idea of the real in Flavin, one can say that he made his work out of color (always direct, always weightless), light, brightness; in short out of all the properties that deprive things of specificity and that—being only properties and thus always in need of specification—are not things themselves. He presented them through the most common source of light in everyday life, the familiar but I think not primary form of the fluorescent tube.

Notes

1. home.howstuffworks.com/fluorescent-lamp.htm (9/7/2005).

2. The influence of Chevreul's *De la loi du contraste simultané des couleurs et de l'assortiment des objets colorés* (Paris, 1839) on the impressionists is nowadays controversial, but it seems to me unarguable that the white used by the impressionists derives from his experiments with measuring daylight; he himself describes the light at midday on the brightest day of the year (midsummer) as a mixture of the three primaries, his color circle proceeding thus outward from white. A white made in this way will also respond to the changes in daylight during the day. However, controversy might be fueled by more recent observations, e.g., "Any white light may be matched in appearance by a mixture of monochromatic lights, and in an indefinite number of ways" (C. L. Hardin, "Color Science," in *Encyclopedia of Aesthetics* [New York: Oxford University Press, 1998], 400).

3. Jeremy Gilbert-Rolfe, *Beauty and the Contemporary Sublime* (New York: Allworth, 2000), 31–32.

4. E. J. Hobsbawm, *The Age of Capital, 1848–1875* (New York: Scribner's, 1975), 52; T. J. Clark, *The Painting of Modern Life* (New York: Knopf, 1985), 149.

5. Guignet of Paris patented the process for manufacturing viridian or transparent oxide of chromium in 1859. Alizarin has a more complex history. A British inventor, William Perkins, was beaten to the patent office by only a few hours by Heinrich Caro, representing Badische Analin- and Soda-Fabrik, where it had been developed by Adolf Bayer, Carl Graebe, and Carl Lieberman between 1865 and 1868. A deal was worked out, and Perkins and Caro had figured out a method of synthesis that was economically feasible—the original Graebe-Lieberman formula was not—by the end of 1869. See Helen Skelton, *A History of Pigment Use in Western Art, Part 2* (Toronto: Dominion Colour Corporation, n.d.), unpaginated. If it is difficult to imagine impressionism without viridian, it seems impossible to imagine it without alizarin. Alizarin was the first synthetic color to wipe out a natural dye: within years of its introduction the indigo trade was finished, industry having found a way for nature's colors to be more fully realized in painting than ever before.

6. Jean-François Lyotard, "The Sublime and the Avant-Garde," in *The Inhuman: Reflections of Time*, trans. Geoff Bennington and Rachel Bowlsby (Stanford: Stanford University Press, 1991), 93.

7. Camilla Gray, *The Great Experiment: Russian Art, 1863–1922* (London: Thames and Hudson, 1962).

8. Donald Judd, "Specific Objects," *Arts Yearbook* 8 (1965), reprinted in *Theories and Documents of Contemporary Art: A Sourcebook of Artists' Writings*, ed. Kristine Styles and Peter Selz (Berkeley: University of California Press, 1966); Barnett Newman, "The Sublime Is Now," *Tiger's Eye* (December 1948), reprinted in *Barnett Newman: Selected Writing and Interviews*, ed. John P. O'Neill (Berkeley: University of California Press, 1992), 170–73; Bruce Glazer, "Questions to Judd and Stella" (1966), ed. Lucy Lippard, in *Minimal Art: A Critical Anthology*, ed. Gregory Battcock (Berkeley: University of California Press, 1995), 154.

9. Judd, "Specific Objects," 116.

10. John Perrault, "Minimal Abstracts," in Battcock, *Minimal Art*, 256–57.

11. Henri Matisse, "On Modernism and Tradition," in *Matisse on Art*, ed. Jack D. Flam (London: Phaidon, 1973), 73.

12. Judd, "Specific Objects."

13. Arthur Danto, in "Uncontrollable Beauty," a panel discussion with Bill Beckley (moderator), Peter Schjeldahl, and myself, at the School of Visual Arts, New York, April 21, 1998. Stella's phrase seems to be one that Danto finds particularly irritating; he attributes it to different causes on different occasions. In *Beyond the Brillo Box: The Visual Arts in Post-Historical Perspective* (Berkeley: University of California Press, 1992), he describes it as "the sullen slogan of Frank Stella"(17) and associates it with Clement Greenberg, who is seen as a kind of Walter Pater figure preoccupied with the moment of looking before interpretation clicks in; but in *The Abuse of Beauty: Aesthetics and the Concept of Art* (Chicago: Carus, 2003), he describes it as possibly related to a kind of philosophy taught at Princeton and Columbia, where "certain of the Minimalists studied."

14. Michael Govan, "Irony and Light," in Michael Govan and Tiffany Bell, *Dan Flavin: A Retrospective*, exh. cat. (New Haven: Yale University Press, 2004), 72.

15. "Apart from *Boogie-Woogie, New York* and the final three paintings (*New York City, Broadway Boogie-Woogie*, and *Victory Boogie-Woogie*), all were begun in Europe" (Yve-Alain Bois, "The Iconoclast," in *Piet Mondrian, 1872–1944*, ed. Angelica Zander Rudenstine [Boston: Little, Brown, 1994], 359). I think the recurrence of "boogie-woogie" suggests that that Mondrian's attention was caught as much by the movement that ran through New York as by the city's skyline or street grid—it is to the point that he liked to dance.

16. Donald Judd, in Dan Flavin, *fluorescent light, etc. from Dan Flavin/lumière fluorescente, etc. par Dan Flavin*, exh. cat. (Ottawa: National Gallery of Canada, 1969).

Anne M. Wagner   Flavin's Limited Light

Many of Dan Flavin's contemporaries found him "spleenish." With reason:
this was someone apt to condemn the many artists and writers he disagreed
with as "dilettanted dada homosexuals" or else "damned fools." The latter
phrase served to name the journalist Hilton Kramer; the former invoked
Robert Morris and his "inbred gang." Together they are enough to demonstrate that Flavin didn't much like the art world system on which he actively
depended, as his frequent contributions to it made abundantly clear. To quote
him directly: "I know of no occupation in American life so meaningless and
unproductive as that of art critic." No wonder Philip Leider accused him of
"bit[ing] the hands that pay the light bills"; at that time the editor of *Artforum*,
Leider was in a position to know. But why, in the years around 1970, was
Flavin so ready to bare his fangs? Why all the snapping and spleen? Surely it
is right to see such displays of animus as a calculated tactic, not simply an occasional foible or a superficial pose. Perhaps one main motive was that they
got results. They effected, so Jack Burnham alleged in 1969, a "journalistic cauterization" that Flavin, "unaided, [had] performed on the body of his own
art." Paradoxically enough, the result was to reduce the likelihood of a reviewer's venturing a hostile response. "Closed-minded, intolerant," prone to

"gratuitous insults," Flavin had earned the reputation, as Burnham put it, "of giving out considerably more punishment than received."[1]

Yet despite this apparently hostile verdict, Burnham counted himself, however improbably, among those select critics who followed and valued Flavin's art. So did many of the artist's other challengers and quasi-foes. One ritual exchange of insults with *Artforum*, for example, ended with Philip Leider's fulsomely declaring, "In an abject, utterly hopeless attempt to have the last word, I should like to affirm my continuing admiration for Mr. Flavin's work."[2] Cauterization had worked. Spleenishness notwithstanding, the artist won the fast allegiance of a spectrum of peers. The critics Peter Plagens, Kenneth Baker, Germano Celant, and Barbara Reise; the artists Dan Graham, Mel Bochner, and Donald Judd: all wrote in his favor. Blessed are the belligerent: aggression reaps rewards.

It is worth asking why. We might look, by way of explanation, to a half-joking list drawn up by Mel Bochner in 1966 (fig. 1). In one column are his friends, both fellow artists and dealers; in the other, the actors who would play them when "Minimal Art: The Movie" made it to the silver screen. With *Pollock* and *Basquiat*

Fig. 1. Mel Bochner, *Minimal Art: The Movie*, 1966, ink and pencil on paper, 6 × 3½ in. (15.2 × 8.9 cm). Collection of the artist.

now behind us, that day may be here sooner that we think. But no new cast list could hope to rival Bochner's original pairings: they are inspired. The gorgeous Monica Vitti would incarnate Eva Hesse, Frank Sinatra the dapper dealer Leo Castelli, and as for the boyish Bochner himself, Peter Fonda was perfect for the role. And Flavin? Jackie Gleason was the man. The suggestion is brilliant. It summons Gleason as a pool-room hustler (1961), or playing Ralph Kramden, know-it-all bus driver (1956–57), or throughout the 1950s and 1960s hosting a weekly variety show (fig. 2). In the last context there was always a caustic monologue, pugnaciously delivered, and then a funny little sideways skip/shuffle, with Gleason intoning, "And awaaaaay we go." If only for a moment the otherwise earthbound body seemed light as a feather and ready to soar. Not only does the comparison insist that Flavin's aggression, like Ralph Kramden's, was mostly comic, but it also reminds us that just like

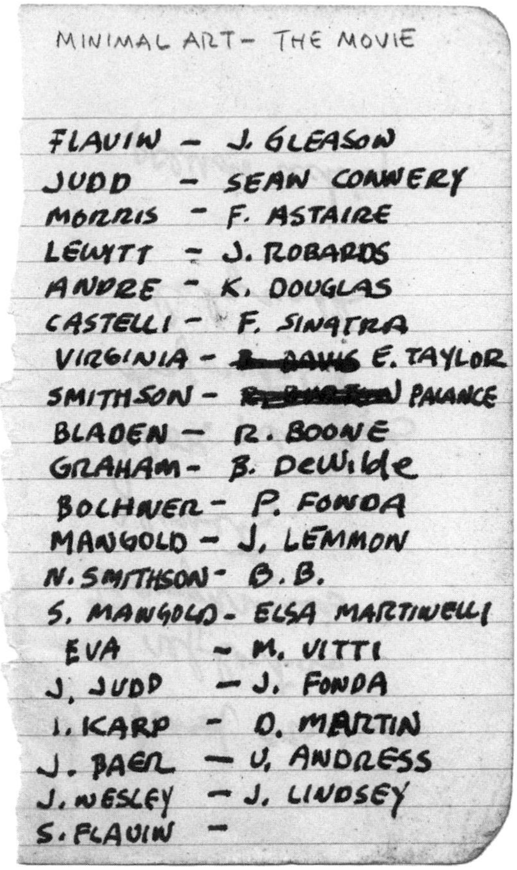

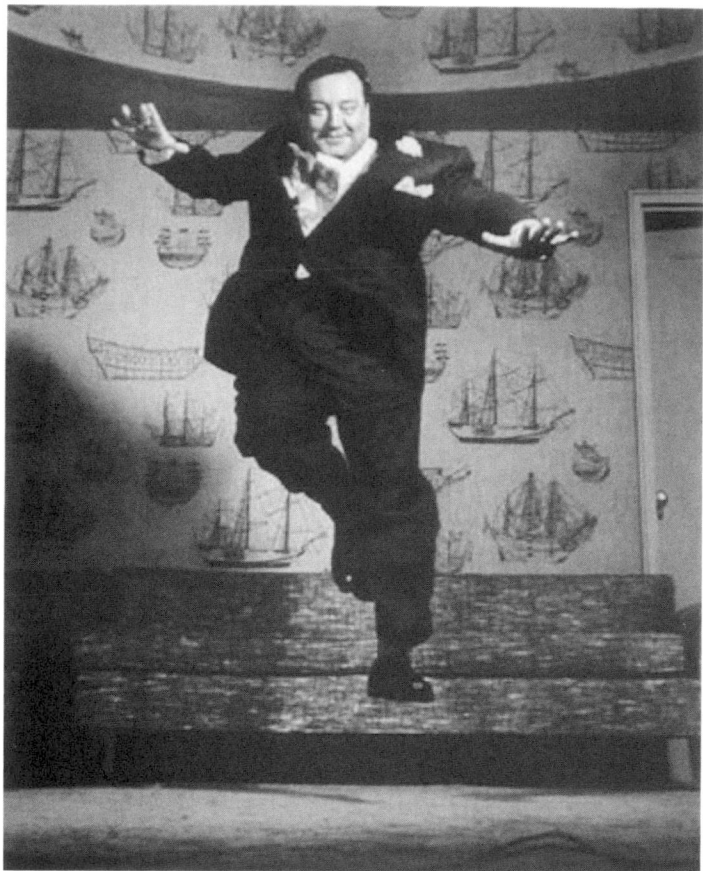

Fig. 2. Jackie Gleason, 1955, photograph. Source: www.haminahamina
.com/Jackie-Gleason-1955.jpg.

his hefty look-alike, the artist could convey a weightlessness that put the lie
to the mundane presence, the material factuality, of his sculptural work. If
Gleason could sometimes seem to shed or transcend his all-too-fleshly body,
Flavin—or at least his work with light—could do the same.

In what follows I want to address some implications of this paradox—the
idea that Flavin's mundane materiality can achieve the limitless, perhaps even
approach the sublime. I am not alone. The transformation has been noted
from the start.[3] Here is a brief sampling of how early critics tried to sum it up.
The *Art News* reviewer Jill Johnston, in January 1965, on the Green Gallery installation of the month before: "One curious effect of the work is the combined quality of an intractably rigid cylinder and that incorporeal radiation
that can't be measured." The *Studio International* reviewer (Dore Ashton), as-
sessing a Kornblee Gallery show of summer 1966: "Rigour in basic form is

erased by pulsating light, producing a strange, and in this case, compelling effect. . . . A cold icon or a lunar symbol?" A second *Art News* reviewer, Elizabeth C. Baker, in 1967, reflecting more generally on the new phenomenon of light art and Flavin's provocative place within it: "Flavin does something for one's idea of light: it is he who makes its mystical qualities uncompromisingly evident, by the very fact of such stark presentation. He deserves credit for jumping straight to this conclusion." If the aesthetic process remarked by all these critics moves (sometimes abruptly) from the literal or factual to the dematerialized, mystical, or symbolic—from the intractable to the incorporeal—then the relevant aesthetic issue comes to concern the metaphorical, even metaphysical, qualities of the artist's work, qualities which exceed the experiential limits of the work of art.[4]

What is notable is not just that the work's installation, its physical presence in the gallery, governed any possible aesthetic reading of its materials—the draconian sense that, as Jill Kornblee herself famously put it, "With Flavin's work, if it isn't up it just doesn't exist"—but rather that its existence as art, when installed, could not be taken simply as a matter of fact. Here lies a crucial distinction with other minimalist materials and practices—for example, with the 137 firebricks that, when arranged in a gallery, become Carl Andre's *Lever* (1966). Mere presence alone—to say nothing of the aggressive hereness secured through the declaratively mundane means of off-the-shelf fixtures (or firebricks)—is for Flavin not the sole effect secured. Certainly the labels which the artist insisted on leaving in position on each metal housing do tell a tale of pedestrian origins in purchases from various metropolitan outlets: in New York City, the National Lighting Supply Company, for example, or the New Jersey–based Worklite Company. The result is a set of materials understood—to quote Barbara Reise—as "rigorously modern and banal." Yet those same mundane fixtures notwithstanding, the light they emitted was something else. According to one observer, it was not "entirely factual." This was because "the positions in which he places his lights are not the same positions they would occupy in an office, laboratory, or other place devoted to the business of ordinary life." And if the light was not quite factual, neither were the shadows it cast.[5]

What are light and shadow when they are no longer factual, yet present nonetheless? And *where* are they, if not somewhere devoted to the business of life? The answer is obvious: the gallery, home to the business of art. Though light is functionally essential there, it normally plays second fiddle to the wares it exposes to view. Flavin's turning of the tables not only transforms fact into fiction, the useful into the ornamental (sometimes spectacularly so), but it also insists that the means and effects of illumination, whether utilitarian or spectacular, should be grasped as having contexts and meanings which are conventional, habitual, and social, thus recognizable. These emerge, albeit negatively, when those governing conventions are somehow broken or obscured. This is a suggestion that Flavin might not have found entirely congenial when stated so baldly. In practice, however, he seems to have routinely put it to the test, under conditions that, though by now familiar, still need spelling out. His main device was the exhibition, as it soon became clear that no single work—even the "ironic" *diagonal of personal ecstasy (the diagonal of May 25, 1963)*, with its "potential for becoming a modern technological fetish"—was conclusive enough in its implications for the artist "to be sure how it would be understood."[6] The end result of such incipient ambiguities was Flavin's turn from the individual object (however fetishistic) to an exhibition strategy based on what we now call installation but what he himself termed in 1969 "careful, thorough composition of the illuminating equipment."[7] This meticulous, even punctilious phrase points to a vocabulary, and a modus operandi, still in the making—one whose purposes and implications were not yet known. In the absence of any stable lexicon, little wonder that Flavin sometimes also called his shows "situations" and even "completed propositions," though not "environments" and never "sculpture."[8] Both the range of epithets and their limits suggest a new reliance on context, where utterly specific architectural and spatial features actively shaped each composition, and where the result was asked to advance some theorem or statement on the relation of light to a particular ambient space.

These investigations meant that by 1966, or so Flavin declared, he himself had begun to temper his earlier fascination with "fluorescent light as image" in favor of a recognition of what he termed the "physical fact of the tube as object in place . . . whether switched on or off." But what sort of object is this, precisely? For while Flavin himself preferred the neologism *image-object,* so as to signal his concern with what he called the "actuality" (not the factuality) of fluorescent light—*actuality* meaning its experiential rather than its literal or physical qualities—some of his most vocal supporters preferred to think of his pieces as brute objects only, leaving image and experience quite pointedly alone. When writing of Flavin, Mel Bochner, for example, invoked Roland Barthes on Alain Robbe-Grillet, appropriating that up-to-the-minute critical verdict to suggest that in *his* use of the factual object Flavin similarly short-circuited metaphor in favor of empirical phenomena: "[The object] is not ambiguous, not allegorical, not even opaque. . . . [F]or him the object is no longer a common-room of correspondences, a welter of sensations and symbols, but merely the occasion of a certain optical resistance." The whole phrase is one to be savored for its period flavor, the idea of "optical resistance" most of all.[9]

Actuality or factuality? Image or object? Transparent or opaque? On or off? It is worth underscoring that when the artist wrote of image-objects he proposed the term as a hyphenated hybrid, neither one nor the other but both. Not unlike the neither-nor of Donald Judd's specific object ("neither painting nor sculpture"), what is proposed here is a contradictory unity. The two nouns make uneasy companions: in fact, it is none too clear what this coinage can mean, at least within a more familiar aesthetic that, in opposing the pictorial and sculptural, also pits the optical and visual *against* the material and tactile—as Flavin well knew. On the one hand, the image-object could hardly pass muster with those colleagues who insisted on his utter literalism. (Here we should add to Bochner's agile ventriloquizing of Barthes Dan Graham's blunt rendition of Flavin's central article of faith: "There is no projected core of inner vision, only the literal projection of each fixture and tube from the ground of the wall.")[10]

On the other hand, however, Flavin's new phrase was equally foreign to the version of modernism that by the mid-1960s had begun to calcify. By those lights, the image-object is an impossibility, a patent contradiction, as can be judged from the hostile response to Flavin offered by Rosalind Krauss in 1969. The two were not on the same wavelength. Krauss sees Flavin's work as essentially graphic, the fixtures as lines, their light as modeling, and the whole effect as "dramatizing again and again the mysterious capacity of line to reproduce visual conditions." Flavin, in other words, does not produce pictures so much as find the physical means to literalize a fundamental aspect of pictorial illusionism. Herein the problem lies. That literalism was fatally apparent, according to Krauss, in one of the two major pieces in the Ottawa retrospective, *untitled (to the "innovator" of Wheeling Peachblow)* (1966–68). Its cornered square format, a main vehicle of the artist's color explorations in the mid-1960s, differed from other uses of that arrangement in that its bottom edge was set directly on the floor. The result, claimed Krauss, is that the "intrusion of the floor area into the visual field of the image appeared like a pictorial device—almost a collage element—to disrupt the illusion by reasserting the actual shape of the room."[11]

Krauss's language is telling. Intrusion and disruption declare that the image-object balance has gotten out of whack. But this is not all. The issue is even more egregious as regards *untitled (to Dorothy and Roy Lichtenstein on not seeing anyone in the room)*, the second major piece in the show (1968; fig. 3). "The other large scale image," Krauss wrote, "—a sequence of nine [the number varied in different locations] vertical, eight-foot tubes, spaced at equal intervals in the doorway between the two gallery rooms and completely barring access to the luminous space beyond them—seemed equally to gesture toward the pictorial. Its particular reference for me was the simultaneous depth and inaccessibility of illusionistic space." But, she continued, the space "in the room beyond is not illusionistic. It is real; and as such it cannot be brought to

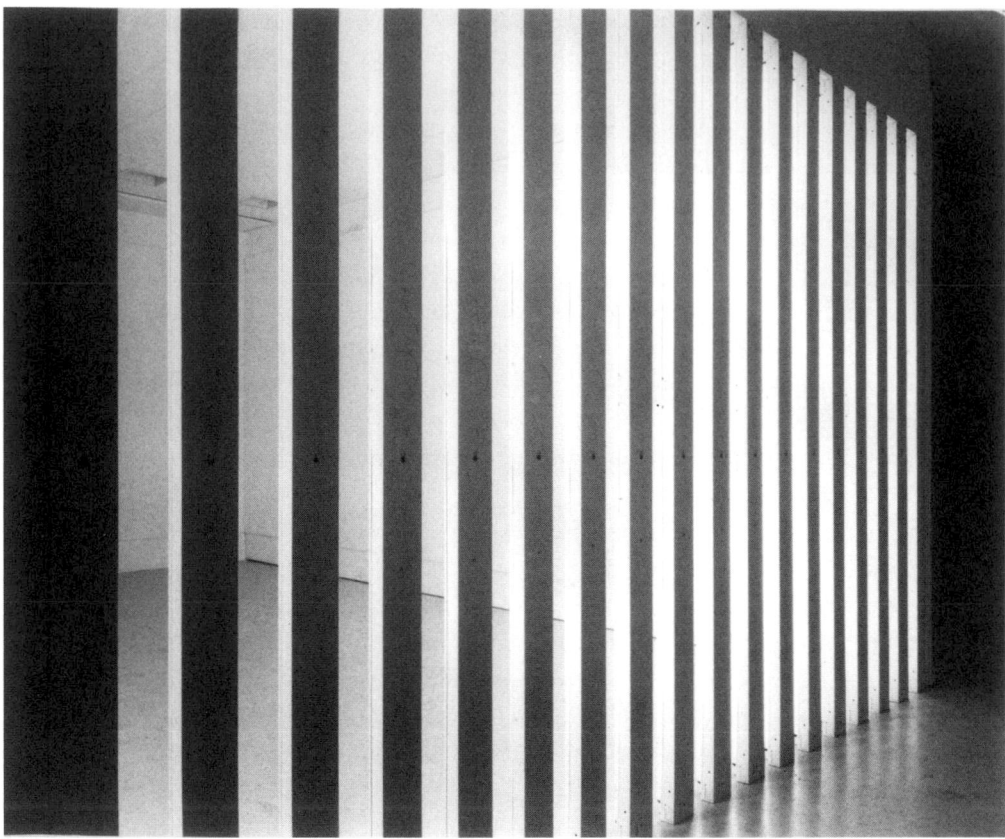

Fig. 3. Dan Flavin, *untitled (to Dorothy and Roy Lichtenstein on not seeing anyone in the room)*, 1968, cool white fluorescent light, 8 ft. (244 cm) high; sixteen fixtures installed in a doorway measuring 8 × 11 ft. (244 × 335 cm). Photo courtesy of Stephen Flavin.

bear on the conventions of painting. It can only be juxtaposed with them, to an end that I see as being . . . conceptually trivial."[12]

For all its hostility, this painful verdict nonetheless rings the changes on the idea of the image-object in a helpful way: in practice *object* now expands to include the spatial real. Yet while Krauss credits Flavin with referencing the key contradiction of depiction—its deceptive depth—she finds the allusion too fragile to be sustained. It is undone by the viewer's knowledge that there is really no illusion at work: where depth should (not) be lies space. The result, says Krauss, is not only conceptually trivial; its trumped-up pictorialism, industrial fixtures notwithstanding, is (shades of Greenberg on Pollock!) "gothic"—too full of "hidden-ness and mystery," despite its reliance on visible sources of radiant light.[13] Such a verdict cannot help but return us to the "common room of correspondences," that run-down location, with its "welter of sensations and symbols," which proponents of the objecthood of Flavin's artwork would prefer us to leave behind.

One way out of this stalemate would be to take seriously the idea of the image-object as Flavin's guiding concept—the balancing act his work aimed at, though did not always achieve. What does he mean by the term? It brings together hardware and software: concrete determinants played off against the pictorial, the immaterial; light objectified as constant and artificial, even while it is emitted by those signature fixtures when configured in an active, even graphic semaphore. The balance was not struck overnight, as his 1960s works attest. This was the decade, after all, when Flavin first plotted out his basic effects and formulas: color relations and spatial placement—locations, intervals, overlaps, angles, projections—were key. Such a job could only be done publicly, in show after show—nineteen solo exhibitions in the 1960s alone. And despite the artist's reliance on drawings to lay out his installations, the exhibitions themselves were inevitably the only sure testing ground for new effects of color, placement, and the rest. Little wonder that at the 1964 Green Gallery exhibition, as Michael Govan notes, Flavin found himself changing bulb colors after the fixtures were in place. If it is essential to re-member that the arrangements we now take for granted as constitutive of Flavin's oeuvre needed such physicalization—needed to be seen and learned from—it is equally useful to discover that some had to be revised or rejected once they could be seen.[14]

Might it not be useful to recover these choppings and changings of mind? Both successes and failures have left their traces in the journalistic topsoil of the time. Flavin may have mistrusted the critics, but their workaday efforts, plus accompanying illustrations, mean that we can say quite a bit about how, in the 1960s, he had his work installed. Thus not only can we grasp something about how he thought it should be encountered, but we can also draw some conclusions about how and why he modified his views. Above all, what was being investigated was the optimal ratio between the opposing qualities of image and object, as those might be rendered through lumens and lamps. Light, for Flavin, was always to be balanced, or at least regulated: his central artifice, it relied on careful deployment and strict control. Remember the soberly qualified title he chose for his first solo exhibition of objects (as op-posed to drawings): *some light*. Writing of the seven "icons" on view there, he declared, "They are constructed concentrations celebrating barren rooms. They bring a limited light." If the celebration of barrenness seems to imagine an art that embellishes emptiness, presumably Flavin could not avoid wonder-ing how to limit light sufficiently, so that the necessary barrenness—a version of the space that he elsewhere (whether tendentiously or hopefully) termed "neutral"—can be maintained.[15]

It is striking how long it took Flavin to work out how to maintain emptiness, and how to limit the light: where, that is to say, to place his fixtures, whether to double or triple, align or angle them, and what those placements might do and mean. We have some evidence of various formats that were eventually abandoned or transformed.[16] Consider his 1964 Green Gallery solo exhibition and the group show held in the same space the following year (figs. 4, 5). Both test out options in ways that must surely have seemed tentative even at the time. Take, for example, the single diagonal that vectors up from the high-gloss floor to lean on the wall in the 1965 show. Or perhaps it vectors down from wall to floor. Though certainly deliberate, the arrangement looks impromptu either way. Unlike the earlier diagonals, what it lacks is an adequate background, and thus the capacity to function imagistically: its spatial projection means that there is no tight framework or stable background to suggest how it should be seen.[17] The same might be said of the wall pieces with floored diagonals, such as *untitled (to Ingrid Nibbe)* (1966), as installed a year later in the Galleria Sperone, Milan (fig. 6), as well as of the floor piece, *gold, pink, and red, red* (1964), which sits so sculpturally in the foreground of the 1964 Green Gallery installation shot (though only in the black-and-white version of the image, oddly enough; see fig. 7). It is easy to overlook its anomalous presence there, if one is accustomed to understanding Flavin's work as

Fig. 4. Dan Flavin's first exhibition at the Green Gallery, New York, November 18–December 12, 1964. From left to right: *the diagonal of May 25, 1963 (to Robert Rosenblum)*, 1963; *a primary picture*, 1964; *pink out of a corner (to Jasper Johns)*, 1963; *alternate diagonals of March 2, 1964 (to Don Judd)*, 1964. Photo courtesy of Stephen Flavin.

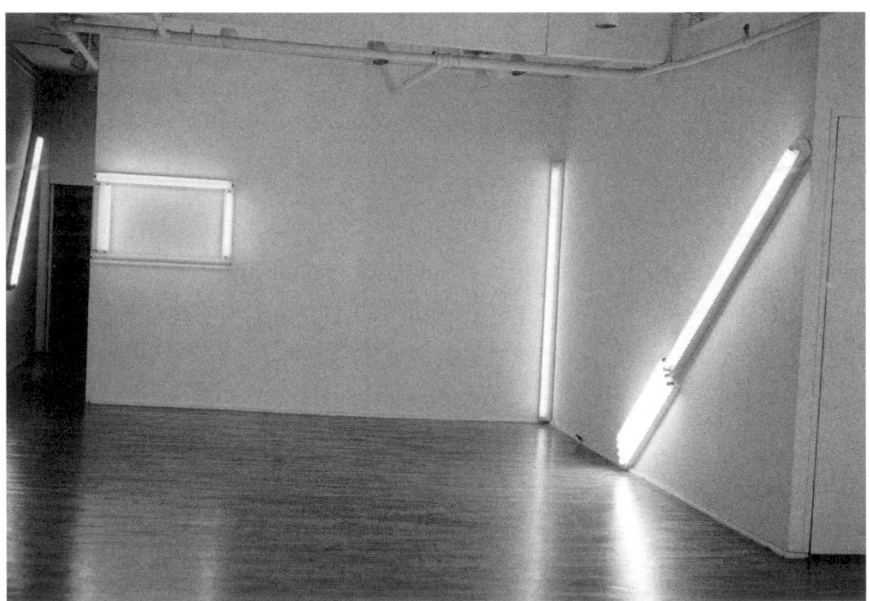

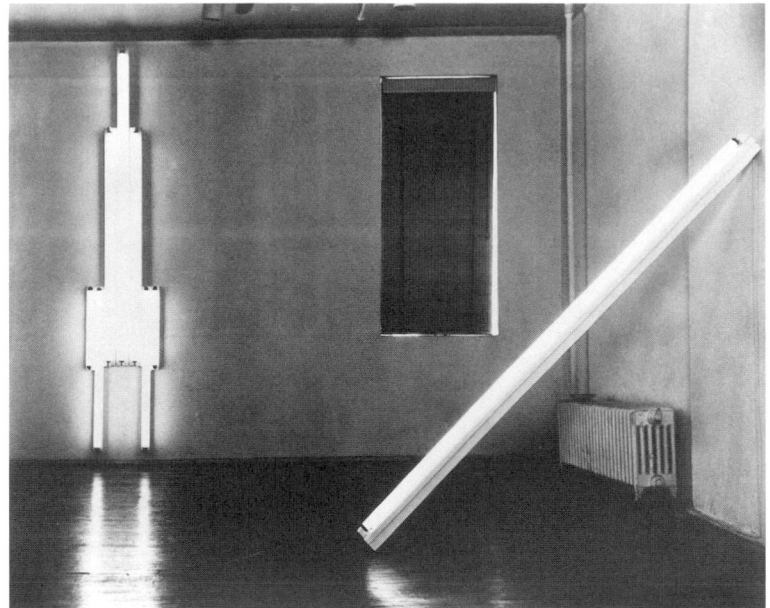

Fig. 5. Dan Flavin, *leaning diagonal*, 1963, in *Flavin, Judd, Morris, Williams,* group show at the Green Gallery, New York, May 26–June 12, 1965. Photo courtesy of Stephen Flavin.

Fig. 6. Dan Flavin, *untitled (to Ingrid Nibbe),* 1966, as installed at Galleria Sperone, Milan, 1967, and reproduced in T. Trini, "Mostre a Milano: Dan Flavin, Galleria Sperone," *Domus* (January 1967): 33.

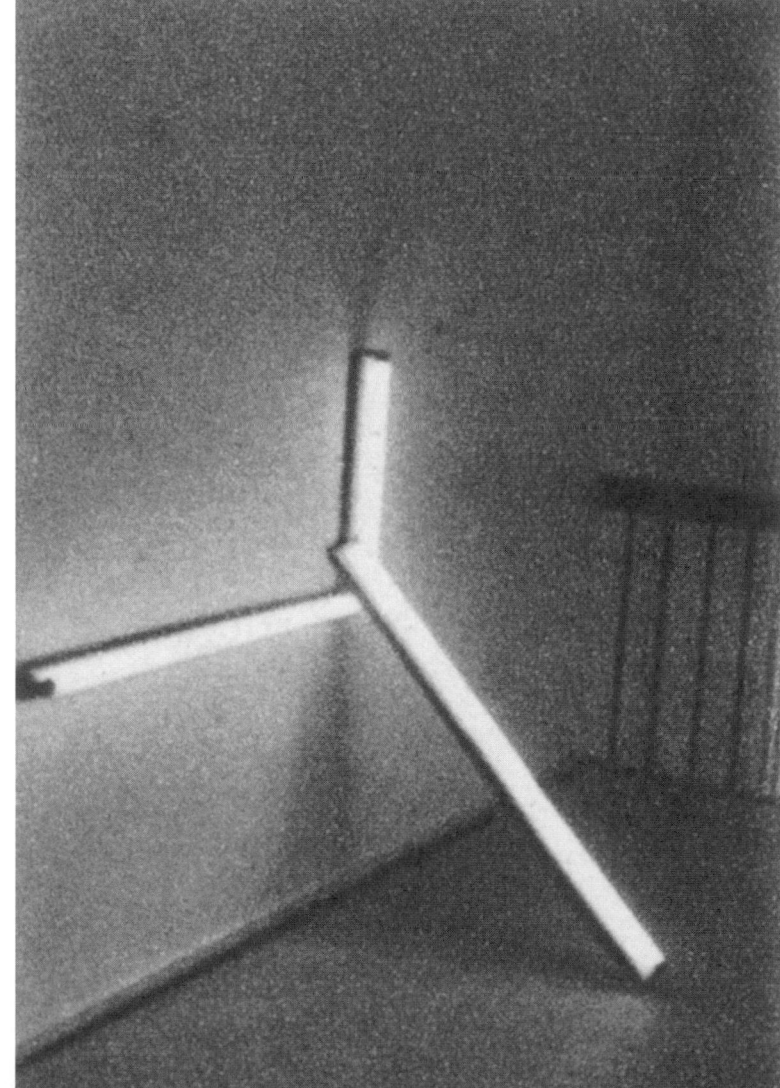

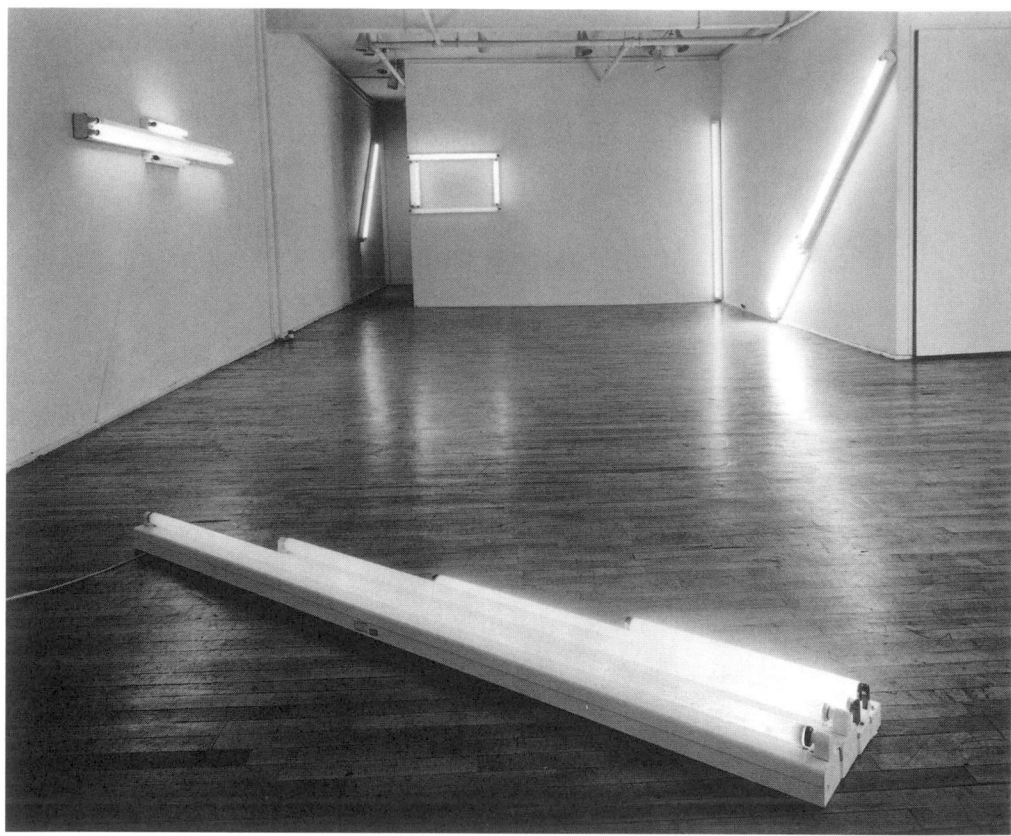

Fig. 7. Dan Flavin's first exhibition at the Green Gallery, New York, 1964, as photographed in black and white. Photo courtesy of Stephen Flavin.

necessarily attached to the wall. In fact, it seems likely that he too came to consider that independent placement anomalous once he had discovered other ways to work on the floor.[18] Not only did he never repeat the idea of a "freestanding" fixture, but he also developed more spatially active alternatives to working "in the round." Floor fixtures came to be used only when linked and interconnected in continuously directed lines, both straight and curved.

The implication here seems obvious: if a fixture is fully spatial as an independent object it cannot easily form an image. Or stated rather differently, for a work to be too spatially present, let alone freestanding, is to let a problematic objecthood prevail. One reason too great a material presence might create difficulties is telegraphed, I think, by what seems incongruous in the 1968 installation that Flavin mounted in the director's office—a space normally occupied by John Weber—of the Dwan Gallery (fig. 8). The arrangement deployed pairings of blue and ultraviolet lights; two were wall mounted, the third bal-

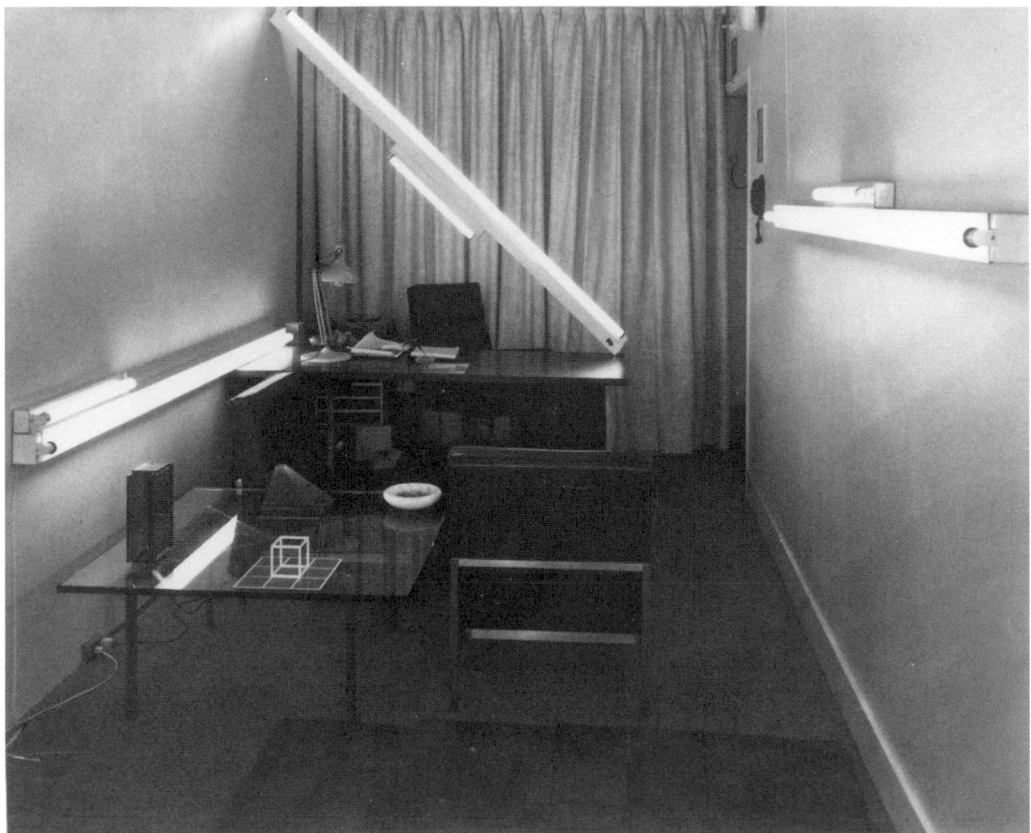

Fig. 8. Dan Flavin, installation in the director's office of the Dwan Gallery, New York, as part of the exhibition *cool white, etc. from Dan Flavin,* 1968. Photo courtesy of Stephen Flavin.

anced, again precariously, between wall and desk. The odd thing is just this almost-mundane encounter of fixtures and furniture: here is the moment when it seems right to insist again, echoing the reviewer I cited earlier, that the positions in which he places his lights are not the same positions they would occupy in an office, laboratory, or other place devoted to the business of ordinary life. Indeed they are not, as we are reminded when we look at John Weber's photograph of the artist fitting his own ample body in under the fixture that cuts across the directorial desk (fig. 9). It would be hard to do any kind of business in a posture like this. Yet though the effects of the light are not so far-reaching as to transform the mundanity—the would-be corporate sobriety—of this workplace, neither do they generate a realist effect. Flavin's term for this particular dialectic was *situational*—in other words, he provided light that was "somewhat useful, but not so useful," colorful, but not so much so to prevent Weber from doing his work. "Realism" would come later, in

1974, when in the context of the Clare Copley Gallery, Los Angeles, Michael Asher subtracted walls, rather than added lights, in order to join usually separate gallery spaces (storage, office, showroom) into the subject, as well as the site, of artistic representation.[19]

The difficulty for Flavin (unlike Asher) as an exhibition artist was precisely how his works connected with their various surroundings, the extent to which some placements or contexts might risk interrupting or suspending the fragile balance he was aiming to secure. "Completed propositions" run unlooked-for risks. Light effects are easily drowned out. Not only did Flavin withdraw an ultraviolet installation from a 1968 show at the Whitney Museum of American Art, citing ambient noise, but twice in the 1960s he refused to recognize exhibitions undertaken without his permission. One of these was an installation at the Galleria Sperone, Milan, his first Italian show. Yet even someone so attentive to presentation clearly could not monitor how editioned

Fig. 9. Dan Flavin at the Dwan Gallery, New York, 1968. Photo courtesy of Stephen Flavin.

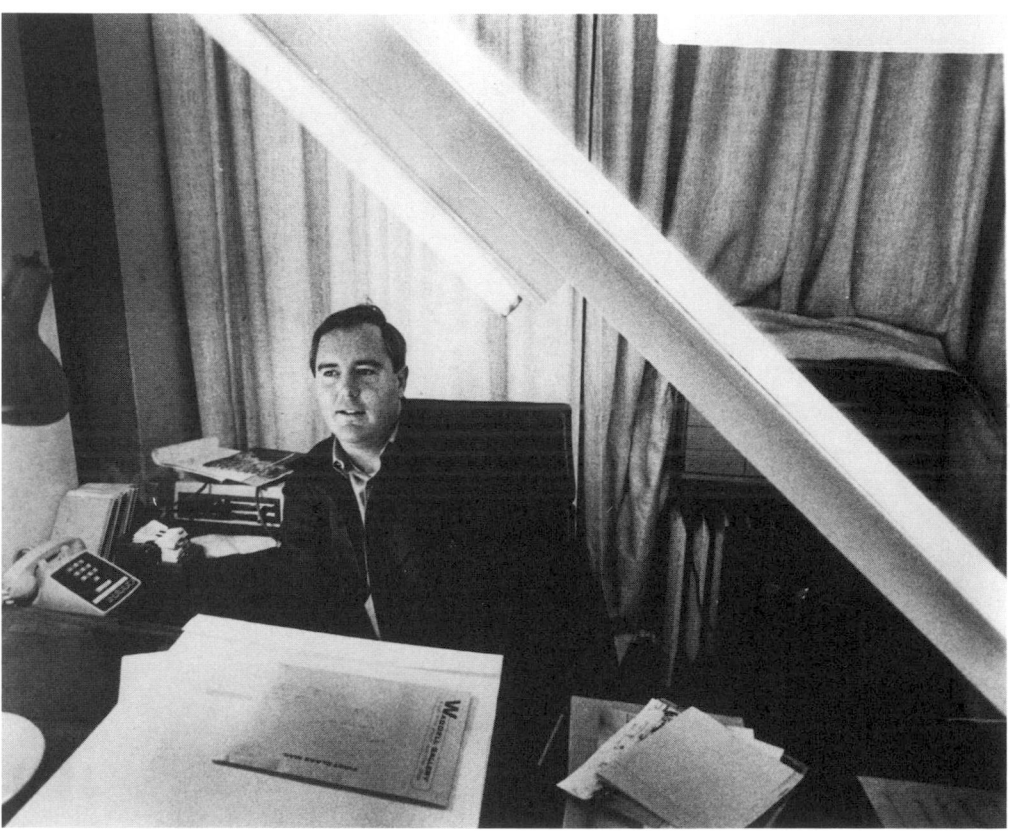

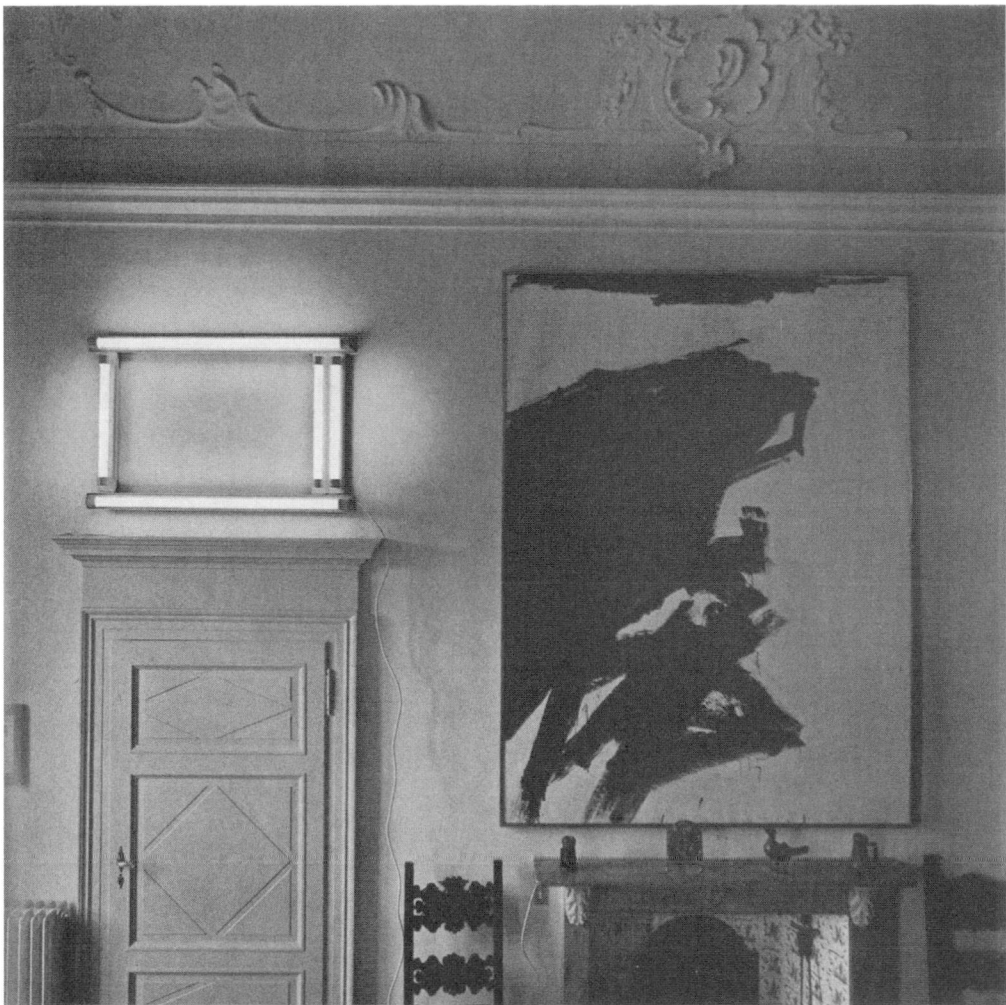

Fig. 10. Dan Flavin, *Ursula's one and two picture*, 1964, as installed in the Panza
collection and illustrated in T. Trini, "Un diario segreto di quadri celebri:
la collezione Panza di Biumo," *Domus* (January 1968): 51.

works were displayed once they had left his hands. Consider how unnecessary, even trivial, his pieces seem as installed in Count Panza di Biumo's Milan
residence (figs. 10, 11): cords slithering and dangling, they look less like art-
works than abandoned appliances, reminders of an absent occupant who has
all too hastily grabbed the bare essentials and headed for the door.[20]

There is no way of knowing how the artist reacted to these images and installations, or if propriety would allow his responses to be cited had they been
preserved. But we do know that Flavin was quite conscious of how his art-

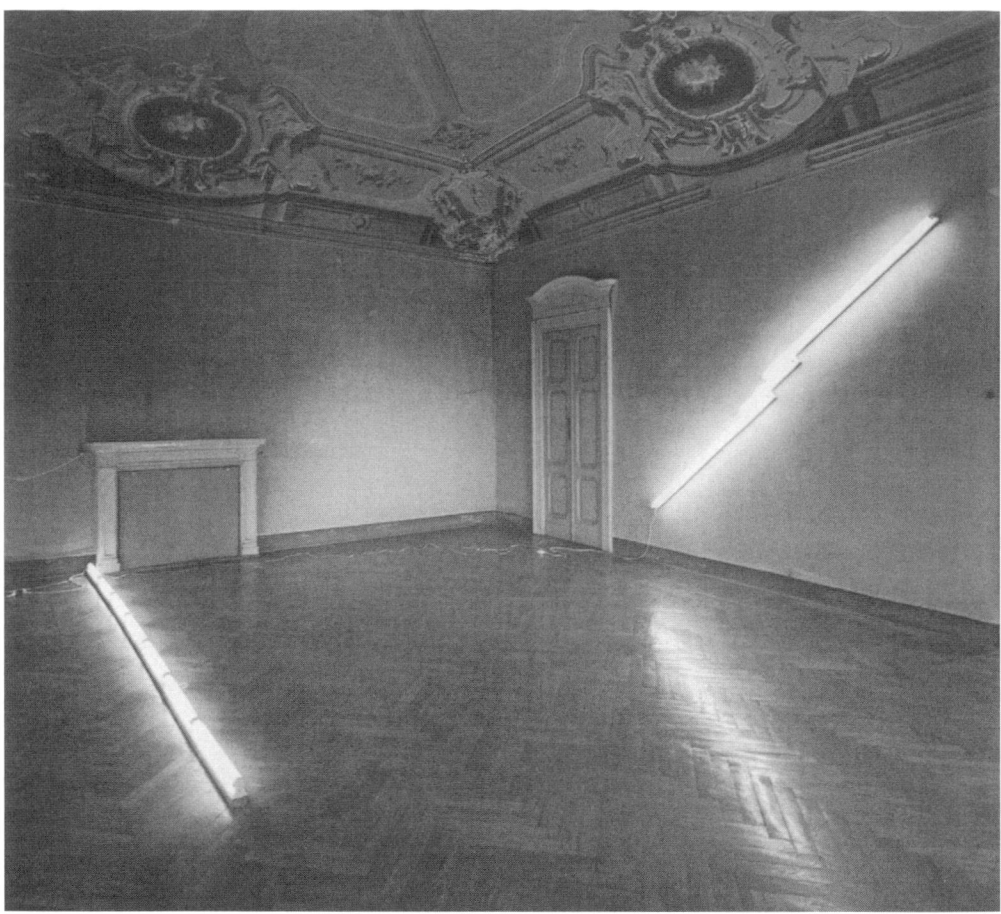

Fig. 11. View of the Panza collection with Dan Flavin's *untitled (to Karin)*, 1966, and an unknown seven-part floor piece, as illustrated in T. Trini, "Un diario segreto di quadri celebri: la collezione Panza di Biumo," *Domus* (January 1968): 52.

works were illustrated by his enemy the press. He particularly objected to the photographs of a spectator standing not beside but within, even behind, his first and best barrier piece, *greens crossing greens (to Piet Mondrian, who lacked green)* of 1966. (A contribution to *Kunst-Licht-Kunst,* one of the first of the many 1960s shows on art and light, it was installed in the so-called El Lissitsky cabinet at the Stedelijk Van Abbemuseum, Eindhoven.)[21] The offending image exists in two published versions (figs. 12, 13): if in one the benighted viewer merely assumes a studied air of aesthetic contemplation, in the other he goes so far as to bend toward the barrier, reaching out as if to give it an exploratory touch. No wonder the artist objected: the gesture says it all. It points to how much the human presence interrupts the wished-for balance and barrenness,

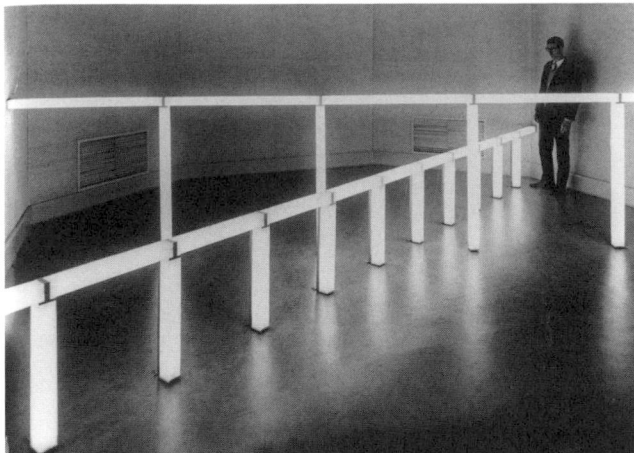

Fig. 12. Dan Flavin, *greens crossing greens (to Piet Mondrian who lacked green)*, 1966, as illustrated in *Perspecta* 11 (1967): 44. Van Abbemuseum, Eindhoven, the Netherlands.

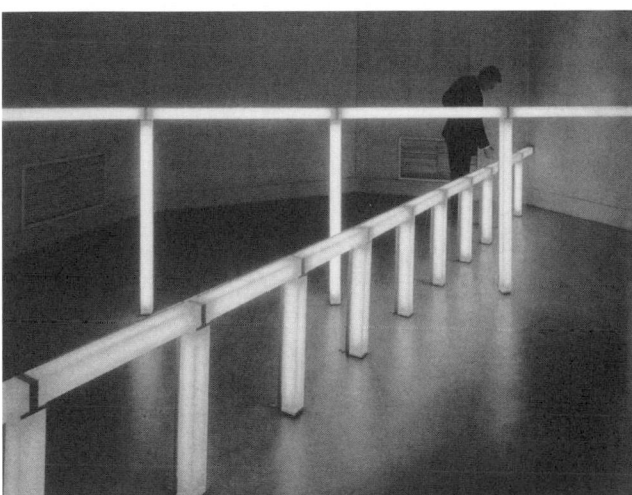

Fig. 13. Dan Flavin, *greens crossing greens (to Piet Mondrian who lacked green)*, 1966, as illustrated in Nan Piene, *Art in America* 55, no. 3 (May–June 1967): 24. Reproduced with the permission of the Van Abbemuseum, Eindhoven, the Netherlands.

where color and fixtures pull together in or as a spatial configuration, yet remain spare and elemental, each quite clearly distinct. Devoid of people, the installation matches an utterly objective presence—two different running fences, which gauge and measure each other, in spatial opposition—with a highly concentrated yet expansive coloristic effect. The latter erases any sense of boundary while forging the two barriers into a single figure, an X. With a viewer present, the fine-tuned dialectic between space and image comes all too abruptly apart.

Is this attitude toward viewers one of the "limits" that Flavin's work labors under and aims to impose? Is the audience basically de trop? Not always: the earliest drawing related to the Eindhoven exhibition, which plans an unexecuted crossed barrier for Kornblee, places it, as a jotted note declares, where it "will inhibit and permit movement of an adult." The paired verbs, with their pedagogical, even disciplinary overtones, seem ripe for analysis à la Foucault. Certainly Flavin's works do sometimes punish viewers with their brilliant, chromatic force: the artist was well aware that his lights, as he phrased it, could sometimes "perform in an abusive way on the eye." But this is not all they do. In a preliminary drawing for the ultraviolet room to be installed in Kassel at *Documenta 4* (1966), the artist can be found imagining light bouncing off pale summer clothes. Which is to say that, wearing its seasonal uniform, the beholder's body is put at the service of, and fragmented by, the bleaching brilliance of ultraviolet rays. Yet one still cannot say that the viewer/participant is fundamental to Flavin's work. As if in keeping with this subordinate status, the documentary photographs published to date have mostly recorded Flavin's pieces devoid of viewers, with the camera assuming the spectator's role. There are exceptions, of course, though surprisingly few have made their way into print.[22]

Fig. 14. Dan Flavin, *three tangented arcs in daylight and cool white (to Jenny and Ira Licht)*, 1969, as illustrated in Germano Celant, "Dan Flavin," *Domus* (February 1973): 47.

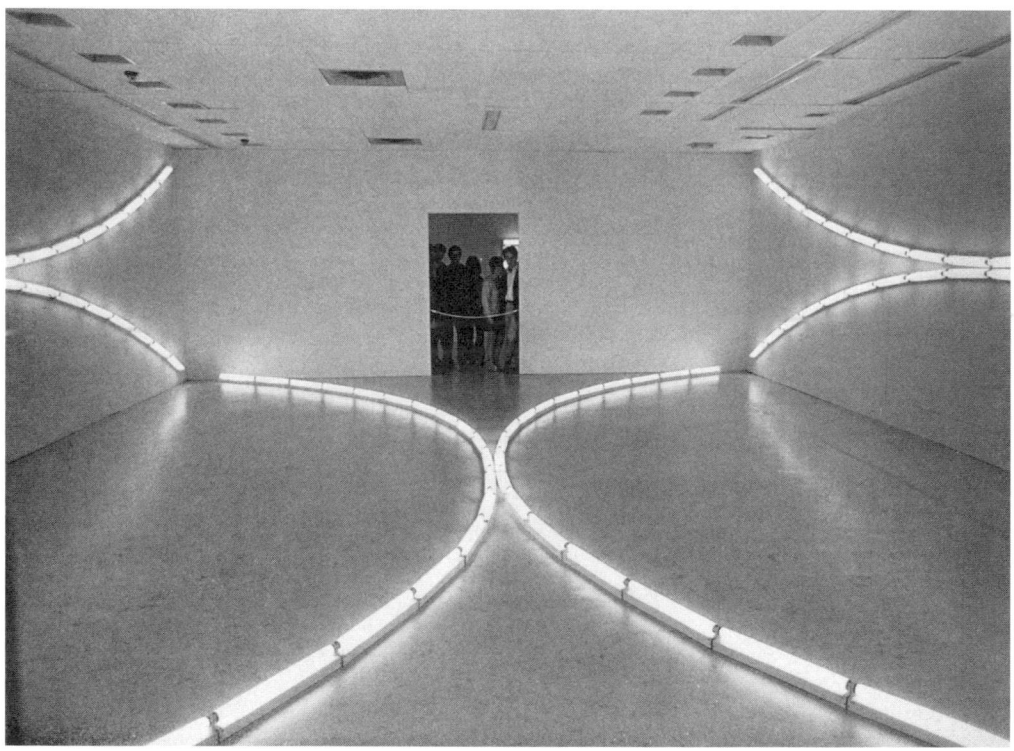

One of the most striking is a photograph taken of *three tangented arcs in daylight and cool white (to Jenny and Ira Licht)* as installed in Ottawa in 1969 (fig. 14). In format and framing it echoes the standard view of the installation and may well have been taken on the same occasion. (I take as the "standard" view the image published in Michael Govan and Tiffany Bell's *Dan Flavin: The Complete Lights*.) In the Govan and Bell image, no audience is present, and thus we assume that the camera vantage we are offered must be equivalent to—must actively stand in for—the absent audience's view. Yet the image in figure 14 says otherwise: five spectators stand in the doorway opposite the camera, now suggesting the independence of its optic from the human view. The human exclusion again seems significant: as with laity barred from the church's inner sanctum (remember Krauss's charge that Flavin's work is gothic), it is as if their mundane presence would undo the powers of the work-as-image, and thus place it too much within the dangerous province of work-as-thing. I myself did not knowingly meet up with Flavin's three platform installations in Grand Central Station in 1976–77, though they remained in place for a decade, but I suspect from surviving documentary photographs that some such risk was encountered there (fig. 15). For once, Flavin's fixtures seem entirely at home. As pallid commuters swim through the pools of light and shadow, actuality and factuality actively collide. The latter wins out.[23]

Fig. 15. Dan Flavin, *untitled*, 1976–77, pink, daylight, and yellow fluorescent light, three sections, each approximately 1,000 ft. (300 m) long; installation in Grand Central Station, New York. Photo courtesy Stephen Flavin.

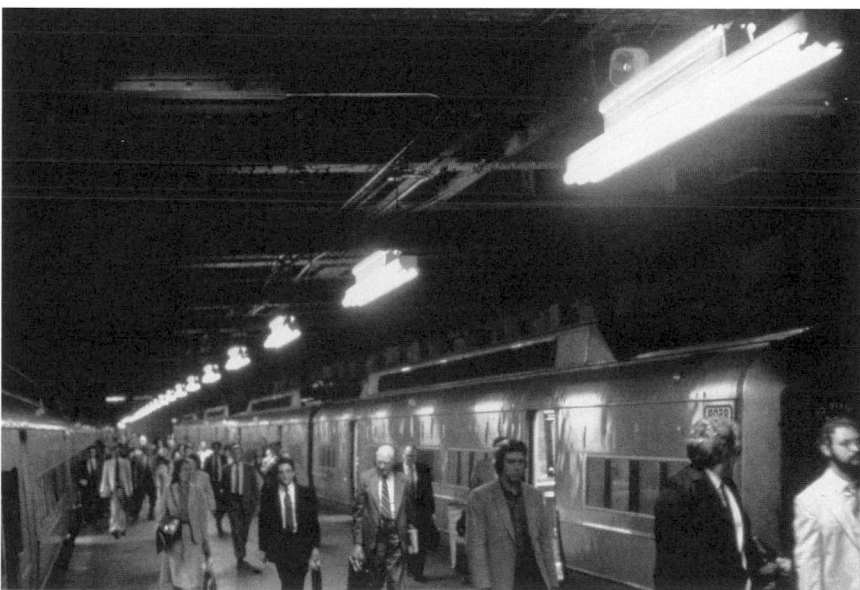

Just as the Ottawa installation alone is not enough to argue that Flavin favored transcendence, the Grand Central piece does not make him a materialist who prefers the station platform to Count Panza's palatial pad. Instead his rather limited success in both settings is enough to insist that for many years his work was really at its best in—as well as actively imagined for—a museum or gallery. After all, these are interiors that in their dedication to endless reinstallation have the most barren rooms of all. And the most abstract. The gallery space, so routinely denuded, just as routinely remerges (thanks to paint and spackle) freshly framed by patient walls.

If the art world context is where the artist himself seems to have felt most comfortable, it is also where his work took optimal form. Image or not, it needs both surface and space. This is one reason why when Flavin planned an exhibition, he most often drew the gallery interior as a perspectival volume opened to vision on its two frontal sides. The aim, he said, was "to poise silent electric light . . . in the box that is the room." Though they may have doors and windows in all the right places, such spatial containers invoke no wider context and summon little more than the most generic sense of place. Space alone, bounded and compact, is what counts, and Flavin (re)produces it in pared-down graphic terms whose chosen language owes an acknowledged debt to constructivist abstraction and the architectural shorthand of de Stijl. "Abstract space," wrote Henri Lefebvre, in his great investigation of spatial transformation under capitalism, "functions 'objectally,' as a set of things/signs and their formal relationships. . . . Formal and quantitative, it erases distinctions."[24] It does so as the space of instrumental rationality, bound up with the exchange of goods and commodities, words and services. And if, according to Lefebvre, it is geometrical, optical, and homogeneous, its communicative means are the map, graph, and plan—the draftsman's means of submitting boundlessness to the appearance of an orderly regime.

Perhaps it goes without saying that abstract space, in Lefebvre's order of things, is envisioned by planners, artists, and architects. I think that Flavin should be counted among them. For his reliance on the gallery is not intent on undoing it so much as exerting an aggressive effort at spatial control.[25] The aspiration was there from early on: "I knew that the actual space of a room could be broken down and played with by planting illusions of real light (electric light) at crucial junctures in the room's composition. For example, if you press an eight foot fluorescent lamp into the vertical climb of a corner, you can destroy that corner by glare and doubled shadow. A piece of wall can be visually disintegrated from the whole into a separate triangle by plunging a diagonal of light from edge to edge on the wall; that is, side to floor, for instance." Abstract space, says Lefebvre, is always "buttressed by non-critical (positive) knowledge, backed up by a frightening capacity for violence, and

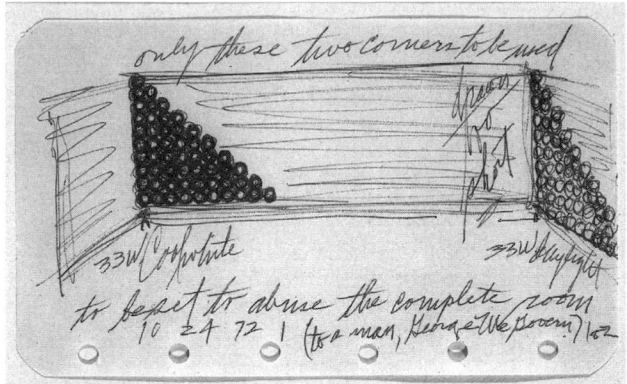

Fig. 16. Dan Flavin, *untitled (to a man, George McGovern)*, 1972, ball-point ink on ring notebook paper, 3 × 5 in. (7.6 × 12.7 cm). Collection Stephen Flavin.

maintained by a bureaucracy which has laid hold of the gains of capitalism in the ascendant and turned them to its own profit." Despite his so often lashing out against his treatment at the hands of the gallery system, Flavin's own dependency on its blank interiors kept him speaking its language to the end.[26]

He did so ambivalently, of course. His art aimed, as he scrawled on his drawing for the 1972 installation *untitled (to a man, George McGovern)* (fig. 16), "to beset to abuse the complete room."[27] There are various ways to read this elliptical insistence; above all we need to lay hold of the contradictory fantasy that gives it its force. If *to beset* is to assail on all sides, it can also mean bejewel or decorate: to surround or set something with jewels or other ornaments. Flavin is speaking of the pleasures offered by his lights, yet ties them to an imagery of pain, and perhaps again to the celebration of barrenness he also espoused. Yet whatever he is suggesting—for surely his phrase presents a set of specific intentions, however cryptically—the formula seems to leave the viewer out. An abused room evaporates the viewer; place yields to placelessness. For what Flavin's work refuses to acknowledge is any claim that it offers *us* a place *in the visible*, even though the camera cannot help finding us there from time to time. This refusal points to the most stringent and aggressive limits on the conception of illumination his work secures. For it is only in emptying or derealizing the room as an inhabited interior—in abstracting it, according to the very art world protocols he so often railed against—that Flavin can imagine ornamentation, illumination, as something his art might be able to provide. That the gallery provides the ideal space for such derealization depends on a constitutive blankness that the artifice of light alone can neither hide entirely nor fully reveal.

Notes

My thanks to Benjamin Young, Katie Hoover-Smoot, and Andrea Nitsche for their generous and efficient help with research.

1. For "spleenish," see Dan Flavin, "some remarks . . . excerpts from a spleenish journal," *Artforum* (December 1966): 27–29; Dan Flavin, "some other comments . . . more pages from a spleenish journal," *Artforum* (December 1967): 20–25. For Hilton Kramer as Flavin's "damned fool," see Flavin "some other comments . . . ," 23. For " dilettanted dada homosexuals" see Dan Flavin, "several more remarks . . . ," *Studio International* (April 1969): 175. He is commenting on Morris and the rest of the artists represented in the Castelli Warehouse show. "I know of no occupation": Flavin, "some remarks . . . ," 28. Leider's phrase comes from an exchange with Flavin in the Letters column of *Artforum* (February 1968): 4. It is clear from the artist's letter that it was Leider who in publishing Flavin's writings first attached the word *spleenish* to them. Flavin responded in injured tones to the suggestion implicit in Leider's insult that he would temper his work or actions with an eye to success or sales. Jack Burnham, "A Dan Flavin Retrospective in Ottawa," *Artforum* (December 1969): 50.

2. Philip Leider, "Letters," *Artforum* (February 1968): 4.

3. In "' . . . in daylight or cool white.' an autobiographical sketch," *Artforum* 4:4 (December 1965): 24, Flavin quoted Kant's *Critique of Judgment* as speaking to his work: "The Sublime is to be found in a formless object, so far as in it, or by occasion of it, boundlessness is represented." This citation, with its declarative affinity with Enlightenment philosophy, was excised when the essay was revised and reprinted in 1969.

4. J. J. [Jill Johnston], "Reviews and Previews: Dan Flavin," *Art News* (January 1965): 13; Dore Ashton, "New York Letter," *Studio International* (August 1966): 102; Elizabeth C. Baker, "The Light Brigade," *Art News* (March 1967): 64. Baker insists that, as she also puts it, "the flat-footed, materialistic, 'minimal' content" of Flavin's work "subsides after a few minutes spent exposed to the liquid fluorescent glow."

5. Jill Kornblee, as quoted in Mel Bochner, "'More Light': Goethe's Deathbed Words or Less Is Less for Dan Flavin (1966–1969)," in Dan Flavin, *fluorescent light, etc. from Dan Flavin/lumière fluorescente, etc. par Dan Flavin*, exh. cat. (Ottawa: National Gallery of Canada, 1969), 25; Barbara Reise, "'Untitled 1969': A Footnote on Art and Minimal-Stylehood," *Studio International* (April 1969): 170; Gordon Brown, "Month in Review. Light: Object and Image," *Arts Magazine* (June/Summer 1968): 54.

6. My analysis here relies on Dan Graham's reading of Flavin's fixtures: his views are frequently repeated in his writing, but paradigmatically formulated in "Art as Design/Design as Art," *Rock My Religion: Writings and Projects, 1965–1990* (Cambridge: MIT Press, 1993), 209–11. The quoted phrases in this sentence, like those in the rest of the paragraph, come from Flavin, "' . . . in daylight or cool white,'" in Flavin, *fluorescent light . . . from Dan Flavin*, 18–19. This essay is a revised version of the article first published under the same title in *Artforum*.

7. Flavin, "' . . . in daylight or cool white,'" 19. This phrasing rewords the termi-

nology used in the earlier version of the essay on page 24. There Flavin refers to "planting illusions of real light (electric light) at crucial junctures in the rooms composition." What is interesting about the earlier formula is its identification of electric light as an "illusion" of real (or natural) light. In citing the passage from the Ottawa catalogue, Beatrice von Bismarck mistakenly traces it to the earlier *Artforum* piece. See her essay "Dan Flavin: Proposals for the Visible," in *Dan Flavin: Installationen in Fluoreszierendem Licht, 1989–1993* (Stuttgart: Edition Cantz, 1993), 19–20 and 26, n. 8.

8. For an approach to the emergence of installation art, see Alex Potts, "Installation and Sculpture," *Oxford Art Journal* 24, no. 3 (2001): 5–24. Potts's goal, which is to provide a distinction between the modes of relation and apprehension of sculpture and installation, does not question the now familiar linkage of the aim of some 1960s and 1970s artists to unseat the fetishism of the autonomous artwork and critique its traditional institutional contexts to the rise of installation. The case of Flavin, I suggest, reveals that a rather different set of purposes were in play. On Flavin's terminology see a letter of June 17, 1967, to Jan van der Marck, director of the Museum of Contemporary Art, Chicago, cited in Dan Flavin, "some other comments . . . ," 23.

9. Flavin, "some remarks . . . ," 28; Bochner, "'More Light,'" 26. The citation is credited to an essay by Barthes entitled "Objective Literature: Alain Robbe-Grillet." Bochner would have doubtless encountered this text as the introduction to *Two Novels by Robbe-Grillet* (New York: Grove, 1965), 11–26. In citing Barthes, he elides and reverses the order of phrases from two paragraphs on page 13.

10. Donald Judd, "Specific Objects," *Arts Yearbook* 8 (New York: Art Digest, 1965), reprinted in Donald Judd, *Complete Writings, 1959–1975* (Halifax: Nova Scotia College of Art and Design with New York University Press, 2005), 181–89; Dan Graham, "Flavin's Proposal," *Arts Magazine* (February 1970): 44.

11. Rosalind Krauss, "New York," *Artforum* (January 1969): 54.

12. Ibid., 54.

13. Ibid.

14. In "Pink, Yellow, Blue, Green and Other Colors in the Work of Dan Flavin," the revised text of a lecture given at the Dia Center for the Arts, New York, February 1996, Marianne Stockebrand reviews some aspects of the artist's development. See www.chinati.org/english2/textonly/newsletters/pink_stockebrand.htm. Michael Govan, "Irony and Light," in Michael Govan and Tiffany Bell, *Dan Flavin: A Retrospective*, exh. cat. (New Haven: Yale University Press, 2004), 56. This essay is also included in Michael Govan and Tiffany Bell, *Dan Flavin: The Complete Lights, 1961–1996* (New Haven: Yale University Press, 2004). In a lecture delivered at the National Gallery in Washington, D.C., on October 23, 2004, Govan stated that *pink out of a corner (to Jasper Johns)* (1963) was initially planned to use a red bulb; the change was undertaken to avoid the red overshadowing the gallery space. See also Tiffany Bell, "Fluorescent Light as Art," in Govan and Bell, *Flavin: Complete Lights*, 116–17, for further discussion of the role of chance in Flavin's installations.

15. The *some lights* show was held at the Kaymar Gallery in New York, March 5–29, 1964. Dan Flavin, *three installations in fluorescent light/drei Installationen*

in fluoreszierendem Licht, exh. cat. (Cologne: Kölnische-Verlagsdruckerei, 1973), 83. In one drawing Flavin used the term *neutral* not once but three times to label the space between fixtures: in writing each inscription, Flavin placed his lettering so as to signal horizontal, vertical, and overhead space. See *The second and final study, the complete plan for a room of green fluorescent light in the Kornblee Gallery, New York, from 7 October to 8 November 1967* (1967), present location unknown; reproduced in Carlo Huber, *fünf Installationen in fluoreszierendem Licht von Dan Flavin. Zeichnungen, Diagramme, Druckgrafik 1972 bis 1975 und zwei Installationen in fluorszierendem Licht von Dan Flavin,* exh. cat. (Basel: Kunsthalle Basel and Kunstmuseum Basel, 1975), n.p.

16. Stockebrand discusses the revisions the artist made to the format of *untitled* (1966), the first square placed across a corner, after its initial exhibition at the Nicholas Wilder Gallery, Los Angeles. Further information is supplied in Govan and Bell, *Flavin: Complete Lights,* nos. 120, 230, 231. The changes make the piece more symmetrical, or as Stockebrand has it, provide "clarity" and "natural simplicity."

17. Stated rather differently, the piece might be described as too sculptural, when *sculpture* connoted "mass and modeling, fitting together, attaching, surrounding volumes of air" (Flavin, interview with Phyllis Tuchman, March 9, 1972, in Govan and Bell, *Flavin: Complete Lights,* 194). While this diagonal has neither mass nor modeling, it is certainly surrounded by volumes of air.

18. Like other early Flavin exhibitions, this show was documented photographically by the artist himself. His color shot of the show eliminates the foreground, and thus *gold, pink and red, red.* In a catalogue note provided by Flavin when *gold, pink and red, red* was shown in Ottawa in 1969, its positioning at the Green Gallery show is explained as strategic, meant "to attract attention away from the prominent end wall of the large gallery, which the artist had decided to avoid using directly" (Flavin, *fluorescent light . . . from Dan Flavin,* no. 98, p. 210. Flavin's decision may also reflect the fact that the end wall contained two windows.

19. Flavin, interview with Phyllis Tuchman, 193; Michael Asher, *Writings, 1973–1983, on Works, 1969–1979* (Halifax: Press of the Nova Scotia College of Art and Design, 1983), 95–100.

20. In a letter to Jean Leering, curator of *Kunst-Licht-Kunst* in Eindhoven, Flavin complained of the "destructive context" created by his work's installation in a 1965–66 show at the Institute of Contemporary Art, Boston, next to a work that created revolving patterns of light. See Paula Feldman, "Dan Flavin: Site Specific Installations in the Netherlands, 1966–68," *Burlington Magazine* (October 2003): 721–24. For Flavin's withdrawal from the Whitney show see Govan and Bell, *Flavin: Complete Lights,* no. 191, p. 277, and Grace Glueck, "Artist, Citing 'Noise,' Withdraws Whitney Exhibit," *New York Times,* July 25, 1968, 30. The first of these unrecognized shows was held at Galleria Sperone, Milan, February 14–March 14, 1967; the second, a group show, *Luminism,* at the George Washington Hotel, New York, May 1967. See Flavin, *fluorescent light . . . from Dan Flavin,* 252. For photographs of the Sperone installation and invitation, see Anna Minola et al., *Gian Enzo Sperone, Torino, Roma, New York: 35 anni di mostre tra Europa e America,* vol. 1 (Turin: Hopefulmonster, 2000), 104,

and T. Trini, "Mostre a Milano: Dan Flavin, Galleria Sperone," *Domus* (January 1967), 33. See also Tiffany Bell, "Fluorescent Light at Art," in Govan and Bell, *Flavin: Complete Lights*, 117. My thanks to Tiffany Bell for pointing me toward Flavin's disowning of the Milan show. For a careful discussion of the fabrication of Flavin's lights, see Bell, "Fluorescent Light as Art," 116–19.

21. Michael Govan notes that Flavin "remarked in anger" at the inclusion of a viewer in the only contemporary photograph of the work. See *Dan Flavin: The Architecture of Light*, exh. cat. (New York: Abrams, 1999), 26–27. "El Lissitsky's cabinet" simply invoked El Lissitsky's *Proun Room* of 1923, which in 1965 was reconstructed, in the same space Flavin would later use, as part of a major exhibition organized by Jean Leering, the curator who also commissioned Flavin's Eindhoven work. See Feldman, "Flavin: Site-Specific Installations," 721, and Henk Puts, "The Lissitsky Collection at the Van Abbemuseum," *El Lissitsky, 1890–1941: Architect, Painter, Photographer, Typographer*, exh. cat. (Eindhoven: Municipal Van Abbemuseum, 1990), 81–83.

22. For the Eindhoven/Kornblee drawing see Saint Louis Art Museum, *Drawings and Diagrams, 1963–1972, from Dan Flavin*, exh. cat. (Saint Louis: Saint Louis Art Museum, 1973), p. 52, no. 67; Dan Flavin, interview with Tiffany Bell, 1982, in Govan and Bell, *Flavin: Complete Lights*, 195. On a drawing illustrated in *Drawings and Diagrams*, p. 62, no. 79, Flavin notes, "ultra-violet 'long wave'/light over everything, each person" and "people will 'transmit' (reflect) violet/ light to each other—especially suited to summer clothing, to Kassel in June, etc." A photograph of the installation, with two spectators, was printed in *Metro* 15 (1971), 29. In a helpful correspondence with me, Tiffany Bell, project director of the Dan Flavin catalogue raisonné, pointed out (email of July 22, 2005) that although his archive includes "quite a few photographs of people mingling with the lights," an editorial decision to choose the clearest images possible meant that they were not included in the catalogue. For the most part, earlier catalogues follow suit, and photos that include people crop up mostly in the contemporary art press.

23. Govan and Bell, *Flavin: Complete Lights*, p. 287, no. 234. For an account of the circumstances of the Grand Central project, see ibid., 337. Taken by Nic Tenwiggenhorn, the photographs reproduced there include one showing a handful of commuters; figure 15, however, shows the river of travelers in full spate. In his 1982 interview with Tiffany Bell, the artist himself makes clear that he considered the installation a "compromise": "almost like a replacement installation for what was there" (interview with Tiffany Bell, 197). In his 1972 interview with Phyllis Tuchman (194), Flavin acknowledged the particular difficulty of working in circumstances like those offered by this commission. In answer to her question, "Would you ever deploy lights on a ceiling?" he replied, "That seems to me to be the territory of utility lighting. Most often it is prejudiced by that utilitarian lighting, so you need not consider it." In the same interview, however, the artist also declares himself a "city boy," saying, "I think it's obvious that what I've done is urban backgrounded." Hence, perhaps, the temptation to accept the Grand Central commission. Its New York location was also doubtless a factor in the choice.

24. Dan Flavin, "Some Artist's Remarks," in *Monuments for V. Tatlin from Dan*

Flavin, 1964–1982, exh. cat. (Los Angeles: Museum of Contemporary Art, 1989), n.p. Dated 1965, although uncredited here, this citation comes from "Dan Flavin," *Art Voices* (Summer, 1965): 72. Henri Lefebvre, *The Production of Space*, trans. Donald Nicholson-Smith (Oxford: Blackwell, 1991), 49.

25. Because my reading of Flavin's spatial attitude differs from the verdict offered by Beatrice von Bismarck, it may be useful to point to where the difference lies. According to her, "Flavin always treats the room gently." See Bismarck, "Dan Flavin: Proposals for the Visible," in *Dan Flavin: Installationen in Fluoreszierendem Licht, 1989–1993*, 20. My own exploration of the artist's view of the room places an emphasis on language in order to approach figural and fantasied aspects of his work.

26. Flavin, "'. . . in daylight or cool white,'" 24; Lefebvre, *Production of Space*, 52. A similar dependency marks the efforts of those artists—Michael Asher and Mel Bochner among them—whose engagement with the real and symbolic space of the gallery operates, as Flavin's did not, from a more explicitly critical or analytical position.

27. The transcription offered in *Drawings and Diagrams, 1963–1972*, p. 86, no. 114, reads, "to be set to abuse the whole room." Although this reading makes plausible sense, it ignores the fact that there is no space between *be* and *set*. I am reading what Flavin actually wrote, rather than what he might have written, or thought he wrote.

Hal Foster   **Dan Flavin and the**
Catastrophe of Minimalism

For years I took Donald Judd too much at his word (why, I thought foolishly,

not take a literalist literally?): that minimalism is absolutely opposed to picto-

rial illusionism and virtual space. But is this account true to the art of Judd, let

alone of his friend Dan Flavin, early or late? What is the fate of the celebrated

opposition between "specific object" and illusionist space in the aftermath of

minimalism—and the role of Flavin in that story?[1]

Like other critics, I have long seen minimalism as a crux between late-

modernist painting, which was the primary point of reference for Flavin,

Judd, and other peers, and postmodernist art, with its new materials, alterna-

tive processes, actual sites, and so on.[2] The key break in this genealogy re-

mains the initial one—the specific object posed against the illusionist space of

painting. (Despite the presence of David Smith, Mark di Suvero, and others,

American sculpture was a relatively weak category in the 1950s, and Flavin

insisted on his difference from it—really his indifference to it—even more

than did Judd.)[3] Yet, opposed to this illusionism, might minimalism also be

propped up by it, bound up with it, even invested in it? In my own literalism

(which was deepened by the literalism of process, body, and site-specific art),

I did not attend enough to how this illusionism, however transformed, is also preserved in minimalism, even expanded by it (think of the reflective surfaces and refractive depths in Judd, or the brilliant color and immersive light in Flavin); and, further, how this illusionism is released everywhere, in the dispersive optical effects of the light-and-space art that followed on minimalism (especially on Flavin) with Robert Irwin, Larry Bell, James Turrell, Doug Wheeler, and others.[4] In short, if the literal in minimalism contested the illusionist in advanced art theretofore, how thoroughly did it do so, and for how long? Was the minimalist break from pictorial virtuality only partial and temporary, a historical ruse on the way to the current triumph of the virtual —which, of course, goes well beyond art?[5] This possibility leads me to ask whether, even as minimalism remains a crux, its aftermath might not also be, at least in part, a catastrophe.

Judd had "illusionist panic" in the way that some men have homosexual panic; it compelled him to project illusionism away from his art and, to a lesser extent, that of Flavin, and so occluded its presence there. "They don't involve illusionistic space," Judd declared of the Flavin "icons" in 1964 (fig. 1), which he described as "blunt" (high praise for him), only to qualify his assessment somewhat with the fluorescent lights: "I want a particular, definite *object*," Judd wrote in 1969. "I think Flavin wants . . . a particular *phenomenon*." Flavin never did sign on fully to the program of "specific objects" (he rarely placed his lights flat on the floor, which his early works did not touch), yet both artists entertained a play between object and phenomenon, material support and illusionist effect; here Judd turned an oscillation within both practices into an opposition between the two. Essential to our experience of a Flavin fluorescent is the rapid relay of our attention between actual fixture, luminous tube, extended glow of color, and spatial diffusion of light, and he knew it: "The composite term 'image-object' best describes my use of the medium" (91).[6]

Flavin once described the oscillation in his work in terms of irony, the high-modernist device par excellence (he was especially taken by James Joyce): "The radiant tube and the shadow cast by its supporting pan seemed ironic enough to hold alone" (87). What does Flavin mean here? Perhaps not only that the pan and its shadow "hold" the radiance of the tube, fasten it down physically—a holding that contrasts with work by Irwin and Turrell where the cause is often obscured by the effects—but also that his viewers are held by the tension between the material object and the immaterial light: each ironizes the other in a way that resists our deciding for one as primary. In this respect Flavin is an ironist more than a literalist, or rather he finds an ambiguity in literalism that holds both work and viewer in tension. In contradistinction to the maxim of Frank Stella, what you see is never quite what you see

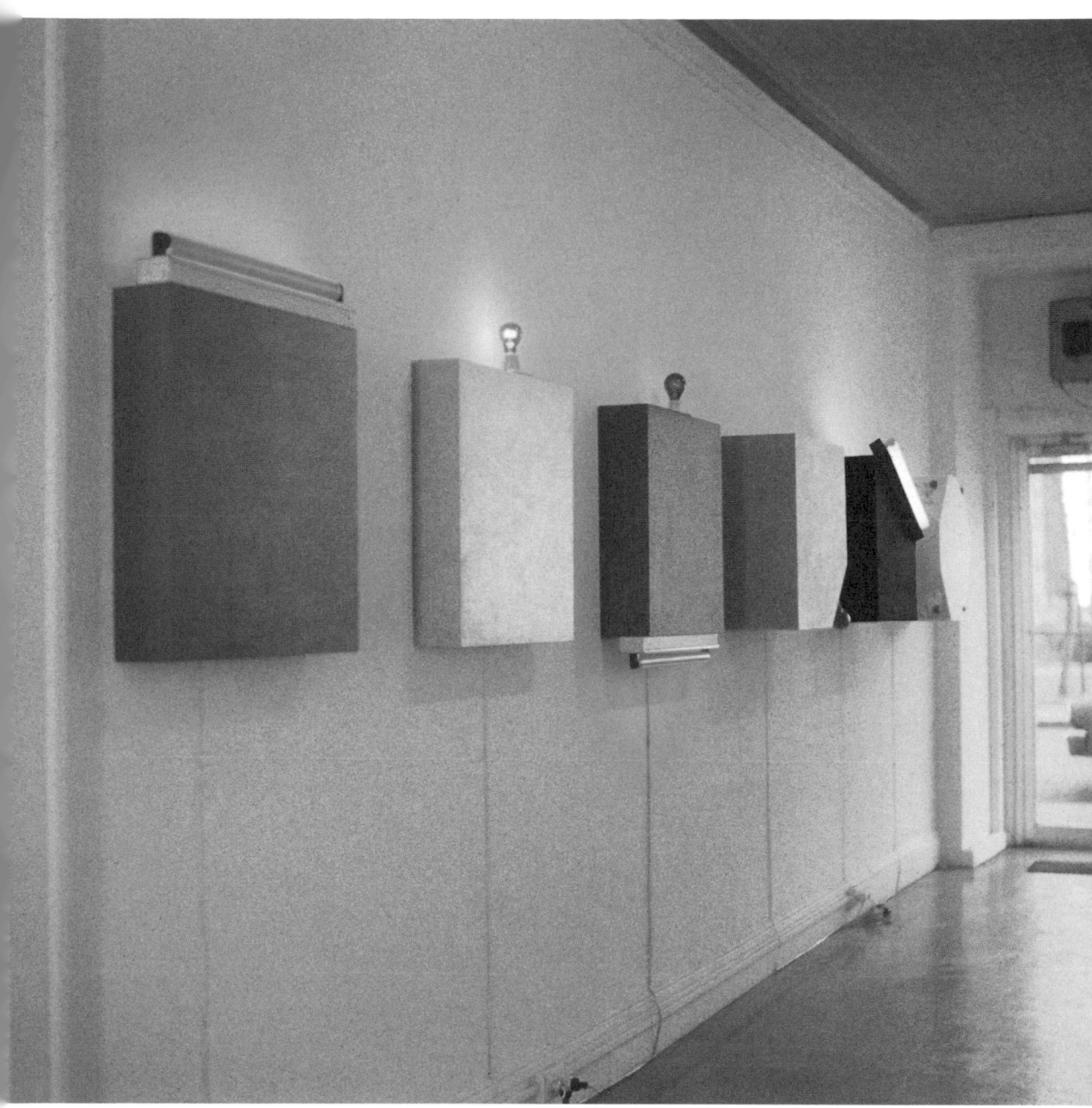

Fig. 1. Installation view of six of the seven Dan Flavin icons at Kaymar Gallery, New York, 1964. From left to right: *icon I (the heart) (to the light of Sean McGovern which blesses everyone)*, 1961–62; *icon II (the mystery) (to John Reeves)*, 1961; *icon III (blood) (the blood of a martyr)*, 1962; *icon VI (Ireland dying) (to Louis Sullivan)*, 1962–63; *icon VII (via crucis)*, 1962–64; *icon VIII (the dead nigger's icon) (to Blind Lemon Jefferson)*, 1962–63. Photo courtesy of Stephen Flavin.

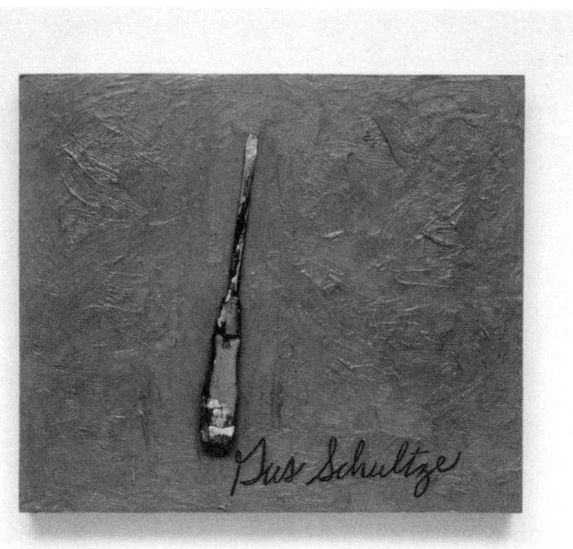

Fig. 2. Dan Flavin, *Gus Schultze's screwdriver (to Dick Bellamy)*,
1960, screwdriver, oil and pencil on Masonite, and
acrylic on balsa, 15⅜ × 17½ × 1¾ in. (39 × 44.4 × 4.4 cm).
Collection Stephen Flavin.

with Flavin: our perception of his colors can change with position or time,
and often we see complementary colors that are not "there" at all. This unde-
cidable aspect of his work is one reason why its tension between illusionism
and anti-illusionism is not a dialectic, a term that suggests a developmental
logic foreign to Flavin (as he thought) as well as a potential resolution that his
irony works to undercut.[7]

For Flavin the struggle with illusionism was chiefly a struggle to hold
"the lamp as image back in balance with [the lamp] as object" (87). A version
of this tension preceded his fluorescent works, too; in fact it was in play ever
since he moved, in the late 1950s, from his fussy watercolors to his tins and
tools smashed against brushy Masonite grounds (which Flavin called, in a
typical riff of Joycean assonance, "plain physical factual painting of firm plasticity" [86]). The mix of abstract painting and found object in these early
works also attests to two principal forces in play in advanced art at the time:
like others in his milieu, Flavin was impressed by Barnett Newman, who later
befriended him (it was in this milieu that Newman was certified as a master),
and he could not avoid the impact of Robert Rauschenberg and Jasper Johns,
whose lineage was underscored by the 1961 exhibition *The Art of Assemblage*
held at The Museum of Modern Art while Flavin was still a guard there

(fig. 2). Curated by William Seitz, this show included a great variety of things —cubist and futurist collages, dadaist objects, late-surrealist and art-brutish works—most of which were seen through the then-current practice of neo-dada and nouveau réaliste assemblages. Either of these lines of influence— "Newman" or "Rauschenberg & Johns"—might have led Flavin to extrude pictorial into actual space, but altogether this "crush of avant-gardism" made the move irresistible (192).

However, a chief motive of this move was not represented in the Seitz show or elsewhere in New York in 1961: the constructivism of Vladimir Tatlin and Alexander Rodchenko. This precedent first came to Flavin by way of a book published in 1962, *The Great Experiment: Russian Art, 1863–1922*, by the English art historian Camilla Gray (it was also important to Carl Andre and Sol LeWitt, who alerted Flavin to it). Among other images of the Russian avant-garde, Gray illustrates the passage in the Tatlin oeuvre from his semi-cubist paintings, via the constructions of Picasso, to his early reliefs like *Bottle* (1913), and then on to his abstract corner- and counterreliefs as well as his celebrated model for the *Monument to the Third International* (1919–20). Three years later, in 1965, Flavin looked back on this constructivist project as the newfound basis of his own "proposal": "This dramatic decoration has been founded in the young tradition of a plastic revolution which gripped Russian art only forty years ago. My joy is to try to build from that 'incomplete' experience as I see fit. *Monument 7* in cool white fluorescent light memorializes Vladimir Tatlin, the great revolutionary, who dreamed of art as science. It stands, a vibrantly aspiring order, in lieu of his last glider, which never left the ground" (84; fig. 3).

The statement is suggestive in several ways. Nearly in neo-avant-garde terms (a concept not available at the time), Flavin sees his proposal as a post-war recovery of an "incomplete" project of a prewar avant-garde; by the same token he does not deny the drastic differences in historical conditions. The Tatlin project was part of a revolutionary transformation in art and society alike, and it commemorated a new political order; the Flavin proposal is for a "dramatic decoration," a far more modest ambition, and it pays homage not to an entire society in the making, but to a failed artist who had withdrawn into the romantic vision of his glider, *Letatlin* (1929–31). Necessarily, then, this recovery is also a retreat, and like the glider the fluorescent pieces remain at the threshold between aesthetic and utilitarian purpose, illusionist and actual space.

This tension between the illusionist and the actual runs deep in modernist art, where it might also attest to the old antinomy between idealism and materialism in modern culture at large. The tension is in play, for example, in Constantin Brancusi, who, along with the Russians, was a signal precedent for

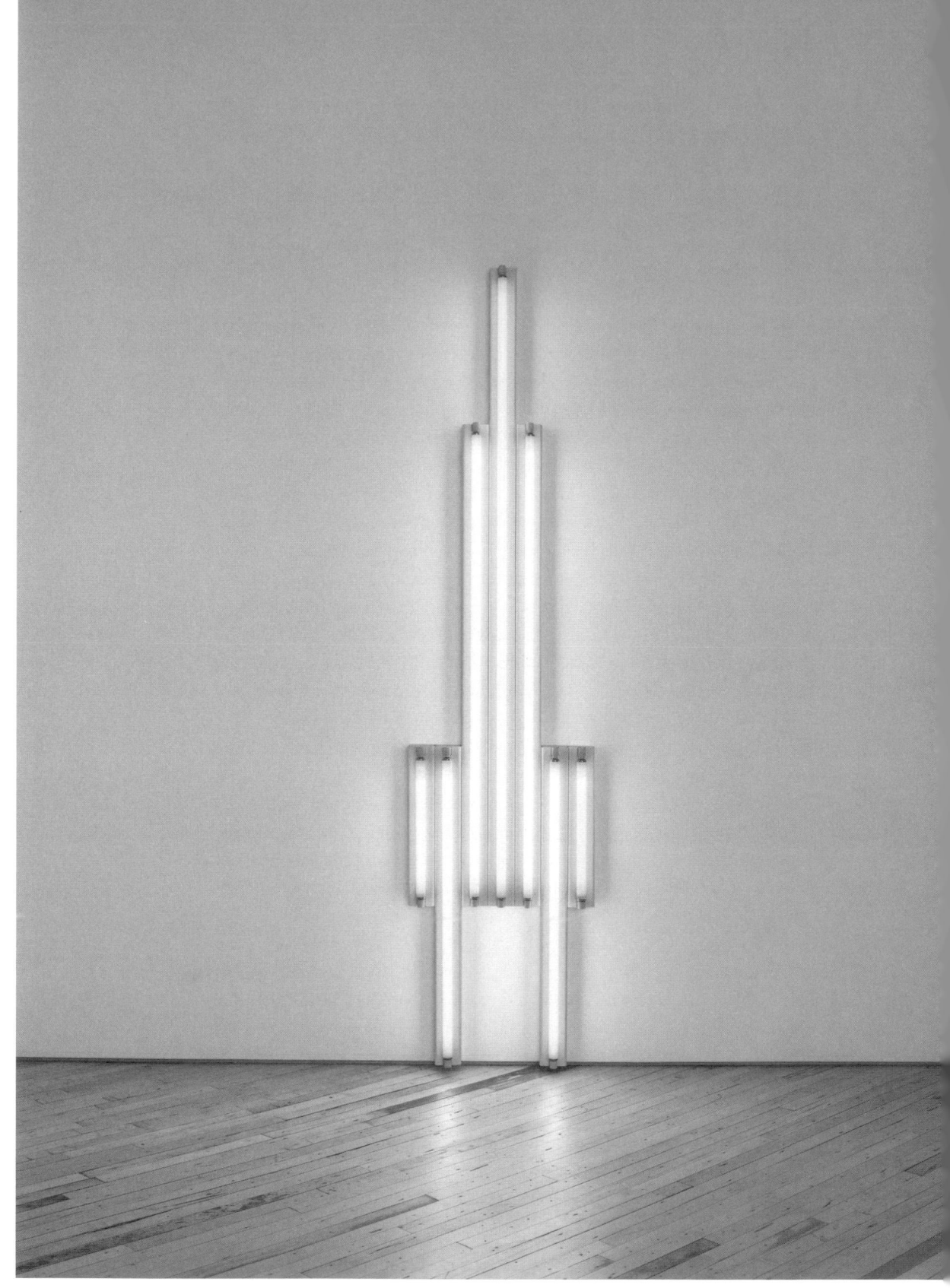

Fig. 3. Dan Flavin, *"monument" 7 for V. Tatlin*, 1964, cool white fluorescent light, 10 ft. (305 cm) high. Dia Art Foundation.

the minimalists (Flavin dedicated his breakthrough piece, *the diagonal of May 25, 1963*, to him), and it is impossible to ignore in Jackson Pollock, especially in the drip paintings that oppose the illusionist to the actual, the opticality of line and color to the materiality of paint and canvas. (Of course some subsequent artists pushed the optical term in Pollock, others the material term, while still others attempted to do both at once, or to develop this contested "legacy" in other ways altogether.) More specific to Flavin is that this tension is also immanent to the two models of the object with which he associated his work: the icon and the fetish. His interest in these categories was hardly novel—among many others, Tatlin was drawn to Russian icons, and Picasso to African fetishes—but Flavin inflects them in particular ways. He used the first term as the rubric for his early paintings with attached lights (first incandescent, then fluorescent): "I had to start from that blank, almost featureless, square-fronted construction with obvious electric light which could become my standard yet variable emblem—the 'icon'" (87). And less often he applied the second term to his fluorescent lights, which he called, in an apparent oxymoron, "modern technological fetishes" (87).[8]

Near the Tatlin reliefs in her book on the Russian avant-garde, Gray illustrates a late-fifteenth-century icon, a *Descent from the Cross* attributed to the "Northern School of Russia." Flavin bought this book on August 21, 1962 (the purchase is recorded in his notebooks), but he might have looked through it previously, for two or three weeks earlier he had made a trip to The Metropolitan Museum, which, in a note of August 9, he had already turned into an artistic epiphany (along the lines of the celebrated visit of Picasso to the Trocadéro Museum in Paris, in June 1907, during the painting of *Les Demoiselles d'Avignon*): "Last week, in the Metropolitan, I saw a large icon from the school of Novgorod [fig. 4]. I smiled when I recognized it. It had more than its painting. There was a physical feeling in the panel. Its recurving warp bore a history. This icon had that magical presiding presence which I have tried to realize in my own icons. But my icons differ from a Byzantine Christ held in majesty; they are dumb—anonymous and inglorious. They are as mute and indistinguished as the run of our architecture. My icons do not raise up the blessed saviour in elaborate cathedrals. They are constructed concentrations celebrating barren rooms. They bring a limited light" (83).[9]

This rich statement intimates what Flavin needed to "recognize" at this juncture. The icon impresses him with its "physical feeling" and its "magical presence" alike, both of which its age seems to bear into the present through a "recurving warp." This great phrase suggests an experience both of historicity and of historicity overcome, of an artifact that declares its auratic distance from Flavin and surmounts it at the same time—precisely because of his

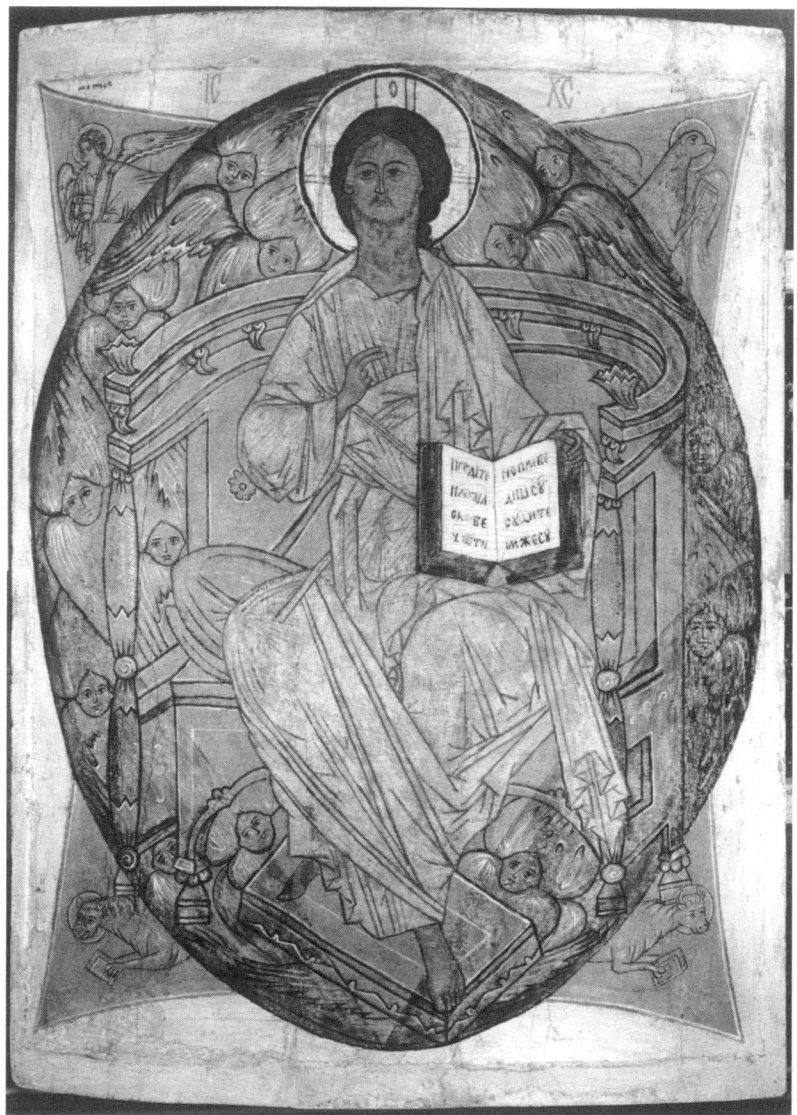

Fig. 4. *Christ in Glory*, icon, Russian (possibly Novgorod) Painter, late 15th century, tempera on wood, 42⅛ × 30⅞ in. (107 × 78.4 cm). The Metropolitan Museum of Art, Gift of George R. Hann, 1944 (44.101).

affinity with it. Clearly he is taken by the ritualistic power of the Russian icon, as was Kasimir Malevich (if not the materialist Tatlin) before him, or indeed as was Picasso with the African fetish.[10] Flavin wants to recover a little of this magic for his own art, though again he is aware of the different conditions: for all his Catholic upbringing, there is no "blessed saviour" for him, only "barren rooms." Yet, in a further twist, it is this very duality of the magical and the physical in the icon that is essential here; of *icon V (Coran's Broadway Flesh)* (1962), Flavin remarked in 1963: "I have tried to infect my icon with a blank magic that is my art" (83).

Perhaps a contemporaneous reading of Tatlin will help to clarify this affinity with the icon. "Let us remember icons," the Latvian artist and critic Vladimir Markov wrote in 1914, mindful of early Tatlin constructions such as *Selection of Materials* (1914); "they are embellished with metal halos, metal casings on the shoulders, fringes and incrustations; the painting itself is decorated with precious stones and metals, etc. All of this destroys our contemporary conception of painting." In this modernist account of the icon, its "physical feeling" (as Flavin puts it) destroys any illusion of the real world in order to conduct "the people to beauty, to religion, to God" (as Markov puts it).[11] The Tatlin constructions, Markov suggests, retain this anti-illusionism but reverse its thrust in a way that directs the viewer not to a transcendental realm of God but to an immanent "culture of materials" (as Tatlin puts it). Perhaps Flavin wanted to hold on to both vectors, the transcendental and the immanent; in any case, equally affected by the Novgorod icon and the Tatlin constructions, he positions his work in the space between them, in the intermediate world of "blank magic" that they define.

A year earlier, in 1913, Markov had also written about African sculpture, or "Negro fetishes" (as such sculpture was often called), as another implicit model, via Picasso, of the new Russian work, and he noted that these very material objects (he describes them as "architectural constructions with only a mechanical linkage") nevertheless carry a profound "spiritual conviction." Here Markov intuits a duality of the physical and the metaphysical that was long a staple of discourse on the fetish (a term used first by Portuguese and then Dutch traders for African objects of worship): for its celebrants the fetish *is* a god, not a representation of one; the divinity resides *in* the thing. (This duality was a scandal for Europeans, who placed fetishism at the bottom of all hierarchies of religion and society for this reason. Such was its function in Kant as in Hegel, and Marx and Freud only played against this usage in their own deployments of the term.) Perhaps Flavin also wanted to highlight this duality of the physical and the magical in his own work when he alluded to his fluorescent pieces as fetishes.[12]

Again, Flavin holds other dualities in tension too, such as the utilitarian and the nonutilitarian: "I can abuse lighting in a sufficiently useful way and still accomplish what I regard as art," he once commented. Supplied by "any hardware store" (91), fluorescent lights were deployed, in the early 1960s as they still are today, in workaday spaces: factories, offices, lunchrooms, subways, train stations (in 1976 Flavin installed lights on two platforms at Grand Central). They are also used commercially, and the colors are unnatural, often gaudy; beyond workaday, the lights can be tacky, and Flavin did not shy away from this association: he once remarked that the fluorescents might evoke "a Brooklyn Chinese restaurant."[13] Sometimes his incandescent icons suggest a campy side as well (with its fleshy tint and flashy lights, *Coran's Broadway Flesh* was titled in homage to "a young English homosexual who loved New York City" [83]).

On the one hand, then, Flavin held that "there is no room for mysticism in the Pepsi denigration" (another great phrase). "My fluorescent tubes never 'burn out' desiring a god" (94). Mel Bochner agreed with this assessment: "Any attempt to posit the objects with a transcendent nature is disarmed by the immediacy of their presence," he wrote in fall 1966. On the other hand, the lights can also be glorious and the effects ecstatic; Flavin often used both terms in the sense of quasi-religious transport (*ex-stasis,* out of self, out of world). Here, then, is another "irony" of different associations held together in tension that "disarms" the viewer as well: evocations of transcendental spaces on the one hand (Flavin designed lights for a church in Milan, finally realized in 1997, a year after his death) and of train stations and subways on the other. Newman zips meet Broadway lights.[14]

Flavin engages other oppositions too—between immediacy and mediation, for example, and materiality and immateriality—oppositions in play almost everywhere in advanced art of the 1960s. And often enough he spoke for both sides of the argument. On the one hand, he claimed, "the physical fluorescent light tube has never dissolved or disappeared by entering the physical field of its own light" (91); on the other, he admitted, the "brilliance" of the light can "somewhat betray its physical presence into approximate invisibility" (91). Once more Flavin wants to hold the different effects in tension: "Regard the light and you are fascinated—practically inhibited from grasping its limits at each end. While the tube itself has an actual length of 244 cm [8 feet], its shadow, cast from the supporting pan, has but illusively dissolving ends. This waning cannot really be measured without resisting consummate visual effects" (87). Yet this tension is difficult to maintain, and often his work appears less site-specific than site-erosive, with light so bright as to dematerialize both support and space, to render them "approximately invisible." An "8-foot fluorescent light pressed into a vertical corner," he acknowledged about pieces like *pink out of a corner (to Jasper Johns)* (1963), "can entirely eliminate the definite structure" (87).

This effect leads me to my primary claim here: with Flavin minimalist anti-illusionism begins to be trumped as an expanded field of illusionism, or, more precisely, with Flavin this trumping becomes available and, for some artists, desirable. This line of advanced art, then, moves beyond the frame of painting and off the pedestal of sculpture into a realm less of specific objects than of pictorial space unbounded and writ large.[15] (In a sense Flavin was "graphic" from the start—he was long interested in drawing, especially American landscapes, which he collected—and the shift here is in the nature of the ground to be marked.) Might his primary achievement—from my present perspective an ambiguous one—be not only to abstract this pictorialism (that was done before him by Pollock and others) but to atomize it?[16] In his minimalism (if that is still the proper term) to literalize is also to pictorialize: Flavin does not negate illusionism so much as he extrudes it into actual space (Dan Graham once called the effect "reverse illusionism"). This diffusion of colored light, Rosalind Krauss wrote in 1969, has "the simultaneous depth and physical inaccessibility of illusionistic space"; "the space 'in the room beyond' . . . bear[s] on the conventions of painting." More intensely than any neo-impressionist, Flavin mixes color in our eyes, and more boldly than any collagist, he treats actual space as an element in a three-dimensional composition. At these times in his work the literal does not correct the illusionist so much as it is subsumed by it.[17]

"As I have said for several years," Flavin wrote in 1966, "I believe that art is shedding its vaunted mystery for a common sense of keenly realized decoration. Symbolizing is dwindling—becoming slight. We are pressing downward toward no art—a mutual sense of psychologically indifferent decoration—a neutral pleasure of seeing known to everyone" (89). Eccentric though Flavin could be, here he conforms to central tendencies in neo-avant-garde practice —toward the anti-auratic and the antisymbolic, toward a "zero degree" of art. Yet, as we know, he did not want to shed "vaunted mystery" altogether. Moreover, "decoration" was not a slight to him, as it was to most abstractionists from Kandinsky and Mondrian in the 1910s and 1920s to all "Greenbergers" in the 1960s. For decoration is valued negatively only if abstraction is pledged absolutely to medium specificity or aesthetic autonomy, and for Flavin it was not. "At times," he said of his icons, "they may be lamp blocks losing their identity to a greater ensemble"; and of his fluorescents, he commented, "The lights are integrated with the spaces around them" (82, 89). For Flavin art as decoration hovered not only between use and nonuse but also between discrete work and architectural ensemble.

This might suggest why Flavin refused any connection with "the term 'environment'": "It seems to me to imply living conditions and perhaps an invitation to comfortable residence. Such usage would deny a sense of direct and difficult visual artifice" (95). Despite his move into actual space, then, he wanted to retain the punctual intensity, the atemporal presentness, of late-modernist painting: "I intend rapid comprehensions—get in and get out situations. I think that one has explicit moments with such particular light-space" (95). For good or for bad, his conception of art as decoration offers the optical effects of a Larry Poons or Jules Olitski painting in the spatial medium of colored light, along the lines that Irwin, Turrell, and company would also pursue: "Regard the light, and you are fascinated."[18]

Flavin achieves this presentness through the brilliance of his lights, to be sure, but also through the systematicity of his arrangements. In the quasi-structuralist fashion of the time, he associated his "system" with language, and in a distinction from the durational dimension of much minimalist art, he insisted that his was not strictly serial; further, Flavin argued, "it is as though my system synonymizes its past, present and future states" (90). This is a strong claim, but it is mostly borne out: even though our perception of a given work might change in time, it does appear to be present all at once, and, as so many arrangements of simple units, each of his pieces can be understood as implicit in every other as well. (In this regard Flavin departs from the constructivist model of art, which sought to be dialectical, and so temporal, in its making and its viewing alike.) Two of his terms for this mode of appearance of his work were *declaration* and *divulgation,* another quasi-religious category that evokes both "revelation" and "enlightenment." In some ways, then, the intensity of this presentness is at odds with the ironies noted above: whereas intensity "fascinates," irony keeps us on edge, even off balance, looking, thinking, moving.

Suspicious of "environmental" art, Flavin was contemptuous of "technological" art, which in 1967 (that is, in the heyday of Experiments in Art and Technology and related activities) he dismissed as so many "concoctions of theatrical ritual, of easy, mindless, indiscriminate sensorial abuse" (93). In particular he decried "a quasi-fetishistic reverence for technological emanations [adopted] as art itself" (93).[19] Yet there is obviously a technological dimension in his own work, which, again, Flavin sometimes aligned with the fetish as well: "A common lamp becomes a common industrial fetish," he wrote in 1964, "as utterly reproducible as ever but somehow strikingly unfamiliar now" (83). Less religious than commercial, the fetish evoked in both descriptions is the commodity, which, in the Marxist account, we endow with a power that it does not possess because we are separated from its production and so mystified by its appearance. The difference between the two uses of the term is that the fluorescent lights are "industrial fetishes" that, though "unfamiliar" as art, are familiar as objects, while the "emanations" of technological art, because they are obscure in manufacture, effect a "quasi-fetishistic reverence." (Marx wrote of the commodity in similar terms.) In a sense the difference is between blank magic and black magic. Yet here again it might be that Flavin wants it both ways: a defetishized object that is transparent in production (another constructivist desideratum) and a fetishistic object that is magical in effect. Perhaps he sensed a common ground with viewers on *both* counts: his fluorescent pieces are at once materially readable as "common lamps" (à la Tatlin) and imagistically consumable as "reproducible fetishes" (à la Warhol).

What does all this have to do with a "catastrophic" aspect of the minimalist aftermath? Etymologically (as I use it here), the term is less dramatic than it sounds: a catastrophe is a "down-turning" (*kata-strophe*), less an outright disaster than a problematic redirection. In my view such a catastrophe begins with Irwin (and others) and builds with Turrell (and others). This is not to deny the importance of these artists; it is simply to suggest that they elaborated minimalism in ways that have produced mixed results, especially in environmental and technological art. "He begins where minimalism stops," an early reviewer remarked of Irwin, "at the edge," and even his early painting in this mode works to dissolve the physicality of its surface and support. To recall the distinction posed by Judd, Irwin is interested in the phenomenon, not the object (the two are no longer in tension here), which, like Turrell, he pursues to the other side of the frame, where the specific is soon lost to light and space, indeed soon overwhelmed by the sublime.

A sense of the stakes here might be evoked through a familiar anecdote about Tony Smith, told in 1966, and his nighttime ride on the unfinished New Jersey Turnpike in the early 1950s, a primal scene "in the expanded field" of art after minimalism, often cited in debates both pro and con. Smith recounts his exhilaration in this strange landscape that was artificial but not-quite-artistic, "mapped out but not socially recognized." His was an aesthetic feeling, he is confident, but one beyond any mere picture or object: "There is no way you can frame it," Smith remarks; "you just have to experience it." Yet, as anticipated by the unfinished turnpike and exemplified by the *Roden Crater* of Turrell, say, is this expanded field truly beyond the pictorial—or is the pictorial relocated here in an apparently frameless *beyond*, a space of technologically heightened experience? In some ways Smith had an intimation of the sublime along the lines formulated long ago by Kant: a first moment in which one is overwhelmed, emotionally, by the sheer scale and force of the event, followed by a second moment in which one recoups, intellectually, such feelings of awe and dread and thereby enjoys a great rush of subjective power. In our time, however, this sublime is highly mediated (perhaps it always was), often supported by massive technological frames, as in the construction of a turnpike (or, for that matter, a *Roden Crater*), and sometimes these frames seem to auto-dissolve—that is, they are not seen or at least remembered as such. Typically, in other words, our sublime is a technological sublime, and its phenomenology a faux phenomenology, and, whatever else artists who stage such experiences might accomplish (or intend), they mystify this condition even as they exploit it.[20]

Smith reaches for correlatives of his turnpike sublime and mentions "abandoned airstrips in Europe" and then, with no hitch in his discourse, a "drill ground in Nuremberg large enough to accommodate two million men." I underscore this overlooked reference not to contaminate the expanded field after minimalism with the architecture of Nazism, but to point to the complications of such transgressions in twentieth-century history at large. For intimated here is that the expanded field is not entirely removed either from the space of "the mass ornament" described by Siegfried Kracauer in 1927 as "*a mythological cult* . . . masquerading in the garb of abstraction" or from the effects of the futurist-fascist sublime described by Walter Benjamin in 1936 as "the artistic gratification of a sense perception altered by technology." In short, what Smith glimpsed (without the pause that our historical distance might grant us today) is that the crux of minimalism allowed not only for a progressive desublimation of painting and sculpture into practices that open onto actual space and everyday life, but also for a problematic resublimation of the pictorial and the sculptural in a technological sublime—a resublimation in which conventional frames often seem to disappear, replaced by mediated formats that often seem transparent. What is delivered, then, are sensations of intensity that, though once radical in art, have become almost normative in spectacle-culture at large, and again, whatever else it might do, such art serves as an aesthetic ally or alibi for this condition.[21]

Already in "The Work of Art in the Age of Its Reproducibility" (1936) Benjamin had noted this effect of immediacy-through-mediation in the cinema of his time: "The equipment-free aspect of reality here has become the height of artifice." In our age this effect is evermore total: it can produce a faux phenomenology so extreme that spaces seem opticalized and bodies all but dissolved. And this effect, already implicit in Flavin, is furthered by Turrell and others, who offer an experience of great spiritual immediacy achieved through intensive technological mediation. Benjamin termed this artifice reality the "blue flower in the land of technology"; he also called it "dream kitsch." In our time Turrell is one master of the mode; another, perhaps the bluest of all blue flowers, is Bill Viola, whose immersive video projections work to render the spiritual and the technological absolutely synthetic. Perhaps this technological sublime can be troped productively, even critically, but to my mind it is not so here, nor is it in the work of younger artists, such as Olafur Eliasson, who follow on Turrell and Viola in this regard.[22]

Notes

I wish to thank Jeffrey Weiss for his invitation to the National Gallery symposium on Dan Flavin, and Tiffany Bell (to whom this essay is dedicated) for her Flavin expertise in general. An initial fragment of this essay was published as "Six Paragraphs on Dan Flavin," *Artforum* (February 2005).

1. I refer, of course, to Donald Judd, "Specific Objects," *Arts Yearbook* 8 (1965), reprinted in Donald Judd, *Complete Writings, 1959–1975* (Halifax: Press of the Nova Scotia School of Art and Design, 1975). I only broach the question of this aftermath here.

2. Almost all these peers (Carl Andre is one exception) began as painters. On this crux see "The Crux of Minimalism" (1987) in my *The Return of the Real* (Cambridge: MIT Press, 1996), 44–46.

3. "Please do not refer to my effort as sculpture and to me as sculptor," Flavin wrote the curator Jan van der Marck on June 17, 1967; "I do not handle and fashion three-dimensional still works, even as to Barbara Rose's Juddianed 'specific objects.' I feel apart from problems of sculpture and painting." See Dan Flavin, *three installations in fluorescent light/drei Installationen in fluoreszierendem Licht*, exh. cat. (Cologne: Kölnische-Verlagsdruckerei, 1973), 95; all page numbers included in the text refer to this publication (and all linguistic oddities are his).

4. Illusionism was also retained, indeed heightened, in much pop art, especially in certain works by Andy Warhol (think, for example, of *Optical Car Crash* [1962]), where it is compounded by the different sort of illusionism carried over from mass-media sources. I did catch this pop version of illusionism, and in "The Crux of Minimalism" I proposed a kind of dialectic of minimalism and pop in this regard—between the specific and the simulacral, the embodied and the disembodied, perceptual presence and mass-mediated representation. And yet, as this is a dialectic, the pop terms are not simply opposed to the minimalist ones but also, in part, internal to them.

5. In large part this virtualization is driven by a deep desire, in advanced capitalist society, for evermore fungible images—a process from which the minimalist aftermath has not proved immune.

6. Judd, *Complete Writings*, 124, 200 (emphasis mine). Though less intense in Judd, this oscillation is active nonetheless. "Object-art would seem to proscribe both allusion and illusion," the twenty-four-year-old Rosalind Krauss wrote in "Allusion and Illusion in Donald Judd" (*Artforum* [May 1966]), only to point to an excess in Judd—of beauty, affect, association—beyond his preferred positivism of interpretation as a "list of physical properties": these works "both insist upon and deny the adequacy of such a definition" (24). As an instance Krauss discusses a 1965 interval piece, a long aluminum bar supported horizontally by short aluminum pieces, all of which are painted purple. From the front, she notes, the colored bars seem to be the luminous figure on the solid ground of the aluminum bar, but this is revealed to be an illusion when one looks from either end: the aluminum bar is hollow and supported by the colored bars. There is also a play with perspective as one walks along the piece. On several levels, then, both illusion and allusion are con-

jured and dispelled, an oscillation that, Krauss argues, Judd develops from the late *Cubi* of David Smith that play with the structure of the frame: "The[se] works," Krauss writes of the *Cubi*, "wed a purely optical sensation of openness (the view through the frame) that is the presumed subject of the work, with an increased sense of the palpability and substance of the frame. Smith in this way embraced the modality of illusionism within pictorial space from painting, and used this to powerful sculptural advantage" (24). Here the virtual is a foil for the specific, the illusionist for the actual, and so on; there is a related "foiling" in Judd as well. In any case, the illusionist persists in the translucency of some of his materials, in the opticality of some of his surfaces, and in the shadowy spaces created by some of his extrusions and recessions; sometimes, too, it seems to emerge in the very seriality of such works. Often, it is true, his seriality is in the service of the specific: especially in plywood pieces the repetition of units prepares the difference of each unit. But this is less the case in other instances, where the serial order tends to virtualize the specific and, in conjunction with the reflective metal, even to dissolve it. Again, for the most part, the illusionist serves to heighten the actual, but this tension was mostly lost in the discursive deployment of Judd, a deployment in the service of specific objects, site-specific works, and so on. For another account of "polarity" in Judd see Richard Schiff, "Donald Judd, Safe from Birds," in Nicholas Serota, ed., *Donald Judd* (London: Tate Publishing, 2004).

7. On Flavin's irony see the essay by Alex Potts in this volume. For Stella's remark, see Bruce Glaser, "Questions to Stella and Judd" (1966), in Gregory Battcock, *Minimal Art: A Critical Anthology* (New York: Dutton, 1968), 158. Flavin participated in this conversation but edited his remarks out of the transcript. A deconstructive (de Manian) kind of analysis, such as that developed by Fred Orton in *Figuring Jasper Johns* (Cambridge: Harvard University Press, 1994), might be also appropriate for Flavin. Flavin wrote of his early fluorescent works, "They lack the look of history. . . . I sense no stylistic or structural development. . . . It is as though my system synonymizes its past, present and future states" (90). Regarding art criticism, his primary bête noire, Flavin also wrote against writing "in the disreputable promo-past tense, of pious, proto-historic figure fabrication by polemical case history" (97).

8. Michel Foucault writes of a similar "empirico-transcendental doublet" deep in modern thought in *The Order of Things* (1966; New York: Vintage, 1970), 318–22; also see "The Crux of Minimalism." The tension is active in twentieth-century architecture too: witness the debate launched by Colin Rowe and Robert Slutsky with their essay "Transparency: Literal and Phenomenal," *Perspecta* 8 (1963). One point of pressure here must be the rise of a post-Fordist economy of consumption based on the "phenomenal transparency" of mediated images. Pollock's "legacy": I allude to Allan Kaprow, "The Legacy of Jackson Pollock," *Art News* 57, no. 6 (October 1958); but also see Robert Morris, "Notes on Sculpture, Part 4," *Artforum* (April 1969).

9. "I smiled when I recognized it": this suggests that Flavin might have looked through the book before his visit, though to my knowledge the icon in the Gray was not the one in the Met. What then did he "recognize" there? Perhaps simply his own affinity with such icons. (It seems that, even before this

visit to the Met, Flavin had begun to title his early series "icons": the first is dated 1961–62, and a note dated March 1962 refers to them as such.)

10. Flavin also did a drawing of an arrangement of his first four icons "with an overt reference to an iconostasis (the screen, adorned with icons, that separates the sanctuary from the nave in a Greek Orthodox church)" (Michael Govan and Tiffany Bell, *Dan Flavin: A Retrospective,* exh. cat. [New Haven: Yale University Press, 2004], 29).

11. Vladimir Markov, *Printsipy tvorchestva v plasticheskikh iskusstvakh. Faktura* (1914), 54, as translated by Christina Lodder in her *Russian Constructivism* (New Haven: Yale University Press, 1983), 13. Markov is not mentioned by Gray, and it is highly unlikely that Flavin knew of his work, yet he too highlights the facticity of his icons: "I use the word 'icon' as descriptive, not of a strictly religious object, but of one that is based on a hierarchical relationship of electric light over, under, against and with a square-fronted structure full of paint 'light'" (88).

12. Vladimir Markov, *Iskusstvo negrov* (1913), 36, translated as "Negro Sculpture" in Jack Flam with Miriam Deutsch, eds., *Primitivism and Twentieth-Century Art: A Documentary History* (Berkeley: University of California Press, 2003), 63; see William Pietz, "The Problem of the Fetish," in *Res* 9, 13, and 16 (Spring 1985, Spring 1987, Autumn 1988), and my "The Art of Fetishism," in Emily Apter and William Pietz, eds., *Fetishism as Cultural Discourse* (Ithaca: Cornell University Press, 1993).

13. "Dan Flavin Interviewed by Phyllis Tuchman" (1972), in Govan and Bell, *Flavin: A Retrospective,* 194.

14. Mel Bochner, "Art in Process: Structures," *Arts Magazine* (September/October, 1966): 39. Michael Govan quotes Joyce on the epiphany, which is indeed pertinent to Flavin: "The soul of the commonest object, the structure of which is so adjusted, seems to us radiant" (Govan and Bell, *Flavin: A Retrospective,* 32). Yet, in Flavin as in Joyce, epiphanic states are sometimes undercut by humorous humiliations. At his most minimalist Flavin separated and opposed the terms of his ironies. For example, *the nominal three (to William of Ockham)* (1963), commemorates the fourteenth-century English scholastic philosopher, who wrote: "Principles (entities) should not be multiplied unnecessarily." Flavin glossed his nominalism in this way: "Reality exists solely in individual things and universals are merely abstract signs. This view led [Ockham] to exclude questions such as the existence of God from intellectual knowledge, referring them to faith alone" (83–84). Yet for the most part Flavin does not oppose "individual objects" and "abstract signs." Again, like the icon and the fetish (and perhaps, for a Christian, like Jesus too, human and divine at once), his lights work to hold such polarities together.

15. This was sensed in the recent retrospective at its National Gallery venue when one moved from the first floor, where the work remained mostly on the walls, to the second floor, where it irradiated the rooms. Of course, this is only one response to Flavin; for a very different reading see "Richard Serra in Conversation with Hal Foster," in *Richard Serra: The Matter of Time* (Bilbao: Guggenheim Museum, 2005).

16. Perhaps Robert Smithson had this effect in mind when he wrote in 1966,

"Flavin's destruction of classical time and space is based on an entirely new notion of the structure of matter" (*Robert Smithson: The Collected Writings*, ed. Jack Flam [Berkeley: University of California Press, 1996], 10).

17. Dan Graham, "Art as Design/Design as Art," in *Rock My Religion: Writings and Projects, 1965–1990* (Cambridge: MIT Press, 1993), 211. In this respect Flavin might be aligned less with the constructivist project of Tatlin than with the color-plane decors of de Stijl. Incidentally, he was always suspicious of the term *minimalism*. Rosalind Krauss, untitled review, *Artforum* (January 1969), 53–54. Some spaces are set apart from the viewer by the fixtures in a way that marks them as "pictorial" in the sense suggested by Krauss (e.g., *untitled (to S.M. with all the admiration and love which I can sense and summon)* [1969]). In his treatment of space Flavin is hardly alone here: in the early-middle 1960s pictorial space burst out of the frame into actual space in a number of ways: think, for example, of the scatter pieces by Robert Morris and others. In a work such as *Threadwaste* (1968) Morris sought to move "beyond objects" altogether—but neither into pure idea (as in much conceptual art) nor into sheer material (as in other process art). He sought the creation of a "field effect" in which the object was often fractured if not dissolved, and the vision of the viewer often disturbed if not deranged. In his own words, Morris wanted "to take the conditions of the visual field" as the "structural basis" of the work and not merely its physical limit. In so doing he attempted to shift the viewer from a focal gaze (as one looks at a painting or a sculpture or indeed a minimalist object) to a "vacant stare" on a visual array; and it was to this end that he arranged materials in a way that could hardly be grasped, in profile or in plan, as an image at all. In works like *Threadwaste* it is as if vision were decentered from the subject, thrown out into the world, and this opticalizing of space is also furthered by artists as different as Warhol and Irwin. See Morris, "Notes on Sculpture, Part 4." On a related derangement of vision in Flavin see the essay by Briony Fer in this volume.

18. In the 1960s the distinctions between these practices were not always clear—though Flavin refused any association with painters like Olitski (cf. page 109). In some sense, to borrow the famous terms of Michael Fried in "Art and Objecthood" (*Artforum* [June 1967]), Flavin split the difference between punctual "presentness" and durational "presence."

19. Flavin continues in his acerbic way: "No one should bother to pay to concede his perception to the pointless audio-visual 'entertaining' punishment haphazardly projected by some of the so-called self-determined multi-media techno-totalitarians, especially since, at home, on any evening, he is already compelled to absorb an 'overload' of much of the same seemingly arbitrary, jarring, messageless mistreatment from television commercials and programs" (93). Perhaps Flavin is sensitive here because his work was sometimes viewed as passive before its own technology: "It is a kind of '1984' passivity," Emily Wasserman wrote, "a lyricizing of basically uninventive, unprofound forms" (*Artforum* [December 1967]: 60).

20. Samuel K. Wagstaff, Jr., "Talking with Tony Smith," *Artforum* (December 1966); reprinted in Battcock, *Minimal Art*, 386. I also allude here to the classic essay by Rosalind Krauss, "Sculpture in the Expanded Field," *October* 10 (Fall

1979), with this revision: the expanded field has proved not to be exclusive of painting; indeed today its space is shot through with the pictorial.

My argument is not the old modernist one that equates authenticity with truth to materials or literal transparency but one that sees the continued relevance of defetishization. I also do not oppose experiences of intensity to, say, those of historicity, complexity, or criticality (they are not so opposed, for example, in Smithson, who also engages the sublime, but in a very different way from Turrell et al.). In "The Crux of Minimalism" I suggested that the very insistence on the phenomenological in minimalism might be symptomatic of its eclipse or at least its radical transformation, as explored concurrently by pop. But, again, if minimalism and pop constitute a dialectic, the phenomenological and the faux cannot be so easily separated. Such is my claim now about Flavin. Today, of course, "minimalism" has become pop—mediated and fetishized—in art and architecture alike.

21. Wagstaff, "Talking with Tony Smith," 386; Siegfried Kracauer, *The Mass Ornament,* ed. and trans. Thomas Y. Levin (Cambridge: Harvard University Press, 1995), 83; Walter Benjamin, "The Work of Art in the Age of Its Reproducibility" (1936), *Selected Writings,* vol. 3: *1935–1938,* ed. Howard Eiland and Michael W. Jennings (Cambridge: Harvard University Press, 2002), 122. This condition has become one norm of contemporary museum practice as well. See Rosalind Krauss, "The Museum of Art in the Age of Late Capitalism," *October* 54 (Fall 1990); and Nicholas Serota, *Experience or Interpretation: The Dilemma of Museums of Modern Art* (London: Thames and Hudson, 2000).

22. Benjamin, "The Work of Art in the Age of Its Reproducibility," 115; Benjamin, "Dream Kitsch," *Selected Writings,* vol. 2: *1927–1934,* ed. Howard Eiland and Michael W. Jennings (Cambridge: Harvard University Press, 1999), 3–5. The "blue flower" here alludes to a figure for the object of desire in the work of the great German romantic Novalis. This description in Benjamin is also apposite today: "What we used to call art begins at a distance of two meters from the body. But now, in kitsch, the world of things advances on the human being; it yields to his uncertain grasp and ultimately fashions its figures in his interior" (4–5). For Benjamin and Kracauer the primary subject-effect of capitalist culture was a complex of attention and distraction, shock and absorption, and they argued that some modernist practices—especially abstract architecture, dadaist collage, and filmic montage—might turn this sensorial complex to critical advantage. At times, too, they suggested a "go-for-broke game" in which this complex might be exacerbated and somehow passed through: "The process," Kracauer writes in "The Mass Ornament," leads directly through the center of the mass ornament, not away from it" (*The Mass Ornament,* 61, 86). It might be argued that this is what artists like Eliasson attempt to do again today—but to what other side?

Contributors

Briony Fer is professor of history of art at University College, London. Her many publications on twentieth-century and contemporary art include *On Abstract Art* (1997) and *The Infinite Line: Remaking Art After Modernism* (2004), both published by Yale University Press.

Hal Foster is Townsend Martin '17 Professor and chair of the Department of Art and Archaeology at Princeton University. Among his recent books is *Prosthetic Gods* (2004).

Jeremy Gilbert-Rolfe is chair of the MFA Program in Art at Art Center College of Design. A painter and the author of several books on art and related topics, he was the 1997 recipient of the College Art Association's Mather Award for Art and Architectural Criticism.

Alex Potts is Max Loehr Collegiate Professor and chair of the Department of History of Art at the University of Michigan, Ann Arbor. His recent publications include *The Sculptural Imagination: Figurative, Modernist, Minimalist* (2000) and *Flesh and the Ideal: Winckelmann and the Origins of Art History* (1994 and 2000).

Anne M. Wagner is professor of modern art at the University of California, Berkeley. Her essays on nineteenth- and twentieth-century art have treated topics as wide-ranging as Courbet's landscapes, Willem de Kooning's drawings, and Eva Hesse's titles. Her most recent book is *Mother Stone: The Vitality of Modern British Sculpture* (2005), published by Yale University Press.

Jeffrey Weiss is curator and head of modern and contemporary art at the National Gallery of Art, Washington, D.C. He has organized exhibitions on various topics in modernist and postwar art, including *Jasper Johns: An Allegory of Painting, 1955–65*, forthcoming in 2007.

Photograph Credits

Alex Potts **Dan Flavin:** "in . . . cool white" and "infected with a blank magic"

1, 8: Photo by Bill Jacobson, New York
2, 3, 9, 10, 11: Photo by Billy Jim, New York
6: Photo by Cathy Carver

Briony Fer **Nocturama:** Flavin's Light Diagrams

8: Photo by Florian Holzherr, Munich
9, 10: Photo by Becket Logan, New York

Jeffrey Weiss **Blunt in Bright Repose**

9: Art © Jasper Johns/Licensed by VAGA, New York, NY. Photo by Dorothy Zeidman

10: Art © Jasper Johns/Licensed by VAGA, New York, NY. Photo by Eric Politzer

Jeremy Gilbert-Rolfe   **Space and Speed in Flavin:** Minimalism, Pop Art, and Mondrian

1, 3, 4: Photo by Billy Jim, New York

2: © 2006 Succession H. Matisse, Paris / Artists Rights Society (ARS), New York

5: © 2005 Andy Warhol Foundation for the Visual Arts / ARS, New York

6: Art © Judd Foundation. Licensed by VAGA, New York, NY. Photographer: Judd Foundation

7: © 2005 The Estate of Fritz Glarner, Kunsthaus Zürich. All rights reserved.

8: Image courtesy Instituut Collectie Nederland

9: Photo: Oren Slor

Anne M. Wagner   **Flavin's Limited Light**

12: Photo: Bichelaer, Geldrop, Holland

Hal Foster   **Dan Flavin and the Catastrophe of Minimalism**

2: Photo by Bill Jacobson, New York

3: Photo by Billy Jim, New York

4: Photograph, all rights reserved, The Metropolitan Museum of Art

Index

Page numbers in *italic* type indicate illustrations.

abstract expressionism, 28, 56, 64, 66–67, 68, 69, 70, 74
abstraction, 75, 143, 146; Flavin's earlier works and, 13, 136; fluorescent works as, 1, 14, 21, 71; functionality and, 71; Gris letter on, 14–15; painting conditions and, 55, 56; representation and, 70–71
abstract space, 70, 126–27
actual space. *See* real space
African fetish, 139, 140, 141
Albright-Know Art Gallery (Buffalo), 21–22*n*4
Allan Stone Gallery (New York), 67, 68
Alloway, Lawrence, 16
ambient space, 49
Andre, Carl, 49, *63*, 80*n*19, 137, 147*n*2; *Lever*, 111
anti-illusionism, 6, 133–34, 136, 137, 139, 141, 142–43
Antonioni, Michelangelo, 31
Apollinaire, 11, *14*
Art and Artists (Bochner), 40
Artforum, 51, 70, 75, 108, 109; Flavin's autobiographical sketch in, 37, 41
artificial light. *See* fluorescent lamps
Art of Assemblage show (Museum of Modern Art, 1961), 55, 136–37
Ashbery, John, 74–75
Asher, Michael, 120
Ashton, Dore, 110–11
assemblage, 6, 70, 137; *Art of Assemblage* show, 55, 136–37; crushed-can series, 9, 10–11, 13, *14*, 15, 21, 31, 56, 136

Austerlitz (Sebald), 25
avant-garde, 36, 53, 62, 68, 139; Flavin's legacy from, 37, 46, 60, 137, 143; readymades and, 56. *See also* constructivism

Baker, Elizabeth C., 111
Baker, Kenneth, 109
Ballantyne, Peter, 27
Barthes, Roland, 112, 113
Bayer, Adolf, 106*n*5
Becquerel, Alexandre, 82
Bell, Larry, 134
Bell, Tiffany, 20, 27, 28, 47*n*8, 48*nn*18,20, 125
Benjamin, Walter, 146, 151*n*22
Benjamin Moore paint series, 64
Bernstein Brothers, 27
Betty Parsons Gallery (New York), 67
Bierce, Ambrose, 49
Bochner, Mel, 26–27, 81*nn*27,28; diagrammatic drawings and, 41, 44; Flavin's gold *diagonal* and, 70; on Flavin's work, 16, 18, 19, 24*n*27, 75, 109, 112, 113, 142; *Minimal Art: The Movie*, 109, *109*; quotations compilation by, 40; serial systems and, 41, 52–53
Bois, Yve-Alain, 101
Bourdon, David, 18, 74, 75
Brancusi, Constantin, 51, 93, 137, 139
Buchloh, Benjamin, 79*n*11
Burnham, Jack, 108, 109
Byzantine art, 35, 60–62, 139

camp aesthetic, 4, 142
Campbell's soup can, 72, 90
Caro, Heinrich, 106*n*5
Castelli, Leo, 44, 109

Castelli Warehouse, 21–22*n*4
Celant, Germano, 109
Center Gallery (Washington, D.C.), 39, 48*n*14
Cézanne, Paul, 31, 32
Chevreul, Michel-Eugène, 56, 83, 106*n*2
Christ in Glory (Russian icon), 139, *140*
chromophobia, 53
Clare Copley Gallery (Los Angeles), 120
color: alizarin crimson, 87; all-green room and, 38–39; art historical/cultural associations with, 98; diagrammatic labeling of, 44, 45, *45*; Duchamp and, 77; Flavin and, 28, 53, 57, 91, 92, 95, 98, 99, 100, 104, 106, 134, 136, 143; fluorescent effects with, 8, 16, 19, *20*, 27, 28, 35, 54, 75, 102, 105, 142, 143; fluorescent prefabricated standardization of, 55, 64, 74; illusion created by, 100–101; impressionism and, 82, 83, 84, 89; Johns and, 72–73, 74; Newman and, 73–74; painting and, 54, 55–56, 64–66; paint technology and, 87; space manipulation with, 100. *See also* paint
commercial materials, 55–59, 63–67, 71, 72, 111; designification of, 92, 96–97, 99; expressive capacities of, 98; fetishes and, 144; house paint as, 57–59, 63–65, 67. *See also* fluorescent lamps
conceptual art, 41, 44, 63, 150*n*17
Congo, 9, *13*
constructivism, 36, 37, 46, 90, 93, 99, 137, 139, 141, 144, 145
critics, 4, 12, 13–14, 16, 39, 42, 74, 108–14; Flavin's critique of, 80*n*24, 108, 115
crushed-can series, 9, 10–11, 13, *14*, 15, 21, 31, 56, 136
cubism, 65

dada, 23–24*n*21
Dan Flavin: The Complete Lights (Govan and Bell), 125
Danto, Arthur, 96
daylight, 24*n*24, 51, 82, 83, 84, 86–87, 88, 99, 102–3, *103*, 104, 105; measurement of, 106*n*2. *See also* white light
de Kooning, Elaine, 26, 27
de Kooning, Willem, 16, 64, 67, 70
Delaunay, Robert, 55, 56
Demus, Otto, 60–61
Descent from the Cross (Russian icon), 139
de Stijl, 126, 150*n*17

Develing, Enno, 21–22*n*4
Dia Art Foundation, 2, 5; staircase, 102, *103*, 103–4, 105–6
diagrams. *See* drawings and diagrams
Diagrams: Dan Flavin/Don Judd show (Center Gallery, 1966), 39, 48*n*14
Diebenkorn, Richard, 70
di Suvero, Mark, 133
Documenta 4 show (Kassel, 1966), 124
drawings and diagrams, 5, 6, 10, 13, 26–46, *30*, *45*; different idioms of, 28–29, 31; exhibitions of, 39, 48*nn*14,15; Flavin's collection of, 34, 143; importance to installation of, 40, 43–44, 52, 115, 123–24; for Kornblee installation, *38*, 38–39; of multiple square-formed icons, *62*, 62–63, *63*; post-installation, 43–44; shorthand notations on, 26, 34, 39
drawings and diagrams from Dan Flavin, 1963–1972 show (Saint Louis Art Museum, 1973), 40, 48*n*15
Duchamp, Marcel, 49, 64–65, 75–77, 78, 80*n*19, 90, 92; diagrams/notes of, 27, 36; Flavin's reaction to, 37; readymades and, 54, 55, 56, 57, 65, 72, 74, 75. *Works: Apolinère Enameled*, 65, 66; *The Bride Stripped Bare by Her Bachelors, Even (The Large Glass)*, 75–77, *76*
Duve, Thierry de, 55, 56, 76–77, 81*n*25
Dwan Gallery (New York), 67, 118, *119*, *120*

East New York Shrine series (Flavin), 221*n*6
electric light. *See* fluorescent lamps
Eliasson, Olafur, 146
empiricism, 89, 112
entropy, 19
European art, 93, 95

Factory studio (Warhol), 61
familiar objects, 82, 91, 98, 99, 141–42. *See also* commercial materials; ready-made materials
fetish, 71, 112, 139, *140*, 141, 144–45
Figuring Jasper Johns (Orton), 148*n*7
First World War, 11
Flaubert, Gustave, 40
Flavin, Dan, *32*, *119;* ambiguity in works of, 51, 53, 71, 98, 112, 134; autobiographical account of, 37, 41, 51, 56, 57, 69, 75; avant-garde and, 37, 46, 60, 137, 143;

brother's death and, 6; central themes of, 10; as collector of drawings, 34, 143; commemorative titles of, 10–11, 14; crushed-can series of, 9, 10–11, 13, *14*, 21, 56; death connotations and, 10, 19, 21, 67; "declaration" and "divulgence" terms and, 144; dedicatees of works of, 3, 6, 9, 12, 21, 33, 36, 50–51, 53, 67, 83, 89, 90, 93, 95, 139; diagrammatic drawings of, *5*, 26, 39–46; dualities and, 141–42; early works of, 6, 13, 31, 136; fetish and, 139; gallery space and, 126–27; Gleason compared with, 109–10, *110*; icons and (*see* icon series); idea of primary and, 98; "image-object" term and, 51, 56, 112–13, 115, 134; impressionism and, 82, 83–84, 88, 89, 91; irony and, 12, 16, 19, 51, 112, 134, 136, 142, 149*n*14; Johns and, 89–90, *90*; major breakthrough of, 1, 3, 11–12; Matisse and, 84, *85*, 88, 89, 92, 95, 98; Mondrian and, 99–103; mortality of work of, 19; Newman and, 67, 69, 88, 89, 136; notekeeping by, 41; œuvre-bridging works of, 2–3, 16; office of, 31–33, *32*; on painters, 57–58; painting and, 53; phenomenological experience and, 26, 27, 35; physical size of, 109–10, 119; poetic drawings of, *7*, 13, *13*; poetry by, 11, 19; politics and, 6, 8, 9, 10, *13*; pop art and, 90–91; rolodex card file of, 41; Russian constructivism and, 35, 37, 137; self view of, 98; serial/permutational work of, 50; spleenishness of, 12, 16, 41, 108–9; sublime and, 110; system of, 143; temporality and, 29, 31; terms for installations of, 25, 112; watercolors and, 6, *7*, *13*, 136. *Works: alternate diagonals of March 2, 1964 (to Don Judd)*, 17, 17–18, *116; Apollinaire wounded (to Ward Jackson)*, 10–11, *14; daylight and cool white (to Sol LeWitt)*, 2, 3, *3; the diagonal of May 25, 1963 (to Constantin Brancusi) (the diagonal of personal ecstasy)*, 35, 50, 51, 53, 61, 69, 77–78, 93, 94, 95, 96, 98, 112, 139; *the diagonol of May 25, 1963 (to Robert Rosenblum)*, *116;* Dia staircase, 102, *103*, 103–4, 105–6; *fluorescent light . . . from Dan Flavin*, 24*n*30; *the gold diagonal (completed)*, 35; *gold, pink, and red, red*, 116, *118; greens crossing greens (to Piet Mondrian, who lacked green)*, 122, *123; Gus Schultze's screwdriver (to Dick Bellamy)*,

136; "Holy Mother of God loaded with Grace please help David Sonja-Dan Flavin," 22*n*6; *icon I (the heart) (to the light of Sean McGovern which blesses everyone)*, 8, *135; icon II (the mystery) (to John Reeves)*, *135; icon III (the blood) (the blood of a martyr)*, *135; icon IV (the pure land) (to David John Flavin)*, 22*n*6, 33; *icon V (Coran's Broadway Flesh)*, 2, *2*, 4, 21–22*n*4, 22*n*9, 33, 141, 142; *icon VI (Ireland dying) (to Louis Sullivan)*, *135; icon VII (via crucis)*, 60, *135; icon VIII (the dead nigger's icon) (to Blind Lemon Jefferson)*, *135; iconostases (for icons I, II, III, and IV)*, 34, 34–35; *Juan Gris in Paris. Adieu Picabia*, 15; *leaning diagonal*, *117; the mechanical interior*, 31; *mira mira*, 31, 35, 56; *monument 4 those who have been killed in ambush (to P.K. who reminded me about death)*, 6, 8, 8–9; "*monument" 7 for V. Tatlin*, 9–10, 36–37, 50, 52, 137, *138; my studio*, 30, 31; *the nominal three (to William of Ockham)*, 4, *5*, 12, 21, 41, 52–53, 70, 149*n*14; *pink out of a corner (to Jasper Johns)*, 89, 90, 116, 129*n*14, 142; *a primary picture*, 19, 20, 21, 53, *116; second diagram for Kornblee Gallery installation 7 October–8 November 1967*, 38; *selections for graphed paper diagram for the Leo Castelli Gallery*, 45; *Song of Songs*, 6, *7; three (to William of Ockham)*, *5; three from meditation (for William of Ockham)*, *5; three tangented arcs in daylight and cool white (to Jenny and Ira Licht)*, 124, *125; to those who suffer in the Congo*, 13; *untitled (1960)*, 30; *untitled (1962)*, 62; *untitled (1976–77)*, *125; untitled (1996)*, 103; *untitled (tenements in the rain)*, 28, *29; untitled (to a man, George McGovern)*, 127, *127; untitled (to Dorothy and Roy Lichtenstein on not seeing anyone in the room)*, 113–14, *114; untitled (to Emily)*, 43; *untitled (to Henri Matisse)*, 84, *85; untitled (to Ingrid Nibbe)*, 116, *117; untitled (to Jan and Ron Greenberg)*, 43, 43–44, *44; untitled (to Karin)*, 122; *untitled (to S.M. with all the admiration and love which I can sense and summon)*, 150*n*17; *untitled (to the "innovator" of Wheeling Peachblow)*, 15, 15–16, 51, 113; *Ursula's one and two picture*, 121; *Vincent at Auvers*, 21, 47*n*5; *Washington Street sculpture*, 21. *See also* fluorescent lamps

Flavin, Judd, Morris, Williams group show (Green Gallery, 1965), *117*

Flavin, Sonja, 36, 43, 44, 48*n*20

Flavin, Stephen, 31, *32*, 43, 46, 48*n*20

Flavin retrospective (1969). *See* National Gallery of Canada (Ottawa) Flavin retrospective

Flavin Studio, 48*n*20

fluorescent lamps, 1–6, *3*, 16–21, *17*, *20*; actuality vs. factuality of, 112–13; ambivalence of, 71, 134; anti-illusionism and, 6; assemblage of, 27, 43, 144; audience's view of, 45, 51, 123–24, 125, 134; authorship and, 74; banality of, 57; blurred distinction between real and ideal and, 99; as both medium and work, 62; brightness of, 84, 87; corridors of, 43–44; critical responses to, 4, 110–14, 125; cumulative experience of, 28; curious nature of, 18–19; defamiliarized position of, 57, 111–12; designification and, 91–92; diagonal placement of, 11, *17*, 17–18, 35, *35*, *50*, 51, 53, 54, 56, 57, 77–78, 102, 104, 112, 116, *116*; diagrams for installation of, 25, 36, 37, 38–39, 42–46, 52, 115, 123–24; duality of, 50, 51–52; early- and late-career aspects of, 53–54; as emblem, 4; familiarity of, 82, 91, 98, 99, 141–42; as fetish, 71, 139, 141, 144–45; first, 35, 139; Flavin's iconic statement on, 11–12; as Flavin's major breakthrough, 1; fluidity of light from, 74, *75*; gaseousness of, 75, 78, 82, 83; history and science of, 82–83, 91; illusionism and, 136; as image-object, 51; impressionist color and, 82, 83, 89; informal rotation of, 57; installation composition and, 52; intensity of, 102; interrelationships between, 52; limited lifespan of, 19, 21, 71, 74; materiality of, 98; minimalist art and, 91–92, 99; multitube architectonic installations of, 19, 21, 27–28; oppositions and, 141–42; paint and, 56–57; as painting surrogate, 54, 59–60, 75, 77–78, 84; physical revisions of, 115–16; pop art and, 91; positioning of, 118–22, 134; preconceptions about, 96, 98; progressional procedure of, 53; as ready-made materials, 27, 31, 49, 54, 55, 59, 71, 74, 75–77; settings for, 126; situations for, 25, 112; sound made by, 51; space-filling effects of, 26–28, 35, 42–43, 53, 69–70, 75, 87, 105–6, 142, 143–44; spectator's importance to, 45, 51; standard lengths and colors of, 27, 50, 57, 64, 66, 68, 74, 99, 142; tackiness of, 142; Tatlin monument series of, 9–10; temporal sense and, 25–26, 45–46; titles given to, 6, 14; uniqueness as art material of, 49–50; unorthodox positioning of, 57, 111–12; visible movement and, 83; white light and, 83, 103, 104, 105

Fonda, Peter, 109

formalism (1960s), 61–62

Foucault, Michel, 148*n*8

found object, 31, 136; readymade as distinct from, 54, 57

Frampton, Hollis, *Untitled*, 65

Freud, Sigmund, 27, 141

Fried, Michael, 59, 80*n*24, 157*n*18

Galleria Sperone (Milan), 116, *117*, 120

Gansevoort Pier, 28, *30*, 31

General Electric, 82

geometric forms, 98

Gilbert-Rolfe, Jeremy, 80*n*20

Glarner, Fritz, *100*

Gleason, Jackie, 109–10, *110*

Gogh, Vincent van, 21, 28

gold *diagonal* (fluorescent lamp), 35, *35*, *50*, 51, 53, 54, 56, 57, 61, 70, 77–78, 93, *94*, 96, 98, 116, *116*; ambiguity of, 112

Göring, Hermann, 16

Govan, Michael, 93, 115, 125, 129*n*14

Graebe, Carl, 106*n*5

Graham, Dan, 46, 109, 113, 143

Grand Central Station installation (New York, 1976), *125*, 125–26, 141

graph-paper diagrams, 43–46, *45*

Gray, Camilla, 36, 60, 90, 137, 139

Great Experiment: Russian Art, 1863–1922 (Gray), 36, 60, 90, 137, 139

Green and White Boxes (Duchamp), 36

Greenberg, Clement, 23*n*19, 70–72, 74, 80*n*24, 107*n*13, 114, 143

Green Gallery (New York), 24*n*24, 27, 46, 53, 54, 74, 110, 115, 116, *116*, *117*, 118

Gris, Juan, 14–15; *Maisons à Paris—Place Ravignan*, 23–24*n*21

Guggenheim Museum (New York), 28

Guignet of Paris, 106*n*5

Hegel, Georg Wilhelm Friedrich, 141

Heidegger, Martin, 96

Helene (Flavin's partner), 43
Hesse, Eva, 44, 109
Hockney, David, 105
house paint, 57–59, 63–65, 67
Hudson River School, 34

icon, 139; extended definition of, 60; fluorescent lamp as, 142; technological, 61
"iconostases" (pencil drawings), 33, *34*
icon series, 6, 8, 31, 33, 50, *62*, 70, 115, 139–41, 143; ambiguity of, 60; illusionist space and, 134, *135;* move from, 34–35, 54; real light and, 60–61; repetition and, 62–63; Russian icons and, 35, 37, 57, 60, 139–41; titles of, 60
illusionism, 54, 88, 95, 96, 99, 100–101, 102; allusion and, 147–48*n*6; anti-illusionism and, 6, 133–34, 136, 137, 139, 141, 142–43
image-object, 51, 56, 70, 112–13, 114, 115, 134
impressionism, 55–56, 80*n*20, 82, 83–84, 91, 99, 102, 103; brushmarks and, 84, 87, 89, 105; daylight and, 83, 84, 86–87, 102
indeterminacy, 89, 104
indigo trade, 106*n*5
industrial objects. *See* commercial materials
Ingres, Jean-Auguste-Dominique, 14
International Day of Protest (1966), 8
irony, 12, 16, 19, 22*n*6, 134, 136, 140
Irwin, Robert, 134, 144, 145, 150*n*17

Jackson State College student killings (1970), 10
Jewish Museum (New York), 4, 6, 8, 10, 16
Johns, Jasper, 49, 57, 70–77; Duchamp and, 75–77, 90; Flavin and, 89–90, *90,* 136, 137. *Works: American Flag,* 90, 93; *By the Sea, 73; Light Bulb, 72; Water Freezes,* 81*n*28
Johnston, Jill, 110
Joyce, James, 134, 136
Judd, Donald, 51, 54, 67, 102; aesthetic terminology and, 104, 113, 145; color and, 95, 100; empiricism and, 89; familiar materials and, 98; first one-man retrospective of, 14–15; Flavin's approach contrasted with, 27, 37; Flavin's first one-man show text by, 4, 49, 104; on Flavin's icons, 60, 134; Flavin's tribute

to, 14–15, 16; on Flavin's work, 39, 109; idea of real and, 95; "illusionist panic" of, 134; minimalist aesthetic of, 84, 91, 92–93, 95–96, 98, 133–34; on Newman's work, 68, 81*n*27; pop art and, 90; reflection and, 134; retrospective (1968) show of, 14. *Works: Untitled,* 97
junk assemblages. *See* assemblage

Kahnweiler, Daniel-Henry, 14
Kandinsky, Vassily, 55, 143
Kant, Immanuel, 141, 145
Kaprow, Allan, 148*n*8
Katz, Paul, 6
Kaymar Gallery (New York), 2–3, 24*n*24, 53, *135*
Kent State student killings (1970), 10
kitsch, 60, 74, 146
Kline, Franz, 28
Kornblee, Jill, 111
Kornblee Gallery, 27, 38–39, 42–43, 52, 110–11, 124
Kracauer, Siegfried, 146, 151*n*22
Kramer, Hilton, 92, 108
Krauss, Rosalind, 41, 42, 113–14, 125, 143, 147–48*n*6, 150*n*17, 150–51*n*20
Kuh, Katherine, 54, 56, 80*n*19
Kunst-Licht-Kunst show (1960s), 122
Kupka, Franticek, 55, 56

Lacan, Jacques, 27
Lefebvre, Henri, 126–27
Leider, Philip, 6, 16, 41, 108, 109
Leo Castelli Gallery (New York), 44, *45*
LeWitt, Sol, 3, 52, 95, 137
Lieberman, Carl, 106*n*5
light: brightness of, 87, 124; Flavin's work and, 67, 91, 92, 98, 106, 111–12, 115, 134, 139; fluorescent nature of, 18–19, 72, 88; human benefits of, 99; icons and, 60–61; industrial signifiers of, 72; painters' use of, 54; as phenomenon, 95–96; reflection of, 58–59, 61, 64; time sense and, 25–26, 27. *See also* color; daylight; white light
lighting fixtures. *See* fluorescent lamps
Lindsay, Vachel, 8–9
Lippard, Lucy, 4, 53, 54
literalism, 133–34
Louis, Morris, 93, 104
Lumumba, Patrice, 9
Lyotard, Jean-François, 88, 89, 106

Malevich, Kasimir, 36, 55, 140

Manet, Edouard, *A Bar at the Folies-Bergère*, 83

Mangold, Robert, 66

Marfa, 28

Markov, Vladimir, 141, 149*nn*11,12

Marx, Karl, 141, 144

Matisse, Henri, 53, 83–84, 87, 88, 89, 95, 98, 99, 102; *Interior, Nice, Seated Woman with a Book*, 84, *86*

McGovern, George, 10

metallic paint, 57–59, *58*, 60–64; original function of, 63–64

Metropolitan Museum of Art (New York), 35, 60, 139, *140*

Mies van der Rohe, Ludwig, 99

mineral colors, 87

minimalism, 12, 63, 133–46; anti-illusionalism and, 133–34, 142–43; Bochner's view of drawings and, 41; catastrophe and, 145; designification and, 92, 96, *97*, 99; dialectic of, 147*n*4; expanded field and, 146; Flavin's relationship with, 1, 3, 21, 82, 83, 84, 88, 91–92, 98, 111, 133, 142–43, 144, 150*n*17; gravity and, 92; Judd's defining essay on, 92–93; pictorial space predating, 62; pop art's relationship with, 89, 90, 91, 99; primary and, 98; ready-made materials and, 32; real space and, 88; resublimation and, 146; specificity of, 27, 91–92, 95, 96, 133

modularity, 67

Mondrian, Piet, 31, 32, 53, 55, 69, 143; Flavin's work compared with, 82, 99–103; studio of, 100, *100*. *Works: Victory Boogie-Woogie*, 100, *100*, *101*, 101–2

Monet, Claude, 87, 102

monochrome, 21, 95

Monroe, Marilyn, 10

monument series, 50

Morris, Robert, 21–22*n*4, 63, 64, 78, 108, 148*n*8; *Threadwaste*, 150*n*17

mosaics, Byzantine, 60–61

Museum of Modern Art (New York), 55, 92, 136–37

National Gallery of Art (Washington, D.C.), 6, 21, 45, 149*n*15

National Gallery of Canada (Ottawa) Flavin retrospective (1969), 4, 6, 113, 125, 126; Apollinaire poem and, 11;

Bochner's collage of citations and, 18; importance of drawings for, 39–49; inclusion of earlier works in, 13–14; Judd's text for, 49, 104; Newman's appearance at, 67

naturalism, 58, 87–88, 99

natural light. *See* daylight

nature, 86, 87, 105

Nauman, Bruce, 51; *Manipulating a Fluorescent Tube*, *52*

neodada, 23–24*n*21, 137

New Jersey Turnpike, 145, 146

Newman, Arnold, 39

Newman, Barnett, 26–27, 103, 106; on American painting, 93, 100; color application and, 73–74; Flavin and, 53, 57, 136, 137; lateral extension and, 89; minimalists and, 99; scale and, 66, 67–69, 70, 90; technique of, 69; time and, 88. *Works: Vir Heroicus Sublimis*, 26–27, 69; *The Wild*, 67–69, *68*; "zip" paintings, 68, 142

"New Realism" (Mondrian), 99

New York City, 101

New York School, 90, 99

Nixon, Richard, 10

nocturama, 25–26, 27

nominalism, 56, 72–73, 75, 149*n*14

Notte (film), 31

nouveau réaliste assemblages, 137

Novalis, 151*n*22

Novgorod icon, 60, 139, *140*, 141

Novgorod school, 35

objet trouvé. See found object

Ockham, William of, 12, 149*n*14

Olitski, Jules, 144, 150*n*18

Order of Things (Foucault), 148*n*8

Orton, Fred, 148*n*7

Ottawa retrospective. *See* National Gallery of Canada (Ottawa) Flavin retrospective

outdoor painting. *See* plein-air painting

paint: impressionists' use of, 83–84, 87, 99; materiality of, 139; objectification of, 70, 73; as ready-made, 54, 55, 59, 64–65; technological advancement in, 87

painting, 53, 54, 55–56, 65–66, 75; commercial paints and, 57–59, *58*, 60, 61, 62, 63–64, 65; "constructing" of, 65–66; Duchamp and, 76–77; Flavin on, 57–58; fluorescent lamp and, 54, 59–60, 71, 75;

Johns and, 72–73, 90; mechanization of, 55, 72; natural light and, 102–3; objectification of, 59, 70, 73; as repetitive practice, 64; scale and, 66–69; space and, 60–62, 69, 75, 100; specific object vs. illusionist space of, 133–34; Stella on, 69; technology and, 84, 86, 87, 88
Panza di Biumo, Count, 121, *121, 122*, 126
Passport (Andre), *63*, 80*n*19
Pennsylvania Station (New York), 91
Perkins, William, 106*n*5
Perrault, John, 93
petrochemical industry, 80*n*20, 87
phenomenology, 26–27, 35, 95–96, 145, 146
Philadelphia Museum of Art, 76, 84
Picabia, Francis, 23–24*n*21, 27
Picasso, Pablo, 65, 137, 139, 140, 141; *Les Demoiselles d'Avignon*, 139
pictorialism, 100, 114, 133, 143. *See also* illusionism
pictorial nominalism, 72–73, 75
Plagens, Peter, 109
plein-air painting, 55–56, 87
pointillism, 55–56
Pollock (film), 109
Pollock, Jackson, 58, 64, 81*n*25, 93, 114, 139, 143, 148*n*8
Poons, Larry, 144
pop art, 83, 89, 90–91, 93, 96, 99, 150–51*n*20; familiarity and, 82; illusionism and, 147*n*4; lightheartedness and, 92; nature and, 105
positivism, 23*n*19
postmodernist art, 133
Primary Structures show (Jewish Museum, 1966), 6, 8, 10
Psalm *21:16–19*, 9

railway, 86, 87, 88
Rauschenberg, Robert, 54, 56, 136, 137
ready-made materials, 32, 63; displaced function of, 71; found objects vs., 54, 57; general traits of, 54; Johns's sculptures and, 72; nature of fluorescent lamps as, 27, 31, 49, 54, 55, 59, 71, 74, 75–77; object sculpture and, 72; paint as, 59, 64–65; paint tube as, 54, 55; standardized materials and, 66–67, 74
real space, 99–100, 102, 104–5, 146
reflectivity, 58–59, 61, 64
Reinhardt, Ad, 53
Reise, Barbara, 109

"Rhyme about an electrical advertising light" (Lindsay), 8–9
Richter, Gerhard, 49
Ripolin-brand enamel paint, 65
Robbe-Grillet, Alain, 112
Rodchenko, Alexander, 36, 95, 99, 137
Rothko, Mark, 26, 59
Rowe, Colin, 148*n*8
Rubin, William, 57, 58–59, 64, 74
Russian constructivism. *See* constructivism
Russian Experiment in Art, 1863–1922 (Gray). See *Great Experiment: Russian Art, 1863–1922*
Russian icons, 35, 37, 57, 60, 139–41, *140*
Ryman, Robert, 53

Saint Louis Art Museum, 12, 43–44, 45, 48*n*15
Salammbo (Flaubert), 40
Sapolin paint, 65
sculpture, 71–72, *72*, 78, 133, 141
Sebald, W. G., 25–26
Seitz, William, 137
Semicraft Lighting Company, 74
"Serial Art Systems" (Bochner), 52–53
serial method, 41, 52–53, 63, 144
Seurat, Georges, 14, 55, 64–65
Several Quotations for Don Judd retrospective (Whitney Museum, 1968), 14
Signac, Paul, 55, 56
Sinatra, Frank, 109
situations (Flavin installations), 25, 28, 112, 119; drawings for, 25, 26–27; encompassing nature of, 26; installation of actual lights in, 36
Slutsky, Robert, 148*n*8
Smith, Brydon, 39–40
Smith, David, 133; *Cubi*, 148*n*6
Smith, Tony, 145, 146
Smithson, Robert, 18–19, 41, 149–50*n*16, 150–51*n*20
some light show (Kaymar Gallery, 1964), 2–3, 115
space: abstract, 70, 126–27; color's manipulation of, 27, 100, 143; fluorescent lamp as, 75, 87–88, 105–6, 143–44; illusion and, 95, 102, 133–34, 143; impressionism and, 89; minimalists and, 88, 134; opticalizing of, 150*n*17; pictorial, 60–62, 69, 75, 100, 150*n*17; pictorial vs. real, 69–70; real, 99–100, 102, 104–5, 146

specificity, 27, 91–92, 95, 96, 99, 113; color effects and, 100, 105, 106; illusionism vs., 133–34
"Specific Objects" (Judd), 92–93, 133, 134
speed, 101, 102, 105, 106
Stable Gallery (New York), 61
standardization, 66, 67
St. Antoine (Flaubert), 40
Stedelijk Van Abbemuseum (Eindhoven), 122, *123*, 123–24
Steinberg, Leo, 92
Stella, Frank, 65, 81*n*25, 89, 98, 134; color application and, 74; designification and, 96; idea of primary and, 98; metallic paintings and, 57–59, 62, 63–64; modularity and, 67; on Newman's technique, 69; pop art and, 90; sketches and, 63, *63*; stripe motif of, 69, 71. *Works:* Aluminum series, 57, 59, 63–64, 67, 69, 74; Black series, 57, 58, 59, 64, 67, 69; *Marquis de Portago, 58*
stripe motif, 69, 71
Studio International (publication), 110–11
sublime, 89, 93, 104, 105, 110, 145–46
"Sublime Is Now" (Newman), 93
sunlight. *See* daylight
Sylvester, David, 72
symbolism, 1, 6, 11

Tatlin, Vladimir, 93, 95, 102, 145; "art as science" creed of, 9–10, 36–37, 137; color and, 100; Flavin's dedications to, 36, 37, 46, 50; light-pieces monument to, 9–10, 21, 52, 137; Russian icons and, 139, 140, 141; specificity and, 99. *Works: Bottle,* 137; *Letatlin,* 137; *Monument to the Third International,* 137; *Selection of Materials,* 141
technical drawings, *35,* 35–36, 123–24
technological icons, 61
technological sublime, 145, 146
technology, 84, 86, 88, 103; art initiatives with, 10, 46; designification of, 91; fluorescent lamps as, 49–50; impressionism and, 87; naturalization of, 105
temporality, 25–26, 28–29, 31, 45–46, 88
three-dimensionality, 95, 98, 143

Tillim, Sidney, 68, 69, 80*n*24
time. *See* temporality
"Transparency: Literal and Phenomenal" (Rowe and Slutsky), 148*n*8
Trocadéro Museum (Paris), 139
Tuchman, Phyllis, 42
Turner, J. M. W., 105
Turrell, James, 134, 144, 145, 146; *Roden Crater,* 145
Twombly, Cy, 53

ultraviolet light, 82, 124

Venezia, Michael, 47*n*6
Verne, Jules, 86
Vietnam War, 6, 8, 10
Villa Panza, 22*n*6
Viola, Bill, 146
visual field, 150*n*17
Vitti, Monica, 109
von Bismarck, Beatrice, 129*n*7, 132*n*25

Wall series (Mangold), 66
Warhol, Andy, 10, 61, 72, 90, 96, 145, 150*n*17. *Works: Brillo Soap Pads Box,* 91, 97; *Gold Marilyn Monroe,* 61; *Optical Car Crash,* 147*n*4
Weber, John, 118, 119
Wheeler, Doug, 134
Wheeling—the "Peachblow" glass, 15
white light: fluorescent quality of, 38, 51, 82–83, 103; impressionists and, 99; Mondrian and, 102–3
Whitney Museum of American Art (New York), 14, 120; Sculpture Annual (1970), 10
Wilde, Oscar, 105
Williamsburg, Brooklyn, 31
working drawing. *See* drawings and diagrams
Working Drawings and Other Visible Things Not Usually Thought of as Art (Bochner 1966 show), 41
"Work of Art in the Age of Its Reproducibility" (Benjamin), 146

"zip" paintings (Newman), 68, 142